Ten Reasons To Lose Faith

And Why You Are Better Off Without It

Rosa Rubicondior

Ten Reasons To Lose Faith

Third Party Copyright.

Third party copyright is acknowledged for work not currently in the public domain, reproduced here for criticism and analysis under intellectual rights fair use regulations.

In the opinion of the author, the minimum necessary for effective criticism and analysis whilst retaining the original context, has been reproduced in this work.

© 2016 Rosa Rubicondior.
All rights reserved.
ISBN-10: 1530431956
ISBN-13: 978-1530431953

Ten Reasons To Lose Faith

I contend we are both atheists, I just believe in one fewer God than you do.

Stephen F. Roberts.

The various modes of worship which prevailed in the Roman world were all considered by the people as equally true; by the philosopher as equally false; and by the magistrate as equally useful.

Edward Gibbon.

Religion was our first attempt at philosophy, just as alchemy was our first attempt at chemistry and astrology our first attempt to make sense of the movements of the heavens. I myself am a strong believer in the study of religion, first because culture and education involve a respect for tradition and for origins, and also because some of the early religious texts were among our first attempts at literature. But there is a reason why religions insist so much on strange events in the sky, as well as on less quantifiable phenomena such as dreams and visions. All of these things cater to our inborn stupidity, and our willingness to be persuaded against all the evidence that we are indeed the center of the universe and that everything is arranged with us in mind.

Christopher Hitchens

One of the great tragedies of mankind is that morality has been hijacked by religion. So now people assume that religion and morality have a necessary connection. But the basis of morality is really very simple and does not require religion at all.

Arthur C. Clarke

Ten Reasons To Lose Faith

Ten Reasons to Lose Faith

Table of Contents.

Introduction.	1
1. The Fallacy of Faith.	5
2. The Fallacy of Holy Books.	33
3. The Fallacy of Apologetics.	79
4. Failures of Logic.	119
5. Absence of Evidence.	151
6. Knowledge, Science and Uncertainty.	159
7. Freedom from Delusion.	187
8. Freedom of Intellectual Honesty.	223
9. Freedom from Fear.	255
10. Freedom to Choose.	291
Bibliography.	309
About the Author.	323
Other books by Rosa Rubicondior.	327

Ten Reasons To Lose Faith

Ten Reasons to Lose Faith

Acknowledgements.

I would like to express my thanks to the following:

Firstly to my life-long partner Catherine, for her patience as I spent probably far too long silently staring at a computer screen with occasional burst of typing, and for putting up with me disappearing occasionally for a few days of solitude when I needed some time alone to concentrate.

Secondly, to Pauline and Therese, for allowing me to find that solitude in their holiday cottage, alone with my thoughts, the birds in the garden, the gurgling and bumps of the central heating and a bottle or two of Chianti.

Thirdly, to my online friend 'Spellchick', who kindly offered to proofread the manuscript and offered invaluable criticisms and suggestions.

Ten Reasons To Lose Faith

Introduction.

Because you are reading this, the chances are high that you fall into one of three groups:

1. **The Believers.** You think your faith is solid, so you want to confirm it by showing yourself you can refute the arguments against it.
2. **The Doubters.** You are having doubts about your faith, so curiosity and honest enquiry have led you to look at alternative opinions.
3. **The Faithless.** You have lost, or never had faith and are looking for arguments to help others lose their faith too.

Whichever group you are in, there is something here for you.

If you are a believer, then you are very welcome! Atheism thrives on good critical arguments. If you can refute the logical arguments and evidence I present here with logical counter-arguments and contradictory evidence then that is just great – please let me know about it! If, however, you find you have to resort to faith to sustain your faith, or you have to resort to the common fallacies and empty arguments to be found in the first five chapters, then you need to ask yourself why? Unless you can answer that question honesty, you are fooling yourself that your faith is a valid way to really know anything. In that case, whoever gave you your faith and told you it is a good thing has deprived you of the right to make up your own mind and accept the world for what it is.

If you are a doubter, then welcome to the world of rational thought, evidence-based opinion and logical argument. With a few exceptions, every Atheist I know went through that stage, however briefly. Most of them still have doubt about a great many things and have learned its value as a spur to learning and personal growth.

If you are already faithless, then you are most welcome to take whatever arguments you need, modify and adapt them as you wish and use them in whatever way you need to – with an acknowledgement of the source, please.

Ten Reasons To Lose Faith

Many people lose their faith. Losing faith, or 'having a crisis of faith', is almost an occupational hazard for those whose livelihood or lifestyle depends on faith. The evidence of the 'Clergy Project'[1] suggests that it is likely that many people who earn their living as ministers of religion lost their faith at some point in their career yet continued in the only job they were qualified to do. They realised they could fulfil whatever social support and spiritual needs their congregation required without actually believing in the supernatural. Rather like actors who don't actually need to be murderers, superheroes or singing nuns to play the part of one, so clergy who have lost faith can still function as clergy, albeit with a lot of rationalisation and not a little guilt.

As I will show in the following chapters, faith is a fallacy. Faith is not a sure and certain way to know the truth nor can it be obtained from holy books. Faith cannot come from the arguments religious apologists use or the false logic routinely taught to the faithful to sustain them in the absence of evidence. The absence of evidence is a major obstacle that cannot be dismissed with the wave of a hand or turned by clever rhetoric into evidence for anything other than absence.

But this book is not just about the reasons why faith is a fallacy and a useless tool for discovering truth; it is also about the personal and societal benefits that come from losing it. The second five chapters deal with the mental liberation that comes from, for example, the humility to embrace doubt and uncertainty. This in turn drives scientific, technological and personal development and learning. The seductive certainty of religion is a false friend that leads only to complacency, ignorance and being satisfied with not really knowing.

Freedom from the mind-controlling nature of faith, especially that of the fundamentalist forms of religion, leads to freedom from fear and delusion; freedom for the real intellectual honesty which comes from accepting that you might be wrong and that being right is not the same thing as settling for a satisfying easy answer.

Lastly, I will show that losing faith provides the freedom to decide for yourself on matters of morality, to take personal responsibility for your actions and to accept that the reason to behave well towards your fellows is because that creates a better, kinder, more caring and inclusive society. Freedom from the

---

[1] (The Clergy Project, 2015)

Introduction

mental straightjacket of conformity to group norms and outmoded received medieval ethics, in order to maintain an in-group versus out-group mentality, will produce a less divided, more tolerant and more peaceful society.

A 'crisis of faith' is seen as a problem by some, especially those with a vested interest, because they haven't yet found reason. Faith is a rejection of rationality. Faith is not a virtue but a sin. It is the abandonment of reason in favour of easy answers with no regard for truth. Faith is an abdication of personal responsibility and a handing over of control to those who tell you what the faithful do.

You can only have confidence in your conclusions and be sure they are your own once you have accepted that the only worthwhile opinions are those to which evidence, deductive logic and honest appraisal have led you. They may or may not be the same as those given to you by people who had their own reason for wanting you to believe what they believe – reasons which were very often not honourable ones – but they will be your own.

As I say with all my books, please do not take my word for anything; please do not accept my opinions without critical analysis, and please do not allow me to tell you how to think or what to believe. If you still want to be told what to think, you still need preachers to talk down to you from a pulpit!

I decided to write this book to put my many years of experience with online religion versus atheism debates, and several years as a blogger about atheism, theology and science, into some sort of logical structure and to help sort out my own thoughts on the subject. I have been an atheist since the age of nine, so because my reasons may have been immature at the time and have developed and been refined over the years, inevitably, like a schoolboy's stamp collection, they needed putting into some sort of order and tidying up a little.

Some of the ten major topics I deal with inevitably shade over into others. For example, fallacies of apologetics are also failures of logic; freedom from fear is also freedom from delusion, but I hope the topics represent the five major objections to faith and the five major benefits from abandoning superstition and going with evidence-based reality instead.

If you enjoy reading this book or want to discover more about the interface between science and faith, you may enjoy reading my 'Rosa Rubicondior' blog at http://rosarubicondior.blogspot.com. This blog is also available by subscription for Kindle for just £0.99 a month. Other books by me, based on this blog, are listed at the end of this book.

1. The Fallacy of Faith.

Faith is a fallacy.

Faith serves no useful purpose. It serves only to rationalise holding irrational beliefs; to make the faithful satisfied with not knowing and left pretending to themselves and others that they know things they do not know. In the absence of any substantive evidence for the physical existence of gods, the last (and often only) resort of a believer is faith.

The dictionary defines faith in this context as:

1. Complete trust or confidence in someone or something.
2. Strong belief in the doctrines of a religion, based on spiritual conviction rather than proof.

For the moment, I am taking a narrow subset of the second definition – belief in the existence of gods because it is a doctrine of religion. I'll look more closely at the broader definition – complete trust or confidence in [gods] – later on. For the time being though, I'll use 'faith' to mean a way to determine the truth of the doctrine of the existence of particular gods which is the central doctrine of all religions.

How do the faithful know their god exists?

What is this faith in the absence of logical proof or physical evidence? How does faith in the absence of logic or evidence, gain the same or greater credibility than real evidence or a real, logically-deduced reason to believe something?

Strangely, since it is supposedly the source of all Christian wisdom and beliefs, the Bible is not much help in understanding how this faith thing is supposed to work. The entire 11th chapter of St Paul's Epistle to the Hebrews is about faith, but it only starts off with a nebulous 'definition', and then has a lot of claims about what people have done through faith, all of them from the Old Testament. One might have expected some more contemporary examples but apparently Paul, or whoever wrote Hebrews, did not know of any.

> *Now faith is the substance of things hoped for, the evidence of things not seen.*
>
> *For by it the elders obtained a good report. Through faith we understand that the worlds were framed by the word of God, so that things which are seen were not made of things which do appear.*
>
> *By faith Abel offered unto God a more excellent sacrifice than Cain, by which he obtained witness that he was righteous, God testifying of his gifts: and by it he being dead yet speaketh. By faith Enoch was translated that he should not see death; and was not found, because God had translated him: for before his translation he had this testimony, that he pleased God.*
>
> *But without faith it is impossible to please him: for he that cometh to God must believe that he is, and that he is a rewarder of them that diligently seek him.* (Hebrews 11:1-6)

The nebulous platitude in the first verse is trotted out *ad nauseum* by Christians but it means absolutely nothing as a practical definition. It might as well read; 'Now faith is pretending to know things you do not know'. What exactly **is** this 'substance of things hoped for'? What on earth **is** the 'evidence of things not seen'? How do we know what these invisible things are, to be able to say with any degree of certainty that this or that is the evidence for them? This is something pretending to be deep that is not even shallow. As a piece of philosophy it would not deserve to be pinned up behind a bar. Why not be honest and say faith is just wishful thinking and the pretence of knowledge?

The Bible fails the faith test on another level. Although believers are required to believe by faith, none of the prophets through whom this 'faith' was supposedly been revealed to mankind were actually required to believe by faith at all. If the accounts are to be believed, they were given evidence in one form or another. They saw burning bushes, heard voices, were 'given signs', 'saw the light' and even the followers of the supposed god-man, Jesus, were supplied with miracles and signs in abundance, allegedly. Not a single example is given in the Bible of a prophet simply believing anything by faith, despite the impressive-looking list used to pad out Hebrews 11.

The Fallacy of Faith

Why was faith alone not enough for these prophets and why are they **more** reliable than we are that we should have faith in them when they required real evidence? Why, if God thinks faith is such a great thing, did he chose prophets who could not rise to the occasion but needed evidence?

The answer is that people are not normally that credulous and gullible. People do not acquire new knowledge by faith but from evidence and reason. What the faithful like to think of as new knowledge is merely confirmation of existing bias. New knowledge does not come from reading the holy books because it had already been accepted that the holy book contained this 'knowledge' when it was read. Opening the book was simply taking it out and accepting that it is the truth, no matter how unlikely.

If you think Jesus' disciples would have believed Jesus was the son of God by faith alone, if he had simply introduced himself as such, try it yourself. Go up to any stranger in the street and introduce yourself as the son or daughter of God and the Messiah come to save them. See how quickly you can gather twelve devoted followers around you as opposed to a group of people concerned for your welfare and worried about what you might do next.

Would you believe a stranger if he told you he was Jesus? Or would you hurry away and maybe give the police a ring?

Islam does little better in its attempt to define faith if this Islamic website is anything to go by[2]:

> *The basis of any religion is faith. Faith is not merely conviction of the truth of a given principle, but it is essentially the acceptance of a principle as a basis for action. Without faith, a man is like a car without a steering wheel, drifting aimlessly upon a sea of doubt and confusion.*

This is, of course, exactly what someone with no evidence, but a dogma to push, would say. It tells us what faith is not, and then makes a claim which any non-believer, indeed I suspect any non-Muslim, will tell you, is nothing more than an unfounded assertion, the entire purpose of which appears to be to reinforce in-group smug self-satisfaction. An almost gleeful revelling in how

---

[2] (IslamWeb.net, 2012)

much better the believer thinks his or her life is compared to those less fortunate fools.

> *What is faith in Islam? It is belief in the Unity of God or Tawheed. This is expressed in the primary Kalimah (Word) of Islam as: "Laa ilaaha illallaah", meaning: "There is no one worthy of worship but Allah."*
>
> *This beautiful phrase is the bedrock of Islam, its foundation and its essence. It is the expression of this belief, which differentiates a true Muslim from an unbeliever, or one who associates others with God in His Divinity.*

This is merely a statement of dogma, entirely dependent on preconceptions about the existence of a particular god with particular qualities. There is no special beauty in the phrase itself, merely in the comfort it brings to believers as confirmation of bias. If there is intrinsic beauty in the phrase, try spotting the intrinsic beauty in the phrase, "There is no one worthy of worship but Thor!" Is there intrinsic beauty and power in that phrase sufficient to form the 'bedrock' of a new religion?

There is no attempt to explain how faith gains this special insight. Faith is simply the acceptance of dogma. "I believe because I believe… and because I believe, what I believe is beautiful and true without question!" This is the self-referential certainty of the smugly self-satisfied.

> *The acceptance or denial of this phrase produces a world of difference among human beings. The believer finds out the right path, knows the truth and chalks out the course of life in the light of reality; the unbeliever chases one illusion after the other and gropes into the dark. For the believers, there is the promise of unhampered progress and resounding success in this world and in the Hereafter; whereas failure and ignominy are ultimately the lot of those who refuse to believe in it.*

Again, these are merely assertions which to an outsider are patently false and which are nothing more than appeals to existing biases, intended to reinforce in-group versus out-group self-satisfaction and contentment.

Like the Bible, there is actually very little attempt in the Qur'an to explain what faith actually **is** or why it should be regarded as trumping evidence. It is taken for granted that 'Allah' exists and faith is spelled out merely in terms of a Muslim's obligations and expressions of confidence in what 'Allah' will do. Simply believing makes this all true, apparently.

Just as a Christian will claim that the Bible proves the existence of God because God wrote or inspired the Bible, so a Muslim will claim the Qur'an proves Allah exists because Allah inspired the Qur'an. The circularity in that reasoning is readily seen by the obvious fact that the claims cannot both be true, but if one claim fails then the other claim also fails because the failure is in the logic of the argument. In fact, this was never a real argument in the first place because both of them rely on two unsubstantiated assertions – this particular god exists and that god inspired the book.

The logical fallacy is in the presupposition of the conclusion. The logic collapses if you change this assumption and replace 'God' or 'Allah' for 'Bottle of Milk' or 'Peanut Butter Sandwich'. This becomes just as absurd to a believer as the holy book 'proof of gods' does to a non-believer and yet the 'logic', such as it is, remains unchanged.

And this brings me neatly to John W. Loftus' *Outsider Test of Faith*.

> *If you were born in Saudi Arabia, you would be a Muslim right now, say it isn't so? That is a cold hard fact. Dare you deny it? Since this is so, or at least 99% so, then the proper method to evaluate your religious beliefs is with a healthy measure of skepticism.*
>
> *Test your beliefs as if you were an outsider to the faith you are evaluating. If your faith stands up under muster, then you can have your faith. If not, abandon it, for any God who requires you to believe correctly when we have this extremely strong tendency to believe what we were born into, surely should make the correct faith pass the outsider test. If your faith cannot do this, then the God of your faith is not worthy of being worshipped.* [3]

Wherever and whenever you were born, if you are religious you would almost certainly have the same faith as your parents. Unless, that is, you had applied exactly the same standard to your parents' faith as you have to all the others. If you had, you are very unlikely to have any faith at all because, like every other

---
[3] (Loftus, 2006)

faith, yours has no evidential basis and so would fail John W. Loftus' Outsider Test of Faith.

In fact, if you were honest, you would admit that you have never really even thought about the other gods and other faiths, let alone applied any of the tests you just assume someone else must have made when they accepted your faith and rejected all the others.

The Outsider Test of Faith, if used honestly in the absence of bias, should reveal the absurdity of 'faith' as the basis for determining the truth of religion. Failure to apply it objectively betrays the cultural biases and in-group versus out-group mentality which underpins all religion. As Richard Dawkins has said, "How thoughtful of God to arrange things so that wherever you happen to have been born, the locally-popular religion is the one true faith!"

By way of illustration of this Outsider Test of Faith, supposing I told you that the other day I met a man in Oxford who told me about someone he had heard about who had lived in Bristol several years ago. The claim was that this man could do things like curing the sick with a touch or just a few words, levitate and walk on water. He could turn things into other things by the power of his thought alone, and he told people they would live for ever with him in the most wonderful place imaginable if they followed him.

No, he had not actually met this man but had met someone who had been told about him by someone who he thought might have met him.

Would you forsake your family and follow this man, certain that this would give you eternal life?

Why not? Do you not want eternal life? Do you not have any faith?

If you are a Christian, that's exactly what you did in respect of what another stranger told you about someone who supposedly lived 2000 years ago in Palestine. Why is your faith a better judge of the validity of that story rather than my story? It has exactly the same evidence that your story does, yet you can dismiss my story with as much ease as a non-Christian can dismiss yours.

So faith alone does not create knowledge; faith merely confirms bias.

The Fallacy of Faith

Since you cannot have faith in something you do not believe in, faith inevitably follows from belief; it cannot precede it or be the reason for it. So, the claim to believe by faith alone must be false and at best a *post hoc* rationalisation of an irrational belief.

A revealing illustration of the operation of confirmation bias in religious apologetics is found in a little-known argument used by St Augustine of Hippo (354-430 CE). It concerned the then hotly debated subject within Christianity of whether Earth is flat like the Bible implies or spherical like science shows. It had been known that Earth is spherical since at least 100 BCE when Eratosthenes (276-c.195 BCE) measured the circumference of Earth. Even then the issue had been merely how big it was, not what shape it was. Yet 500 years later, Christian scholars were still arguing that Earth must be flat because the Bible said so.

Augustine of Hippo is still regarded as one of the founders of Western Christian theology and a leading thinker. Unfortunately, he committed the great error in apologetics of making a testable prediction which could be falsified.

In *De Civitate Dei* (City of God), Book XVI, Chapter 9, he wrote:

> *But as to the fable that there are Antipodes, that is to say, men on the opposite side of the earth, where the sun rises when it sets to us, men who walk with their feet opposite ours that is on no ground credible. And, indeed, it is not affirmed that this has been learned by historical knowledge, but by scientific conjecture, on the ground that the earth is suspended within the concavity of the sky, and that it has as much room on the one side of it as on the other: hence they say that the part that is beneath must also be inhabited. But they do not remark that, although it be supposed or scientifically demonstrated that the world is of a round and spherical form, yet it does not follow that the other side of the earth is bare of water; nor even, though it be bare, does it immediately follow that it is peopled.*
>
> **It is too absurd to say, that some men might have taken ship and traversed the whole wide ocean, and crossed from this side of the world to the other, and that thus even the inhabitants of that distant region are descended from that one first man.**[4] [My emphasis]

So, here we have a leading and highly respected Christian theologian, who is still widely respected and whose writing is required reading for would-be theologians today, telling us that there could not be people on the far side of Earth. Being descendants of Adam (actually according to the Bible they would be descendants of Noah but Augustine seems to have overlooked that detail) they would not have had time to get there.

But, there **were** people living on the far side of Earth. We now know this beyond any shadow of doubt. Clearly, if Augustine had been right about all people being descended from Adam and not having had enough time to get there, they must be descended from someone else, or Earth is much older than theologians of the day concluded from the Bible.

Augustine made a prediction based on the Bible and the prediction was falsified!

Does this cause Bible literalists to revise their beliefs? Does it lessen their respect for the founding fathers of their religion? Of course not! Inconvenient facts which do not confirm bias are selectively given a much lower weighting or dismissed altogether, whereas, because Augustine also said things they agree with, these amazing arguments are enough to elevate Augustine to the status of a saint.

Perhaps the most accurate definition of 'faith' is that used by Peter Boghossian in *A Manual For Creating Atheists* – pretending to know things you don't know.

> *Not everything that's a case of pretending to know things you don't know is a case of faith, but cases of faith are instances of pretending to know something you don't know.[5] For example, someone who knows nothing about baking a cake can pretend to know how to bake a cake, and this is not an instance of faith. But if someone claims to know something on the*

---

[4] (St Augustine of Hippo, 5th Century CE)

[5] The exceptions to this are those people who are not pretending. These individuals are either delusional, or they're victims of a wholesale lack of exposure to alternative ideas and different epistemologies. In the latter case, many people in the Islamic world fall into this category. For example, most of the people in Saudi Arabia are not pretending to know something they don't know about the Koran. They've never encountered nor been given an opportunity to genuinely engage in competing ways of understanding reality. In a very real sense, they're epistemological victims. Additionally, anyone reared by fundamentalist parents deserves credit for the exceptional struggle from indoctrination to enlightenment. [Peter Boghossian's footnote].

> *basis of faith, they are pretending to know something they don't know. For example, using faith would be like someone giving advice about baking cookies who has never been in a kitchen.*[6]

Boghossian gives several examples to illustrate the true idiocy (it really is difficult to think of a better adjective) of faith. Some of them are:

> *"My faith is beneficial for me." = "Pretending to know things I don't know is beneficial to me".*
>
> *"I have faith in God." = "I pretend to know things I don't know about God".*
>
> *"Life has no meaning without faith." = "Life has no meaning without pretending to know things I don't know".*
>
> *"Teach your children to have faith." = "Teach your children to pretend to know things they don't know".*
>
> *"She's having a crisis of faith." = "She's having a crisis of pretending to know things she doesn't know." Alternatively, "She is struck by the fact that she's been pretending to know things she doesn't know."*

It is a simple exercise to think of many more examples where substituting 'pretending to know things I don't know' for 'faith' sounds quite absurd and even more than a little delusional. Whoever managed to sell the idea that faith is a good thing and a virtue? More to the point, perhaps, how on earth did they get away with it?

'Faith' is in fact no use at all for determining the truth of anything. I'll illustrate this with a few examples.

Imagine for a moment that you are a defendant in a courtroom, charged with committing a serious crime – something that, if convicted, would mean your liberty would be at stake.

Your defence team have brought in a forensics expert to testify that there is unarguable evidence that you did not commit the crime but someone else did. They have produced eye-witnesses who swear that you were somewhere else

---

[6] (Boghosian, 2013)

when the crime was committed. There is independent evidence to prove it. Character witnesses have testified that you would never do anything of the sort.

By contrast, the only witness brought by the prosecution is the detective who arrested you. He has sworn in court that he has faith in his own judgement and is as certain as it is possible to be that you committed the crime. He has not evidence but he has no doubt at all that you are guilty. He has defended this with the assertion that faith is a virtue; that those without faith are deficient; that faith and faith alone is the only way to determine the truth and faith trumps all the evidence. He has produced lots of religious literature which says just that to justify his claim and even called on an evangelical Baptist pastor, a Hasidic Rabi and a Wahhabi Imam to testify on the power and virtue of faith. They both quote from their respective holy books, prophets and teachers to support that claim.

Who would you prefer the jury to believe?

Is there anyone, even the most ardent of faith-heads, who is going to accept that they must be guilty despite all the contrary evidence, because faith trumps evidence? Would anyone even be prepared to accept a guilty verdict even if the defence had offered no evidence of innocence and the prosecution had relied solely on the faith of the arresting detective?

If you were on the jury panel, would **you** convict or acquit? I suspect the answer, at least for a fair and intelligent adult, would be 'not guilty', or at the very best, 'not proven'. The very question even seems absurd, and yet it is precisely the same argument made to justify belief in a particular god, and almost invariably the god that your parents believed in.

Perhaps the more important question is whether the detective and prosecutor should keep their jobs.

The second example of how faith is used to support an irrational *post hoc* conclusion entirely unrelated to the real world evidence, is that of the simple, everyday task of crossing a road.

If faith is at least as good a way to determine the truth as is real evidence, then why does no one depend on it when they cross a road? Anyone who does not need constant, responsible supervision will normally look both ways to check for evidence of approaching traffic, and only when that evidence is absent will they cross the road. Then they bet their lives on the reliability of that absent evidence.

There is probably a very good evolutionary explanation for this tendency to check the evidence before making a life or death decision. Those who did not check had a greatly reduced likelihood of passing on their genes, so the genes for not bothering about evidence would tend to lose out in competition with their counterparts which regarded evidence as important.

So, when it comes to life and death decisions in real life, normal people not only rely on evidence but look for it and regard it as the best available basis for the decision. Importantly, they regard absence of evidence of cars as perfectly reliable evidence of the absence of cars. Why would they not? What would be the purpose of looking for evidence then regarding its presence or absence as evidence of the same thing?

Absence of evidence of approaching traffic is perfectly good evidence of the absence of approaching traffic. This is not a faith-based decision; it is just as much an evidence-based decision as is a decision based on the presence of evidence?

Again, in the real world, evidence, not faith, is the only sane thing on which to base important decisions. This, of course is because we know very well that evidence is a higher standard of proof than is faith, requiring as it does a prior belief in the required conclusion – which alone should render it useless. When important decisions are required, the higher standard of evidence wins every time and the idea of doing otherwise is almost too ridiculous to contemplate.

For the same reason, no sane, rational person would believe in fairies or invisible hippopotamuses by faith alone and dismiss absence of evidence as not evidence of absence.

For example, I could claim that my loft is full of undetectable hippopotamuses I could claim I know this by faith. But we both know there are no undetectable hippos in my loft, do we not!

We know this because faith is not good enough and the probability of there actually being invisible hippos in my loft is so low as to be functionally zero.

In fact, if I seriously started to make that absurd claim I would rightly be considered certifiable and a possible danger to myself or others. The idea is just too absurd to even consider.

But when it comes to belief in the presence of gods, because there is no evidence, a much lower standard of proof becomes acceptable to the believer. The standard of 'proof' that would get you killed crossing a road, wrongly convicted of a crime or considered insane, is suddenly elevated to the status of a virtue and worn with pride. People even dress accordingly, adopt special hair-styles, wear symbols to show off their dependence on it and refuse to eat certain perfectly good food! Some people even allow it to dictate their entire life.

The uncertain and unreliable nature of faith is why the well-known phenomenon of losing one's faith is a perpetual occupational hazard in theological circles. Struggling with a crisis of faith is considered a right and noble thing for any cleric who has either suddenly or gradually come to realise that actually his or her faith was not enough to sustain belief in the face of doubt; that it could all be pretence of knowing something he does not know.

Seen from the position of a rational materialist, it seems strange that losing faith by allowing the fact of no evidence to dictate an opinion is even regarded as a problem. It seems strange that other clerics see this as a regular occurrence needing special measures and contingencies to support those who have doubts or have lost faith, yet never seem to question just why it should occur at all. Surely, if faith were at least as good as evidence or, as many clerics will claim, superior to it, these crises of faith would never happen, would they?

Do you know of anyone of sound mind who has a sudden crisis of faith about electricity continuing to work, day following night or water flowing downhill?

Imagine a scientist having a 'crisis of faith' in gravity or the Laws of Thermodynamics! Scientists will constantly question what they think they know and will actively seek ways to falsify even the most fundamental of scientific principles. This is not regarded as a 'crisis' or problem to be coped with by seeking reassurance from colleagues or spending time in meditation, struggling with it. Doubt is the lifeblood of science. Doubt and uncertainty are the great virtues of science and the things that give it its power. Certainty is the thing to be avoided. The moment a scientist claims to know the answer to a problem by faith alone, would be the moment he lost credibility as an objective scientist.

There are many, many examples of town and city councils saying prayers before a meeting, but for your sake and the sake of your fellow citizens, be sure to sack the lot of them at the next opportunity if they ever start to hear the voice of God telling them what financial or planning decisions to make rather than looking at the facts.

And yet clerics, monks and nuns have these crises of faith frequently, and may leave their religion because of it. For every atheist who suddenly 'finds God', or rather for every self-proclaimed 'former atheist' who suddenly claims to have 'found God', there are probably hundreds of former clerics or devout Christians and Moslems who lost God and found reason. Perhaps the difference between a religious person having a crisis of faith and a religious person ceasing to be religious is that losing faith is no longer regarded as a problem; the realisation that depending on faith is a crisis of rationality.

All opinion polls and measures of movements in public opinion throughout the developed world shows that there is an inexorable and accelerating movement away from faith and towards non-belief, often via disaffiliation from the established churches. Incidentally, the fact that complete non-belief is often preceded by disaffiliation is a clue to why 'faith' has such a strong psychological hold on people, as we shall see later.

Almost nowhere will you find examples of a mass movement from non-belief to belief. The real measure of the abandonment of faith in favour of reason is in these figures, not in the highly suspect examples of 'former atheists' who suddenly appear on the scene, often as fully-formed evangelicals complete with professional-looking websites with of course a donate button and all the phony and fallacious standard apologetics and techniques of sophistry that, as an atheist, he or she would have seen through in a moment. In very many of these cases, either the 'former atheist' is using a private definition of 'atheism' or they are frankly lying for effect, probably for money and often because they have a trashy book to sell.

Even the recently beatified, and at the rate her elevation to the Catholic sainthood is being rushed through, maybe even a Catholic saint by the time this book is published, the late Catholic nun, Mother Teresa of Calcutta (real name Anjezë Gonxhe Bojaxhiu), admitted to a friend that she doubted God was there. As Christopher Hitchens showed in *The Missionary Position*, this doubt lay behind everything that Ms Anjezë Bojaxhiu did. Her entire life was dedicated to two things:

- Allowing people to suffer in the perverse hope that, in experiencing what Jesus supposedly experienced, this would make Jesus appreciate her enough to reveal himself to her.
- Creating a new Catholic order in her name so God would notice her and show her he really existed.

In effect, Ms Bojaxhiu was a reluctant atheist struggling to be a believer.

The following quotes are taken from letters to friends, which she wanted destroyed on her death but the Vatican ordered should be kept as potential saintly relics. The wishes of the dead are of no consequence when saintly relics are needed.

> "I spoke as if my very heart was in love with God -- tender, personal love," she wrote to one adviser. "If you were (there), you would have said, 'What hypocrisy.'"

> "Please pray specially [sic] for me that I may not spoil His work and that Our Lord may show Himself -- for there is such terrible darkness within me, as if everything was dead. It has been like this more or less from the time I started 'the work.'" (1953)

> "Such deep longing for God -- and ... repulsed -- empty -- no faith -- no love -- no zeal. (Saving) souls holds no attraction -- Heaven means nothing -- pray for me please that I keep smiling at Him in spite of everything." (1956)

> "If there be no God -- there can be no soul -- if there is no Soul then Jesus -- You also are not true." (1959)

> "Darkness is such that I really do not see—neither with my mind nor with my reason—the place of God in my soul is blank—There is no God in me—when the pain of longing is so great—I just long & long for God. ... The torture and pain I can't explain." (c.1961)

> *"I utter words of community prayers -- and try my utmost to get out of every word the sweetness it has to give -- but my prayer of union is not there any longer -- I no longer pray."*
>
> *"Jesus has a very special love for you. As for me, the silence and the emptiness is [sic] so great that I look and do not see, listen and do not hear."* – To the Rev. Michael van der Peet, September 1979. [7, 8]:

How then do religious people, in the face of this seemingly obvious fallacy, rationalise what they call faith? The first step seems to be to persuade themselves, or at least to allow themselves to be persuaded that, despite all the evidence to the contrary, faith gives unquestionable knowledge. The following example is one of many such examples found within a few minutes searching online:

> **Question:** *Why does God require faith? Why doesn't God "prove" Himself to us so there is no need for faith?*
>
> **Answer:** *Our relationship with God is similar to our relationship with others in that all relationships require faith. We can never fully know any other person. We cannot experience all they experience nor enter into their minds to know what their thoughts and emotions are. Proverbs 14:10 says, "The heart knows its own bitterness, and a stranger does not share its joy." We are incapable of even knowing our own hearts fully. Jeremiah 17:9 says that the human heart is wicked and deceptive, "Who can know it?" In other words, the human heart is such that it seeks to hide the depth of its wickedness, deceiving even its owner. We do this through shifting blame, justifying wrong behavior, minimizing our sins, etc.*
>
> *Because we are incapable of fully knowing other people, to some degree faith (trust) is an integral ingredient in all relationships. For example, a wife gets into a car with her husband driving, trusting him to drive safely, even though he often drives faster than she would on winter roads. She trusts him to act in their best interest at all times. We all share information about ourselves with others, trusting they will not betray us with that knowledge. We drive down the road, trusting those driving*

---

[7] (Reuters, 2007)
[8] (Crabtree S. , 2007)

> *around us to follow the rules of the road. So, whether with strangers or with intimate friends and companions, because we cannot fully know others, trust is always a necessary component of our relationships.*
>
> *If we cannot know our fellow finite human beings fully, how can we expect to fully know an infinite God? Even if He should desire to fully reveal Himself, it is impossible for us to fully know Him...*[9]

The first thing to note here is the unquestioned assumption in the question itself. This is not a website designed to make people question anything fundamental about the existence of this god or about the efficacy of faith as a means to determine this existence. It is a website designed to make readers feel satisfied with their pre-existing bias.

The 'answer' to the question posed then proceeds with the same assumption in the question and so never really answers it. The first sentence is of course nonsensical and irrelevant because we see physical evidence of the existence of other people, whether or not we have confidence in them, so faith tells us nothing about their existence. This false analogy then continues through the rest of the apologetic.

The final paragraph, truncated for the sake of brevity, stretches the analogy beyond breaking point. We do not need to know everything about a human being to know they exist, however, if we are going to 'have faith' (read: have confidence in) their ability to drive safely we need to know they can drive. We also need to have some idea about how well they do it and if they have any history of good or bad driving. We do not simply 'have faith' in them, nor do we accept their existence without evidence.

No-one not in need of full-time responsible adult supervision would get into the passenger seat of a car and simply have faith that there was a competent driver in the empty driving seat. Acceptance of the existence of a god and assumptions about its qualities, however, is exactly analogous to that piece of insanity. Not only do the faithful have confidence in their god's existence without evidence, they have confidence in its abilities without evidence.

In fact, knowledge of the existence of another human is a necessary condition for any 'faith' we might have in them. The gibberish about knowing the mind

---

[9] (GotQuestions?org)

The Fallacy of Faith

of another person or knowing our own mind has no bearing on our knowledge of their existence. IT seems designed, consciously or otherwise, to avoid the question and excuse that avoidance with lots of platitudes and Bible quotes. The intention here seems to be to reassure the reader that this god agrees with them, not to show them how faith proves it actually exists. When you run out of logic, throw in a Bible quote or two and appeal to authority.

In fact, of course, all these websites do is to start from the assumption that the particular god exists whether the Christian, Jewish or Muslim version, in pretty much the form and with the character the readers require. Faith is simply assumed to be a virtuous and powerful tool for confirming what they already purport to know.

It is probably highly significant that people who believe by faith alone seem to need this constant reassurance. So much of religion seems to be about believers gathering together to reassure one another that a particular god is real and really is as they believe it to be. For most actively religious people, active appears to mean going to a place of worship to join in this collective reassurance, like group therapy. As Dan Barker has pointed out, if scientists needed to gather together weekly to sing songs about how they truly believed in gravity, we could not help but conclude that they actually had some doubt about it.

Faith is not only an inconstant friend to those who rely on it, it is also singularly inept as a means of discovering real-world truth, so is only ever used for matters of religion and never for solving real-world, every-day problems like working out whether it is safe to cross the road, for determining matters like guilt or innocence in courts of law, discovering cures for illnesses and infections, or making financial and planning decisions.

It is quite possible to imagine a devout but scientifically illiterate person concluding that how aeroplanes stay up is probably all to do with God and so we need faith to keep them in the sky. It would be another matter entirely if the cabin crew or maintenance staff believed that. Imagine the pilot trying to land the plane by gradually losing faith.

All religions extol the 'virtues' of faith, or more accurately perhaps, all religious clerics whose livelihood, privileges and power depends on a large body of faithful followers, extol the 'virtues' of faith. What they rarely extol is the virtue of following the evidence wherever it may lead. And yet faith is never anything more than a *post hoc* rationalisation of an evidence-free belief.

It is essentially arrogant. Quite how it differs in any practical sense from the Christian 'sin' of vanity is hard to see. The person claiming to know something by faith alone is essentially claiming the power to determine the truth by belief alone. They are claiming that because they believe it to be true, it must be true. It even amounts to the belief that somehow reality depends on your belief in it; that it only becomes real because you believe in it, almost as though your beliefs create reality.

To hold onto faith-based beliefs on nothing more substantial than that they must be true because you believe them, is to assume that your beliefs cannot possibly be wrong – but that people who have other faith-based beliefs can be.

And yet this arrogance is used to justify belief in a god who allegedly taught humility.

If faith really is such a good way to determine the truth then those who argue for it should be able to explain why it only works for their particular faith. Every different religion has people believing it by faith because they have no evidence, yet clearly they cannot all be right. If faith was really such a great way to determine the truth then people who depend on it, no matter the beliefs of their parents or the culture they were raised in, should arrive at the same truth as those whose parents had different beliefs or who come from a different culture, yet they never do.

Children of Christian parents do not wake up one morning to discover that they have become Muslims just by faith; children of Muslims do not become Shintoists and Shintoists do not become Hindus by faith alone. No-one now becomes a believer in Horus, Apollo, Thor or Mithra by faith. Why not, if faith was once such a great way for the followers of these earlier gods to know they existed and were just as their priests and shamans said?

The evidence of the geographical distribution of different religions is evidence that faith alone is not the determinant of religious belief but is a consequence of it. It is evidence that something other than faith is the cause of religion and that faith is not any basis for determining what is and what is not true.

The Fallacy of Faith

The fact that faith is used by religious people to rationalise their belief in something despite the lack of evidence for it, or even in the face of the evidence against it, can be seen by considering the following questions from the point of view of someone who believes their particular god created the entire Universe and everything within it. The question is, who or what created the evidence you have such little 'faith' in? Why do you need something other than or even in place of this evidence?

This becomes even stranger when asked of those who believe they have a holy book they believe their god created, dictated or inspired which trumps the evidence they also believe it created. There is the assumption somewhere that their creator god created inadequate or even misleading evidence in the physical, scientifically detectable, measurable and verifiable Universe, yet never made a mistake in the holy book.

The only reason to doubt the evidence they believe their god created is because it doesn't equate to what the holy books says. Why this arbitrary decision to go with the holy book and assume it trumps the physical evidence? Did their god deliberately lie in the physical evidence? Do they conclude that it must have lied because they have 'faith' that it only told the truth in a book? A book moreover with a known history of compilation from lots of difference sources, none of which now exist; a book containing known factual and historical errors and contradictions, and in the case of the Bible, evidence of later additions and which is at best a translation of a translation. They have faith in these highly dubious sources and in the one-off honesty of a liar?

The standard excuse, and an excuse that many people who are not convinced by the claim that faith trumps evidence find shockingly dogmatic, is that the holy book is the Word of God and is therefore infallible, whilst evidence is merely a human interpretation and might be wrong. What God says is so; what man says may or may not be so. The circularity of assuming not only the existence of the respective god but that a book is its infallible word for no other reason than that the book contains that claim, then using that assumption as though it were now an established fact, is profoundly dishonest. It is indistinguishable from the claim that facts can exist merely by fiat; that something must be true because it has been declared to be true.

Yet despite this intellectual dishonesty, creationists routinely resort to it to wave aside inconvenient evidence whilst simultaneously claiming to have lots of evidence to support creationism. As is so often the case, evidence is carefully selected for special emphasis or instant dismissal depending on how well it fits the 'faith'. Evidence does not inform faith; rather faith informs the selection of evidence.

So why this cavalier, selective and essentially dishonest attitude towards the physical evidence the faithful believe their god created?

The answer to this conundrum can probably be seen in the accounts of so many former devout Christians who asked themselves these questions and decided they had nothing to fear from going with the evidence wherever it might lead them. Very many of them found it led them away from belief in a god and to acceptance that there is no need for a god in the explanation.

Faith often requires the faithful to compartmentalise their thinking so they can hold two or more mutually exclusive facts, simultaneously. Perhaps the most obvious example of this is the belief in both freewill and the existence of an infallible, omniscient god. The inconsistency of these two beliefs can be seen by asking the simple question, if God knows what you will have for breakfast, can you chose to have something else? An omniscient god would know in advance what your choice will be and will have known it for eternity. Its omniscience will guarantee the infallibility of that knowledge which it will have had since before your birth. So, can you exercise freewill and choose something else, so rendering God fallible, or are you bound by God's omniscience?

Clearly, you cannot do both. Either this omniscient infallible god exists or free will does; not both. Yet the entire Christian and Muslims faiths depend on believing both things simultaneously. If God is not omniscient and infallible then God is not perfect; if God is perfect then we do not have freewill and our actions are pre-ordained by God's infallible omniscience. With no free will we have no responsibility for our actions so nothing for God to forgive and no value in our worship of this god. With no freewill, we have no more responsibility for our actions than the computer I am typing this with is responsible for the words I type. If I make a mistake or get something right why would I punish or reward this computer?

A related inconsistency is the belief, common to most religions, especially the Abrahamic religions, that prophecies are possible. All three Abrahamic

The Fallacy of Faith

religions are supposedly based on revelations through various prophets. But, to prophesy the future, the future must be fixed and unchangeable. Everything in a Universe in which accurate prophecies are possible is a predictable Universe because a prophecy is nothing more than a prediction.

Yet the exercise of freewill (and incidentally, the known to be unpredictable results of chaos) makes the Universe unpredictable. You cannot have freewill in a predictable Universe. To exercise freewill is to make a choice about the future, but, just as with an infallible omniscient god, the future cannot be both predictable and a matter for free choice.

Again, freewill, supposedly a gift from God, is entirely inconsistent with other claims about that god and the Universe it supposedly created. Yet the faithful are able to hold these mutually exclusive beliefs simultaneously and make them central to their entire belief system.

A third example of the faithful being required to hold diametrically views simultaneously is in the supposed need and efficacy of prayer. Given the claims about the infallible, omniscient and omni-benevolent nature of gods, as we have seen above, this must mean that the future is not only known but that that future is maximally good.

We could of course debate, probably endlessly, about what 'maximally good' actually means and what future would have that quality, but this should not be a problem for an omniscient god. Such a good would know exactly what this maximally good future is going to be and, being omni-benevolent and omnipotent, will be ensuring it happens. If not, then what is this god doing exactly?

But then, what is the purpose of prayer? There should be nothing you can tell this god that it does not know already, so the purpose of prayer cannot be to inform this god. Such a god will have ensured that the future is the best possible future, so the purpose of prayer cannot be to persuade it to change its mind. To attempt to do so presupposes that you think this god's plan needs changing to a better one of your own devising.

Why ask gods to prevent or put right wrongs? Does the god who supposedly gave humans our moral codes not know when something is wrong and needs humans to point it out? Does it not know it is happening or does it not know it is wrong? Clearly, asking a god to right a wrong must assume one or the other, or both.

At this point, most Christians, Jews and Muslims will start talking about free will and how God has granted this to mankind. Notwithstanding that I showed above how this is inconsistent with belief in an omniscient, inerrant god, this also implies that, by exercising freewill, humans can override God's plan, so rendering prayer ineffective. If God cannot intervene to prevent the effects of human freewill then he is not omnipotent. If he could intervene but always chooses not to then why ask him to change the future?

Whatever justification, in terms of influencing gods, that prayers might be believed to have, all of them assume that humans can persuade gods that humans know best. Clearly, if gods are as their believers claim, this is nonsensical and supremely arrogant, and relegates gods to mere online mail order catalogues.

And yet almost all religious activity consists of believers gathering together at set places and times to collectively petition gods, though rituals, prayers and songs, to change their minds. Places of worship are even designed to channel prayers and project them upwards to some supposed abode of these gods up in the sky.

To an outsider, this even sounds very much like a blasphemy. How dare humans tell gods that they have got things wrong, are out of touch or do not even know right from wrong?

Yet we find that assumption in the Bible even. There is no doubt in the Bible that God should be prayed to at all times and petitioned to provide 'our daily bread' and forgive us for the wrongs we have done. It even tells us to ask God to 'lead us not into temptation' despite the assurance that "cannot tempteth he any man". (James 1:13)

The Bible is even more explicit that we can change God's mind with prayers. In Mathew 21:21-22 we read:

> *Jesus answered and said unto them, Verily I say unto you, If ye have faith, and doubt not, ye shall not only do this* which is done *to the fig tree, but also if ye shall say unto this mountain, Be thou removed, and be thou*

> *cast into the sea; it shall be done. And all things, whatsoever ye shall ask in prayer, believing, ye shall receive.*

So, whatever you ask for in prayer you will receive, or so the author of Matthew tells us Jesus said. And there's that faith thing too. With enough 'faith' you can literally tell a mountain to do it and it will jump into the sea. Later on we are told that the truly faithful can drink poison and handle venomous snakes without being harmed. (Mark 16:18).

The Qur'an is no less emphatic that Allah answers prayers but requires a few things in return. Never-the-less, Allah will presumably defer to your better judgement and change his perfect plan on request.

> *And when My servants ask you concerning Me, then surely I am very near; I answer the prayer of the supplicant when he calls on Me, so they should answer My call and believe in Me that they MAY walk in the right way.*(Qur'an 2:186).

Faith then is nothing more than an unsatisfactory rationalisation; a psychological strategy to justify irrational beliefs for which, if there were any real evidence, no-one would claim to believe by faith. But it is a strategy which itself requires compartmentalised thinking and coping strategies to be able to hold diametrically opposite beliefs simultaneously.

Depending on faith cannot honestly be described as a virtue. Having faith is not a virtue but a sin. It is the sin of abdication of personal responsibility for objective reasoning and the abandonment of reason in favour of received opinion. Faith puts your mind under the control of those to whom you have handed it because you found that easier than thinking for yourself. If the truth sets you free, faith makes you a prisoner, because faith cannot discover the truth but locks you into received dogma.

What then are the consequences of this faith-based belief, of firmly-held convictions based on nothing more substantial that a personal conviction that you cannot be wrong?

On a personal level, buying into received faith inevitably means buying into someone else's opinions without question, so handing over your independence and responsibility for your own opinions to someone else. The probability is that you do not even know the person whose opinions you are buying in to, because the person or people whose opinions you have bought into will have bought into someone else's faith.

Faith and the abandonment of personal responsibility that goes with it, leads to grotesque abuses in the name of whatever faith is involved. Once people abandon personal responsibility for their beliefs and especially their actions and put that responsibility into the hands of an assumed deity, or more likely the priesthood of this assumed deity, almost anything becomes possible.

Mix in with that the idea that gods define morality and therefore anything gods mandate become morally good by definition, and you get the Srebrenica massacre, the Holocaust, the Rwanda genocide, the Thirty Years War, the Spanish Inquisition, the slave trade, witch burnings, Crusades, the Hamidian massacre, the Noakhali genocide, and many, many more examples of people killing other people because that was what God wanted.

Believing by faith in something they have only the opinions of others to go by, and deferring to the authority of those who claim special insight and knowledge not available to the rest of us, puts the faithful under the control of the unscrupulous and the megalomaniacal. A priesthood which purports to reveal the mind of gods to the faithful is a priesthood which commands the will of the faithful, and yet this entire power-base is nothing more than an illusion. Faith, as we have seen above, is nothing more than imagination and wishful thinking. It has no substance and no basis in reality.

As Christopher Hitchens said, "…the pattern and original of all dictatorship is the surrender of reason to absolutism and the abandonment of critical, objective inquiry."

With this power, a manipulative priesthood can control entire populations. Harnessing this to political power in an unholy alliance in which the rulers support and grant privileges to the priesthood, and the priesthood sanctify and bless the rulers has been the *modus operandum* of despotic dictatorships the world over. When you hear a politician or a priest talk about a nation being a 'Christian country', an 'Islamic country', a 'Hindu nation' or a 'Jewish state', be afraid. What they are boasting about is that they are in charge with the absolute and corrupting power to control and manipulate that belief by faith alone puts into their hands.

The Fallacy of Faith

There was a very good reason why the American Founding Fathers, probably the first revolutionary leaders to truly give to the people the power they had taken on their behalf and to hedge it about with protections against it being usurped by the scheming of priests and corrupt politicians, insisted on building a 'wall of separation' between church and state. Freedom nestles in the freedom to dissent, to disagree; to have beliefs others do not have and be entitled to them as free and equal citizens before the law. A free nation cannot be a Christian, a Jewish or an Islamic nation; a free nation can only be a secular nation.

In his final letter to American atheists shortly before his death, Christopher Hitchens wrote:

> .....*I have found, as the enemy [impending death] becomes more familiar, that all the special pleading for salvation, redemption and supernatural deliverance appears even more hollow and artificial to me than it did before. I hope to help defend and pass on the lessons of this for many years to come, but for now I have found my trust better placed in two things: the skill and principle of advanced medical science, and the comradeship of innumerable friends and family, all of them immune to the false consolations of religion. It is these forces among others which will speed the day when humanity emancipates itself from the mind-forged manacles of servility and superstition. It is our innate solidarity, and not some despotism of the sky, which is the source of our morality and our sense of decency.*
>
> *That essential sense of decency is outraged every day. Our theocratic enemy is in plain view. Protean in form, it extends from the overt menace of nuclear-armed mullahs to the insidious campaigns to have stultifying pseudo-science taught in American schools. But in the past few years, there have been heartening signs of a genuine and spontaneous resistance to this sinister nonsense: a resistance which repudiates the right of bullies and tyrants to make the absurd claim that they have god on their side. To have had a small part in this resistance has been the greatest honor of my lifetime: the pattern and original of all dictatorship is the surrender of reason to absolutism and the abandonment of critical, objective inquiry. The cheap name for this lethal delusion is religion, and*

we must learn new ways of combating it in the public sphere, just as we have learned to free ourselves of it in private.

Our weapons are the ironic mind against the literal; the open mind against the credulous; the courageous pursuit of truth against the fearful and abject forces who would set limits to investigation (and who stupidly claim that we already have all the truth we need). Perhaps above all, we affirm life over the cults of death and human sacrifice and are afraid, not of inevitable death, but rather of a human life that is cramped and distorted by the pathetic need to offer mindless adulation, or the dismal belief that the laws of nature respond to wailings and incantations.

As the heirs of a secular revolution, American atheists have a special responsibility to defend and uphold the Constitution that patrols the boundary between Church and State. This, too, is an honor and a privilege. Believe me when I say that I am present with you, even if not corporeally (and only metaphorically in spirit...) Resolve to build up Mr Jefferson's wall of separation.

And don't keep the faith.[10]

So what has faith done? What are the achievements we can give due credit to 'faith' for?

For sure we can point to some great works, the works of social reformers, the abolitionists and anti-segregationists; the composers of great religious music; the artists of great religious works of art. We can point to the architects and builders of great cathedrals and mosques and the humble little churches containing the work of thousands of unknown and unnamed stone masons, carpenters and artisans, and hold these up as evidence of the power of faith.

But the great social reformers were, almost without exception, rigorously opposed by other people motivated by faith in the same god and equally able to cite relevant texts from the same holy books as the reformers. What both sides in the debate were doing was to try to lend credence to their own pre-existing biases.

---

[10] (Hitchens, Hitchens' address to American Atheists, 2011)

The Fallacy of Faith

Noble though the aims of the reformers were, their motivation came from something outside the holy books which they believed by faith; they simply cherry-picked the parts that agreed with them. The outside influence was, of course, their underlying humanity, their innate sense of right and wrong and maybe the need to have the respect and esteem of their social peers.

A more realistic assessment of many of these great achievements, often regarded as the great achievements of civilisation which set us apart from the 'uncivilised' or more accurately under-developed, people of the world, is that they were the products of fear and anxiety. They came from an overweening need to placate and gain favour with the god who could, on a whim, inflict death and destruction and who, unless entirely satisfied to an almost impossible level of satisfaction, with the devotion to and adoration of him, would inflict an eternity of unimaginable horror.

Of course, the motivation of needing to earn a living at a time when wealth was concentrated in the hands of powerful patrons all keen to demonstrate their own piety, was by no means insignificant. Great works were not done for the love of the work but because they had been commissioned. It is not necessary to be a devout Christian to depict scenes from the Bible as reputedly atheist artists such as Raphael have shown. It is not necessary to be a Christian to write jingles like 'God Bless America' as the secular Jewish atheist, Irving Berlin showed and it was not necessary for atheist Ralph Vaughan-Williams to be a Christian to write hymn tunes.

The supply or works of art, literature, music and architecture today are not diminishing as secularism and atheism grow and religions diminish.

In summary then, we have seen how faith cannot be the path to knowledge or belief because belief must precede faith. We have seen that faith is merely confirmation bias dressed up in fancy clothes to look virtuous when in reality it is the sins of arrogance and indolence. And we have seen that faith is an abdication of personal responsibility and a surrender of personal freedom not to gods but to their priesthood.

We have seen how faith enslaves the mind and can be a corrupting power in the hands of the unscrupulous because it abandons responsibility for personal accountability and provides something to blame. And we have seen how the faithful can be and often are, manipulated and controlled and persuaded to commit atrocities believing them to be the will of gods and how faith places the people under the control of rulers in alliance with priesthoods.

And we have seen that faith achieves nothing that could not be achieved without it.

But the danger of faith is in the permission it gives the faithful and how this permission can be granted to extremists by moderates confirming for them that faith is a respectable, even admirable way to know the minds of gods. We will see the effects of this in the next chapter.

2. The Fallacy of Holy Books.

But does this faith not come from a holy book written by people who knew the truth?

Well, no it does not. It is only through the fallacy of faith that the faithful are able to rationalise this piece of circular reasoning. It takes a pre-existing belief in the sacredness of the holy book to believe it can be evidence of its putative author. The idea that an omnipotent god would write such a convoluted book as the Bible just to get an essential message across to mankind is almost laughable. As Richard Dawkins said:

> *Imagine you are God. You're all-powerful, nothing is beyond you. You're all-loving. So it is really, really important to you that humans are left in no doubt about your existence and your loving nature, and exactly what they need to do in order to get to heaven and avoid eternity in the fires of hell. It's really important to you to get that across. So what do you do?*
>
> *Well, if you're Jehovah, apparently this is what you do. You talk in riddles. You tell stories which on the surface have a different message from the one you apparently want us to understand. You expect us to hear X, and instinctively understand that it needs to be interpreted in the light of Y, which you happen to have said in the course of a completely different story 500-1,000 years earlier.*
>
> *Instead of speaking directly into our heads – which God has presumed the capability of doing so – simply, clearly and straightforwardly in terms which the particular individual being addressed will immediately understand and respond to positively – you steep your messages in symbols, in metaphors. In fact, you choose to convey the most important message in the history of creation in code, as if you aspired to be Umberto Eco or Dan Brown.*
>
> *Anyone would think your top priority was to keep generation after generation after generation of theologians in meaningless employment,*

rather than communicate an urgent life-or-death message to the creatures you love more than any other. [11]

You could add too that this message is so important for the whole of mankind that you wait some 250,000 years after you have created humans before telling anyone. Then you select an obscure Middle Eastern tribe to tell it too in such a way that it is going to take another 3-4,000 years before everyone even hears about it, let alone actually reads it. Meanwhile, all those who have not heard or understood the message are either getting a free pass into Heaven anyway, so do not need to hear the message, or are going straight to Hell because of your incompetence. Yes, that all seems very sensible; and such a loving thing to do!

Despite the assertions of Bible literalists who themselves depend on nothing but the received opinions of others, there is no evidence that any of the Bible was written by actual eye-witnesses to the events described any more so than the Greek and Roman myths, the Arthurian legends or the legends of Irish heroic figures like Niall of the Nine Hostages or Cú Chulainn were written by eye-witnesses.

There is evidence too that the authors of much of the Bible often did not know the history of the times in which they set their stories. For example, as was pointed out by Thomas Paine in *The Age of Reason*, in Genesis 14:14 we are told:

> *And when Abram heard that his brother was taken captive, he armed his trained servants, born in his own house, three hundred and eighteen, and **pursued them unto Dan**.*

And yet in Judges 18:27-29 we are told:

> *And they took the things which Micah had made, and the priest which he had, and came to Laish, to a people that were at quiet and secure: and they smote them with the edge of the sword, and burnt the city with fire. And there was no deliverer, because it was far from Zidon, and they had no business with any man; and it was in the valley that lies by Bethrehob. And they built a city, and dwelled therein. **And they called the name of the city Dan, after the name of Dan their father, who was born unto Israel: howbeit the name of the city was Laish at the first.***

---

[11] (Freedom From Religion Foundation, National Convention Address, 2012)

Whoever wrote that part of the Genesis story did not know that Dan was called Laish at the time in which his story was set. This mistake places the authorship of at least this part of Genesis sometime after the death of King Solomon.

Similarly, in Genesis 37:25 we have a story including camels and a spice trade with Egypt:

> *And they sat down to eat bread: and they lifted up their eyes and looked, and, behold, a company of Ishmeelites came from Gilead with their camels bearing spicery and balm and myrrh, going to carry it down to Egypt.*

However, as the archaeologists, Israel Finkelstein and Neil Asher Silberman of Tel Aviv University point out in *The Bible Unearthed: Archaeology's New Vision of Ancient Israel and the Origin of Sacred Texts*, camels were not used as beasts of burden before about 1000 BCE and the spice trade with Egypt was not established until much later, at the time of the Assyrian Empire:

> *Indeed, excavations at the site of Tell Jemmeh in the southern coastal plain of Israel – a particularly important entrepôt on the main caravan route between Arabia and the Mediterranean – revealed a dramatic increase in the number of camel bones in the seventh century. The bones were almost exclusively of mature animals, suggesting that they were from traveling beasts of burden, not from locally raised herds (among which the bones of young animals would also be found). Indeed, precisely at this time, Assyrian sources describe camels being used as pack animals in caravans. It was only then that camels became a common enough feature of the landscape to be included as an incidental detail in a literary narrative.*[12]

The story teller has simply assumed things at the time in which he set his story were more or less the same as the time he lived in. Had this story been written by an eye-witness there would have been no camels, no trading caravan and no spice trade for him or her to witness.

There are other similar mistakes in the Old Testament stories that give away the fact that it was written later and by people who did not know the history, geography and politics of the time they were writing about. For example,

---

[12] (Finkestein & Silberman, 2002)

Exodus has the Israelites escaping from Egypt and Pharaoh's army by crossing the Red Sea into Sinai. However, Sinai was then as now part of Egypt and would have been patrolled by Egyptian troops. There is no possibility that some three million people could wander about in part of Egypt without the Pharaoh being aware of them, especially since the story says that they followed a pillar of smoke by day and a pillar of flame by night – not the best way to hide.

We have the strange story in Genesis 26 that tells of a famine and Isaac going to Gerar to see Abimelech, king of the Philistines. The author was apparently unaware that the Philistines did not become established along the coastal plain of Canaan until after 1200 BCE and never reached their peak of power until the eleventh and tenth centuries BCE. Moreover, Gerar was a small, insignificant village even in the early phase of the Philistine domination and did not become a large fortified stronghold until the Assyrian administration in the eighth and seventh centuries BCE. The author had simply assumed that a familiar landmark had always been there and was vaguely aware that the Philistines had once been a power in the land.[13]

It is not just in the Old Testament that we find these errors of ignorance either. Perhaps the most famous example in the New Testament is the account in Acts of the sudden conversion of Saul of Tarsus, the alleged Jewish hunter and persecutor of Christians, into the Christian evangelist Paul, who spread Christianity over much of the Eastern Mediterranean world. Apart from being an almost textbook description of an hallucination caused by the well-documented neurophysiological condition, temporal lobe epilepsy, the story contains a major geo-historical error.

According to the Bible, Saul was going to Damascus with a letter of authorisation from the Jewish Temple Authorities in Jerusalem to arrest Christian 'heretics' and bring them back to Jerusalem for trial. This writ or letter and the purpose for which Saul was on 'the road to Damascus' when this life-changing event allegedly occurred, are mentioned several times (Acts 9:1-3, 9:13-14, 22:4-5, 26:10-12). One might be tempted to think that the need to repeat it so often betrays a certain anxiety on the part of the author.

---

[13] (Finkestein & Silberman, 2002)

The Fallacy of Holy Books

In the Roman Empire at that time the custom was that local religious laws were the responsibility of the local religious authorities in that province. The Roman governor merely had an oversight in local matters and would have been the final arbiter in the case of disputes but generally had a hands-off approach. There are echoes of this in the story of the trial of Jesus where the Roman Governor decides there has been no offence in Roman law but hands Jesus over to the religious authorities for trial under religious law and 'washes his hands' of the affair.

So, the Temple Authorities in Jerusalem would have been responsible for religious matters throughout the province and would have had powers in the province to enforce laws against blasphemy, working on the Sabbath, etc.

The problem is that Jerusalem was in the Roman province of Judea, but Damascus was in the province of Phoenicia, far to the north, and with no history of Judaism and no connection with the Temple in Jerusalem. There was no Roman crime of Judaic heresy at any time or place in the Roman Empire and the religious writ of any provincial sectarian authority would only run in that province.

A writ from the Jewish Temple Authorities in Jerusalem would have had no validity in Damascus either in around 40-50 CE, when this story is supposedly set, or at any time in history.

Until it became officially Christian and began suppressing other religions, the Roman Empire was, like the Greek and Egyptian Empires, polytheistic and tolerant of other religions. The very idea of religious intolerance is a relatively modern, monotheist theocratic idea. Any neo-Christian Jewish 'heretics' in Damascus would have enjoyed the protection of Rome; it would have been any would-be kidnappers who would have had something to fear. Had there been such a Roman crime of being a heretical Jew, the Christians in Damascus would have been arrested by Roman soldiers and tried by the Roman governor there, not in Judea.

Very clearly, whoever wrote Acts invented at least this part of the Paul myth; probably to give it additional credence and appeal to the early Christians it was being written for. Just like modern Christians and Muslims, they would have wanted to think their founders were persecuted, but the author was unaware of the geography of the Middle-East and the limits of legal powers of some assumed Jerusalem Temple Authority. The purpose of making their founders the victim of Jewish persecution and conspiracy was almost certainly to distinguish Paul's particular Gentile sect from other more Jewish messianic and competing ones. There is evidence that this Pauline sect was trying to broaden its appeal to non-Jews by, for example, the lifting of the requirement to be circumcised – probably a major inhibition when trying to recruit European adults with no tradition of infant circumcision.

From these examples we can see several instances of the Bible clearly **not** being the work of eye-witnesses. Indeed, there are probably very few serious Bible scholars who would argue anything other than that much of the Bible was written long after the events described in it. In the case of the Old Testament, much of it appears to have been written in around 500-600 BCE while the New Testament was written between about 100 and 300 CE.

Significantly, there are no instances of the word 'Jesus' used to describe a messiah, religious leader of god in any written record or monumental inscription. The word is never used in the entire first century of the supposed Christian era! So, if as many Christians will claim, they get their faith from the Bible, they actually get their faith from people who, like them, got their faith from someone else.

We do not know who actually wrote most of the Bible. According to biblical scholars, some of Paul's letters may have been written by him though several almost certainly were not, and none of the Gospels were written by the people later credited with writing them. So to take the Bible on faith is to accept the word of strangers who did not witness what they describe and who got it themselves from other strangers. Some of these strangers even pretended to be someone they were not.

Given that what might seem to be Bible-based faith is actually unquestioning faith in the tales of strangers, try this test:

Imagine you are standing at your front door and someone you have never met before comes along and tells you that he has just seen a man walking on water, turning water into wine, curing cripples and feeding thousands with a few morsels of food. Would you simply believe him by faith and let his story change your whole life, or would you at least want evidence of his claims, even if you did not entire dismiss the credibility of them?

Which of the miracles supposedly performed by Jesus, or the events associated with his life and death, or the accounts of Muhammad flying around on a winged horse would you believe if a stranger told you he had seen them performed by someone just a few days ago? How much less believable would you find these stories if this stranger told you he had not actually seen these things himself but had heard about someone who had?

How does that differ because someone once wrote these claims down? How did a stranger writing it down turn an unbelievable story with no evidence, into a story you can believe by faith with unquestioning confidence and allow to determine your life?

The answer of course is that it does not. People who imagine they believe by faith because the Bible convinced them are delusional. They believe because a stranger told them they should and someone sold them the idea that this was a virtuous thing to do. Almost certainly, in fact, they have simply accepted the cultural beliefs their parents and peers had and, to go along with cultural pressure and expectation, have pretended to know things they do not know.

Try this test on an assortment of friends, either atheist or followers of other religions, including Christianity and Islam. First read this traditional story of Muhammad's 'Night Journey':

> ...the Night Journey took place ten years after Muhammad became a prophet, during the 7th century. Muhammad had been in his home city of Mecca, at his cousin's home ... Afterwards, Prophet Muhammad went to the [Sacred Mosque in Mecca].While he was resting at the Kaaba, the angel Jibril (Gabriel) appeared to him followed by Buraq [a winged horse-like creature from Arabic mythology, often depicted with a human face]. Muhammad mounted Buraq, and in the company of Gabriel, they travelled to the "farthest mosque" [traditionally believed to be the Al-Aqsa Mosque on the Temple Mount] in Jerusalem. At this location, he dismounted from Buraq, prayed, and mounted Buraq, who took him to the various heavens, to meet first the earlier prophets and then Allah. God instructed Muhammad to tell his followers that they were to offer prayers fifty times a day. At the urging of Moses (Musa), Muhammad returns to God and eventually reduces it to ten times, and then five times a day as this was the destiny of Muhammad and his people. Buraq then transported Muhammad back to Mecca. [14]

Now give your friends three choices about this story. In their opinion, is this:

1. An account of a hallucination?
2. Pure fiction?
3. True?

You can almost guarantee that only the Muslims will agree that this is a true story. Almost all others will select one of the other two choices.

The conclusion can only be then that this story and other similar stories appearing in the holy books are not themselves the reason for their believers' faith. These stories are not the cause of faith but rather pre-existing faith determines our opinion of them. In many if not most cases, the stories are so unlikely that few but the faithful will simply accept them as true, least of all unquestionably true.

Does anyone actually believe the stories from Greek mythology where gods spoke to people and commanded storms and earthquakes; where obtaining fleeces made of pure gold were the object of epic voyages under the protection of a goddess who spoke; where giants stood on mountaintops to hold the sky up or carried Earth on their shoulders?

The Greek myths make fascinating reading if for no other reason than that they give us a glimpse of how Bronze Age people saw the world as they spread out and explored the Aegean, the Mediterranean, the Black Sea and beyond. But like the Bronze Age authors of the Hebrew myths, this was a magical, demon-haunted world of giants and mythical beasts, of sea monsters and strange humanoid races living on remote islands. But no one now takes these myths seriously.

Does anyone believe the following creation story from Norse Mythology is literally true?

> *The first world to exist was Muspell, a place of light and heat whose flames are so hot that those who are not native to that land cannot endure it. Surt sits at Muspell's border, guarding the land with a flaming sword. At the end of the world he will vanquish all the gods and burn the whole world with fire.*

---

[14] (Wikipedia, 2016)

The Fallacy of Holy Books

Beyond Muspell lay the great and yawning void named Ginnungagap, and beyond Ginnungagap lay the dark, cold realm of Niflheim. Ice, frost, wind, rain and heavy cold emanated from Niflheim, meeting in Ginnungagap the soft air, heat, light, and soft air from Muspell.

Where heat and cold met appeared thawing drops, and this running fluid grew into a giant frost ogre named Ymir.

Ymir slept, falling into a sweat. Under his left arm there grew a man and a woman. And one of his legs begot a son with the other. This was the beginning of the frost ogres.

Thawing frost then became a cow called Audhumla. Four rivers of milk ran from her teats, and she fed Ymir.

The cow licked salty ice blocks. After one day of licking, she freed a man's hair from the ice. After two days, his head appeared. On the third day the whole man was there. His name was Buri, and he was tall, strong, and handsome. Buri begot a son named Bor, and Bor married Bestla, the daughter of a giant.

Bor and Bestla had three sons: Odin was the first, Vili the second, and Vé the third. It is believed that Odin, in association with his brothers, is the ruler of heaven and earth. He is the greatest and most famous of all men.

Odin, Vili, and Vé killed the giant Ymir. When Ymir fell, there issued from his wounds such a flood of blood, that all the frost ogres were drowned, except for the giant Bergelmir who escaped with his wife by climbing onto a lur [a hollowed-out tree trunk that could serve either as a boat or a coffin]. From them spring the families of frost ogres.

The sons of Bor then carried Ymir to the middle of Ginnungagap and made the world from him. From his blood they made the sea and the lakes; from his flesh the earth; from his hair the trees; and from his bones the mountains. They made rocks and pebbles from his teeth and jaws and those bones that were broken.

Maggots appeared in Ymir's flesh and came to life. By the decree of the gods they acquired human understanding and the appearance of men, although they lived in the earth and in rocks.

> *From Ymir's skull the sons of Bor made the sky and set it over the earth with its four sides. Under each corner they put a dwarf, whose names are East, West, North, and South. The sons of Bor flung Ymir's brains into the air, and they became the clouds. Then they took the sparks and burning embers that were flying about after they had been blown out of Muspell, and placed them in the midst of Ginnungagap to give light to heaven above and earth beneath. To the stars they gave appointed places and paths. The earth was surrounded by a deep sea. The sons of Bor gave lands near the sea to the families of giants for their settlements.*
>
> *To protect themselves from the hostile giants, the sons of Bor built for themselves an inland stronghold, using Ymir's eyebrows. This stronghold they named Midgard.*
>
> *While walking along the sea shore the sons of Bor found two trees, and from them they created a man and a woman. Odin gave the man and the woman spirit and life. Vili gave them understanding and the power of movement. Vé gave them clothing and names. The man was named Ask [Ash] and the woman Embla [Elm]. From Ask and Embla have sprung the races of men who lived in Midgard.*[15]

I doubt that anyone now believes that this is a literal description of how the world was created, and yet it is no more fantastical than the myth incorporated into the early part of the Jewish Pentateuch that was later incorporated in the official holy book of Christianity, the Bible, and patronisingly called the 'Old Testament'.

But what is there in this story that would make it less credible than the Canaanite and Mesopotamian myths that became mixed up to form the Hebrew creation myth common to Islam, Judaism and Christianity? The only difference is that parents and authority figures do not tell children that this story is literally true and they'll upset a god if they doubt it. In other words, children are not taught to have faith in the truth of books with this story in it.

We know that the biblical flood myth had its origins in an earlier Mesopotamian myth recorded in the Epic of Gilgamesh, and was probably incorporated into Hebrew origin myths during the 'Babylonian Captivity'. We

---

[15] (McLaughlin, 2012)

know that the story is mythical for the simple reason that it is inconceivable that, if all people all over the world share this common origin just a few thousand years ago, that everyone not influenced later by Christianity would have forgotten about it almost completely.

To accept that the Noahcian myth is historical fact we would have to accept that everyone else not only forgot all about Noah, including his name, even though he was the founder and saviour of the human race and our common ancestor, but they forgot all about the god who destroyed all life and who spoke to our common ancestors who witnessed this awesome power.

Yet not a single non-Abrahamic culture even remembered this god and, apparently, invented all manner of false gods in its place with false origin myths, false tales of what these gods did. They then wrote entirely new (and fictional) holy books themselves that contained nothing of this god or the flood he destroyed all living things with.

Bible literalists insist that this flood happened about 4000 years ago, in other words in about 2000 BCE, yet there is conclusive archaeological evidence that Egypt had a well-developed religion, complete with priesthoods, temples, inscriptions, ritual burials monuments, statues and other artefacts by 3000 BCE and that this continued unbroken until Alexander the Great overthrew the native rulers.

There is not a single record in this detailed history of a global flood and repopulation by newcomers. The religion of Egypt in 1000 BCE was clearly a derivative of that in 3000 BCE and had no relationship to the Hebrew cult of Yahweh.

The same case can be made for China and India where there is a continuous and unbroken history of civilisation and development of religions not derived from Yahwehism but from earlier, native religions. In the case of China there is a clear and unbroken record of the development of written Chinese going way back before the supposed flood. Why would newcomers moving in from the Middle-East to a land now devoid of human life, adopt the local Chinese script and religion when there would have been no survivors to teach it to them?

The tale of the Tower of Babel is an equally implausible tale from Hebrew mythology which seeks to explain why there are so many different languages in the world and yet, whilst it might have satisfied parochial Late Bronze Age Canaanite hill farmers, simply does not make any sense given what we know today of the origin, evolution and distribution of languages.

This part of the Bible also contains one of the more glaring contradictions. We are told after the Ark story, that Noah's sons, Shem, Ham and Japheth, each had several sons who founded in their turn all the nations of Earth, each with their own tongue.

> *Now these are the generations of the sons of Noah, Shem, Ham, and Japheth: and unto them were sons born after the flood...*
>
> *By these were the isles of the Gentiles divided in their lands; every one after his tongue, after their families, in their nations...*
>
> *These are the sons of Ham, after their families, after their tongues, in their countries, and in their nations...*
>
> *These are the sons of Shem, after their families, after their tongues, in their lands, after their nations.*
>
> *These are the families of the sons of Noah, after their generations, in their nations: and by these were the nations divided in the earth after the flood.* (Genesis 10)

That is about six generations or so, by which time all those nations had been populated from just three men! Note how these nations had their own tongues (not tongue, singular; tongues, plural). So, that's the Bible's first attempt at explaining why there are different languages.

Now turn the page, and what do we find?

> *And the whole earth was of one language, and of one speech.* (Genesis 11:1)

Whoever wrote that had not read the previous story about how everyone is descended from Noah's sons and spoke lots of different languages.

And in six generations starting from just three men and their wives, there was a sufficiently large population to undertake a major construction project, complete with all the support needed to maintain a large number of builders, apparently. This was in the days when Heaven was just above the sky directly about the Middle-East, of course...

And yet, to believe these stories, we have to buy into the belief that, although every other human group forgot them, the Hebrews remembered them in absolute word-perfect detail. Why would a god who wanted people to learn lessons from these supposed events, arrange it so that only one small tribe of Middle-Eastern hill farmers remembered them?

Anything more than the most superficial reading of the Bible readily yields other clues that it was not written by eye-witnesses to the events in it and in several instances there was not even any pretence of being an eye-witness account. Very many of the stories were clearly written as retrospective 'histories' or accounts of current beliefs and some considerable time afterwards. Betraying the compiled nature of the Bible, there are often several contradictory attempts to describe the same event.

For example, we frequently find the phrase 'unto this day' or something similar, showing that there has been a considerable lapse of time between the event and the telling of it. There is no pretence of contemporaneousness and every indication of retrospection.

In Deuteronomy, which is traditionally believed to have been written by Moses along with the rest of the Pentateuch, on no better evidence than that the Jewish historian, Flavius Josephus said so in his *Antiquities of the Jews,* we find:

> *So Moses the servant of the* LORD *died there in the land of Moab, according to the word of the* LORD*. And he buried him in a valley in the land of Moab, over against Beth-peor; but no man knoweth of his sepulchre* **unto this day**. (Deuteronomy 34:5-6).

And Moses was supposedly alone with God at the time. Not only do we have to believe that Moses wrote about his own death and burial, but, by using the phrase, 'unto this day', he was telling us he wrote it some considerable time later. Very clearly, the author of this part of Deuteronomy was neither pretending to be Moses, nor to be an eye-witness. He was telling a tale.

And yet Deuteronomy is supposedly a first-hand account of how God gave the Laws to Moses and is the source of centuries of persecution of homosexuals amongst others, despite this glaring evidence that it was no such thing and probably was never intended to be taken as such.

This verse also tells us this is a story, not an eye-witness account in another way. If 'no man knoweth' how did the author know? Are we to believe the author when he says himself he does not know what he is implicitly claiming to know? The only way to resolve this paradox is to accept that the author was writing a story. He knew what happened in the same way that J. K. Rowling knew Harry Potter's secret thoughts or what he said to Hermione when they were alone.

This problem occurs in the New Testament too, in the so-called Gospels. For example, of the women who supposedly found Jesus' tomb to be empty, we find in Mark 16:8:

> *And they went out quickly, and fled from the sepulchre; for they trembled and were amazed:* **neither said they any thing to any man**; *for they were afraid.*

And yet the author of Mark somehow knew about it. What we have in Mark is an account that was never intended to be taken as an eye-witness account but a story. It is fine to write in fiction, or an embroidered account of a historical event padded out with fiction for effect, but an account in which the author himself admits he is claiming to be true something he could not know, cannot be taken as either infallible or even reliable.

It cannot be a source of faith because it is clearly fiction.

The same problem arises in one of Christianity's favourite passages in the New Testament in the story of the 'woman taken in adultery' (John 8:7-11):

> *So when they continued asking him, he lifted up himself, and said unto them, He that is without sin among you, let him first cast a stone at her. And again he stooped down, and wrote on the ground.*

> *And they which heard it, being convicted by their own conscience, went out one by one, beginning at the eldest, even unto the last: and* ***Jesus was left alone, and the woman standing in the midst.***

The Fallacy of Holy Books

*When Jesus had lifted up himself, **and saw none but the woman**, he said unto her, Woman, where are those thine accusers? hath no man condemned thee? She said, No man, Lord. And Jesus said unto her, Neither do I condemn thee: go, and sin no more.*

There were no eye-witnesses to this event, yet the author of John knew exactly what was said!

This passage is widely believed by Bible scholars to have been a later interpolation and does not appear in earlier copies yet it forms the basis both of claims that Jesus somehow did away with the old Laws of Moses and introduced new ones.

The problem of it being dismissed as an interpolation in a source of absolute truths is not the only problem for the faithful in this passage. Remember, the Bible is supposedly about an inerrant god and Jesus is supposed to be a sin-free manifestation of that god, yet here, in effect, not only is Jesus saying God's Laws are wrong and adulterous women should not be condemned, but there are other problems hidden away there too.

If all human beings are born sinners and so need to be saved from sin, how can these laws be enforced if the enforcers need to be free from sin? Did Jesus not think that one through, or was it the author of John who did not understand the implications of his tale? Or was it some later interpolator who just did not think it through well enough?

And what of 'sin-free' Jesus? According to his 'new rule' he should have cast the first stone, should he not? Why did the earthly manifestation of God not follow God's instructions? Had adultery been decriminalised for a day or did Jesus think God's laws are unjust?

Clearly, these few verses in John raise all sorts of insurmountable issues and obstacles for anyone making a serious case for the Bible being able to be taken as a reliable source of truth and consisting of literal truth as related by eye-witnesses, but even if that story is dismissed as an interpolation there are other indications in the New Testament that the authors did not fully accept the Old Testament as the word of a perfect and inerrant god who defines morality and justice. Take this passage

> *Now the birth of Jesus Christ was on this wise: When as his mother Mary was espoused to Joseph, before they came together, she was found with child of the Holy Ghost. Then Joseph her husband,* **being a just man, and not willing to make her a public example***, was minded to put her away privily. But while he thought on these things, behold, the angel of the Lord appeared unto him in a dream, saying, Joseph, thou son of David, fear not to take unto thee Mary thy wife: for that which is conceived in her is of the Holy Ghost.* [My emphasis.] (Matthew 1:18-20)

The Old Testament is uncompromising in its insistence, according to the laws supposedly given by God to Moses, that adulterous women should be publicly shamed and stoned to death (Deuteronomy 22:18-22), yet Joseph, 'being a just man' decides not to comply with God's Law! Clearly, the author of Matthew believed the public shaming and stoning of adulterous women would be unjust.

It gets even worse for those trying to sell the Bible as a reliable account and the basis for living one's life when one examines the different and contradictory account of the alleged crucifixion and resurrection of Jesus. For a book in which this is supposedly the central part of the Christian story and the entire basis of the faith, these accounts are irredeemably contradictory and clearly as fictional as the account of the death and burial of Moses in Deuteronomy.

As Thomas Paine said in *The Age of Reason*:

> *I lay it down as a position which cannot be controverted, first, that the agreement of all the parts of a story does not prove that story to be true, because the parts may agree and the whole may be false; secondly, that the disagreement of the parts of a story proves the whole cannot be true.*

A great deal has been written about these contradictions and the *Easter Challenge* which Dan Barker issued in his book, *Godless: How an Evangelical Preacher Became One of America's Leading Atheists*[16]. Briefly, the challenge is to take all the different accounts of the discovery of the empty tomb and turn it into a single narrative that covers all the things claimed. To date, I have never seen a sensible answer to this challenge that does not involve absurdities like time travel or two mutually exclusive claims both being simultaneously true.

---

[16] (Barker, Godles: How an Evangelical Preacher Became on of America's Leading Atheists, 2009)

The Fallacy of Holy Books

For example, the tomb cannot have both been open (Mark 16:4, Luke 24:2, John 20:1) and closed (Matthew 28:2) when the women approached it; the women cannot have both told people about what they saw (Matthew 28:8, Luke 24:9, John 20:18) and not told anyone (Mark 16:8).

To make matters worse, Paul (1 Corinthians 15:5) relates how Jesus first appeared to Cephas (Peter) then to 'the 12', yet other narratives have Judas dead by now so there were not 12 at that point. Bible scholars believe a great deal of the writing attributed to Paul actually predates the Gospels so this may well have been written before Judas had been demonised and portrayed as the traitor of the cause.

This piece of what can only be described as poor editorial control gives us a clue to what was going on as the Jesus myth grew and diversified as different sects vied for members. There are a few scraps of an early 'Gospel of Judas' which was excluded from the Bible by the Council of Nicaea, which strongly suggests that Judas could have been the leader of one such sect and that the contradictory accounts of his betrayal and death were attempts to discredit him – pieces of political propaganda intended to sow distrust and dissent.

First Matthew's version:

> *When the morning was come, all the chief priests and elders of the people took counsel against Jesus to put him to death: And when they had bound him, they led him away, and delivered him to Pontius Pilate the governor.*
>
> *Then Judas, which had betrayed him, when he saw that he was condemned, repented himself, and brought again the thirty pieces of silver to the chief priests and elders, Saying, I have sinned in that I have betrayed the innocent blood. And they said, What is that to us? see thou to that. And he cast down the pieces of silver in the temple, and departed, and went and hanged himself.*
>
> *And the chief priests took the silver pieces, and said, It is not lawful for to put them into the treasury, because it is the price of blood. And they took counsel, and bought with them the potter's field, to bury strangers in. Wherefore that field was called, The field of blood, unto this day.*
> (Matthew 27:1-8)

So, Judas regrets what he has done, confesses and asks for forgiveness – not that that means much apparently – gives the money back and kills himself. The priests then use the money to buy a plot of land to bury strangers in and it gets called the Field of Blood because it was bought with blood money. Incidentally, note that 'unto this day' phrase.

When we get to Luke's account however, something really strange has entered the tale:

> *Then entered Satan into Judas surnamed Iscariot, being of the number of the twelve. And he went his way, and communed with the chief priests and captains, how he might betray him unto them.*
>
> *And they were glad, and covenanted to give him money. And he promised, and sought opportunity to betray him unto them in the absence of the multitude.* (Luke 22:3-6)

Curious indeed! Remember, according to the Christian narrative, Jesus was sent by God specifically to be sacrificed because 'He so loved the world'. The crucifixion was all part of God's plan to save mankind so anything or anyone who helped this happen was doing what God intended, were they not?

But here we suddenly have Satan helping to ensure God's plan to save mankind worked and using Judas to do it through! Why would Satan do that? Someone has lost the plot completely here. The point of the story has been abandoned or forgotten; the objective now is to blacken Judas's name at all costs.

In fact, it is Judas' 'betrayal' that actually made the plan come together, if you buy into the claim that this was all part of God's plan. But if it was not God's plan then the whole crucifixion thing becomes meaningless and the basis of Christianity evaporates! But that's not the main point here.

Neither John nor Luke, like Mark before them, has anything more to say about Judas. Judas is a traitor and that's enough. John bends over backwards, almost obsessively, to refer to Judas's treachery every time he mentions his name, but we learn nothing more of his fate.

It is not till we get to Acts that we learn more. Apparently, the author of Acts had a source outside the alleged 'eye-witness testimonies' of the four Apostles. Bear in mind what Matthew told us above.

The Fallacy of Holy Books

And in those days Peter stood up in the midst of the disciples, and said, (the number of names together were about an hundred and twenty,) Men and brethren, this scripture must needs have been fulfilled, which the Holy Ghost by the mouth of David spake before concerning Judas, which was guide to them that took Jesus. For he was numbered with us, and had obtained part of this ministry.

Now this man purchased a field with the reward of iniquity; and falling headlong, he burst asunder in the midst, and all his bowels gushed out. And it was known unto all the dwellers at Jerusalem; insomuch as that field is called in their proper tongue, Aceldama, that is to say, The field of blood. (Acts 1:16-19).

Did you spot the differences?

In this version, Judas buys the field, not the chief priests. There is no repentance; no returning the money and no meeting of the chief priests to decide what to do with it. Judas does not hang himself but falls headlong and 'bursts asunder' and his bowels gush out. The field is now called the Field of Blood because of Judas's blood spilt on it, not because the priests bought it with blood money. In fact, the only thing in common between these two tales is the name of Judas, where the money came from and the name of the field.

Both these stories cannot possibly be right. Either Judas or the priests bought the field, not both. Either Judas returned the money or he bought a field with it, not both. Either Judas hanged himself or he fell headlong and burst asunder, not both. And either the field is called the Field of Blood because of Judas's blood spilled on it or because it was bought with blood money by the priests, not both

A narrative so essential to Christianity is hopelessly garbled and contradictory in the Bible, probably because there were several different attempts to write better and more convincing 'histories' for nascent Christian sects, and because of early competition and schisms

The tale has already become a tool for political propagandising even before someone decided to gather together various books, 'testimonies', statements of belief and letters, edit them, and put them together in a book they were never intended to be put together in. To make matters worse, they then presented this badly edited compilation as the inerrant, infallible word of God.

The disagreement of the parts of a story proves the whole cannot be true!

So, the Bible fails badly as a reliable source in which anyone can reasonably have any confidence or faith, either as a historical account or a source of knowledge about the will of the god described in it. Indeed, it is so hopelessly muddled and contradictory and, as we will see later, so full of primitive notions of what the Universe is really like, that it cannot possibly have been written or inspired nor even in any way endorsed by the god described in it unless it was wilfully deceiving us. That alone should render it no more reliable than any other compilation of myths and documents.

Indeed, the Complete Works of Shakespeare, the Collected Novels of Charles Dickens, the poetry of Robert Frost or Robert Burns, and even the humorous writings of Terry Pratchett, probably contain more understanding of the human condition; more humanity and more innate morality than the Bible with its casual misogyny, brutal savagery, endorsement of slavery, racism, genocide and infanticide, and blatant threats in lieu of rational arguments and civilised discourse.

Is the Qur'an then any better? Is it more reliable as a source of knowledge of 'the will of Allah' and a source of confidence in what Allah will or won't do?

Ask any Muslim what the Qur'an is and who wrote it, and you'll be told almost without exception, that it is Allah's word as revealed in divine revelations to Muhammad through Allah's messenger, the Archangel Gabriel (Jibril). You will be told that it is eternal and unchanging and is an exact replica of one that Allah has in Heaven.

You might even be given the simplistic answer that Muhammad literally wrote it. This only happened once, apparently. Although this revelation was spread over some twenty-three years, there is no record of Allah revealing the same thing several times, least of all the entire Qur'an. This is an important point to bear in mind – there was only one revelation, albeit spread over several years.

You'll most likely be told that the proof that the Qur'an is Allah's revealed word is the fact that Muhammad was illiterate and yet was able to write the

Qur'an in perfect classical Arabic; that Allah literally guided his hand. This is, of course, the 'lie to children' version. Very few Quranic scholars believe Muhammad literally picked up a pen or a quill and wrote the Qur'an as dictated by a divine messenger.

The accepted version amongst Islamic scholars is that Muhammad never actually wrote anything of the Qur'an. Instead, the words came to him as 'revelations' over a period of some twenty-three years and were taught to his followers as oral traditions, only being written down after his death, on the instructions of the first caliph, Abu Bakr when some of those who had memorised the Qur'an were killed in a battle and he realised there was a grave risk of it being lost altogether if it remained an oral tradition.

Tradition has it that. Zayd ibn Thabit was the person charged with collecting the Qur'an together because "he used to write the Divine Inspiration for Allah's Apostle". The actual writing was done by a group of scribes working under Zayd. The final manuscript remained with Abu Bakr until he died. However, the document was not written from memory but was collected together from various pieces of writing on parchment, palm-leaves and thin stones, and from people who knew it by heart. Zayd was the final arbiter on what should and what should not be included. After Abu Bakr died, Hafsa bint Umar, Muhammad's widow, was entrusted with the manuscript.

So this manuscript is the actual first Qur'an according to this tradition. Note that a great deal has been recorded concerning who compiled it and how. Nowhere in that process though did Muhammad have any say in this nor did he approve the final document, having been dead for some years.

The orthodoxy of this first approved copy was further reinforced when in about 650, the third Caliph Uthman ibn Affan ordered a committee headed by Zayd to use Abu Bakr's copy and prepare a standard copy of the Qur'an, to resolve slight differences that were emerging in the Levant, Iran and North Africa as Islam expanded. It is not clear why a committee was needed because, if Zayd had done his work correctly, the copy entrusted to Hafsa bint Umar should have been sufficient anyway, but within twenty years of Muhammad's death, the Qur'an was standardised by a committee and other versions are believed to have been destroyed.

The standard Qur'an was actually compiled and written down not by Muhammad but by a committee headed up by Zayd ibn Thabit, an associate of Muhammad! This is a long way from being divinely revealed fully formed and perfect, and actually not very far removed from the way the Bible was compiled.

This of course destroys the argument that the fact that an illiterate man suddenly 'wrote' the Qur'an is proof that it came from Allah, but, like other religions, Islam seems capable of believing two or more mutually incompatible things simultaneously. But, whichever version you prefer, both end up with a supposed single original Qur'an. The belief is that this was then used as the master copy from which other copies were made, initially as personal copies for important figures.

Moreover, in the Qur'an, there is an explicit and unambiguous declaration, supposedly by Allah, that he personally will protect and guard the Qur'an.

> *Indeed, it is We who sent down the Quran and indeed, We will be its guardian.* (Qur'an 15:9).

So the Qur'an then, even more so than the body of Muhammad himself if ever it were to be found, is the most precious thing imaginable to a Muslim. Their entire religion comes from the words in it and the words are the words of Allah himself. The entire power and authority of the early imams and caliphs comes from it. It is at the very centre of the Muslim Universe and some even argue that, along with Allah, it has always existed and was never created, merely revealed.

It is inconceivable that such a sacred object would be casually disposed of, thrown out with the rubbish or cast aside and forgotten, to decay into dust and disappear. It is almost inconceivable that it would be stolen or broken up and the pages recycled or used for some less important writing. It is inconceivable that some disaster like a fire, a flood or an earthquake would have destroyed it without at least some record of this disaster being made.

And it even supposedly has the indestructibility of being protected by Allah.

So the obvious question then is where is this original Qur'an? Where is the book originally compiled under Uthman ibn Affan from the Abu Bakr first edition given to Hafsa bint Umar, Muhammad's widow, to look after? Neither the Abu Bakr edition, nor the final committee-compiled edition exists!

In short, where is the most precious; most sacred object imaginable to any Muslim; a book protected by Allah himself, the original Qur'an? Did they just lose it but forgot to record that fact? Did it just go missing but nobody noticed? Did Allah fail to protect it and allow it to decay or be destroyed?

So, given that history, none of which is seriously disputed by Islamic scholars or Quranic historians, from where comes the confidence that it is indeed the complete word of Allah as revealed by Jibril to Muhammad? Non-Muslims will immediately begin to think of other possible explanations for the Qur'an's origins and reasons to doubt that claim. Muslims, on the other hand, base their entire religion on the claim; some will even go so far as killing those who do not accept the unproved and unprovable claim by faith.

Quite obviously and unarguably, faith in the Qur'an does not come from the Qur'an but by prior acceptance of the claim. Faith does not come from the Qur'an; acceptance of the Qur'an as sacred comes from pre-existing and essentially arbitrary faith. In reality, the believer has chosen to believe and has set himself up as the final judge in this matter, or more likely, to have been frightened into belief and made afraid to doubt.

How many Muslims will admit to having judged the claims of Islam and assented to them? How many Christians will admit to having done the same with the Bible or Jews with the Torah?

For books which the faithful believe to be communications from God to impart knowledge to humans, one might expect the Bible and Qur'an to contain new information not then available to the people who wrote them down, yet, looked at objectively, both books could probably be accurately dated by the level of scientific knowledge in them, or rather the degree of scientific ignorance

Despite the implausible claims to be able to discern modern science in both the Bible and the Qur'an, these can easily be dismissed, often with little more than a cursory glance. It is noticeable that the claims are invariably claims about science we already know about and that those claims were never made before humans discovered the actual science. In years of asking, no-one has yet been able to look in the Quran or the Bible and predict what the next major scientific discovery will be.

Just a few examples should suffice to illustrate the wide gap between what the faithful claim this or that verse says, and what it actually says. In many cases, the claim is for science that is not actually what science says. It is often apparent that, at best, these claims are made by people who do not understand the science and often seem not to understand the holy book. At worst, as is common in apologetics, they are deliberate misrepresentations of the holy book or science or both.

For example, this claim taken from a Christian apologetics site[17] that the Bible says that time had a beginning:

Cited Bible Passages:

> *Who hath saved us, and called us with an holy calling, not according to our works, but according to his own purpose and grace, which was given us in Christ Jesus before the world began* (2 Timothy 1:19).

> *In hope of eternal life, which God, that cannot lie, promised before the world began* (Titus 1:2.)

> *But we speak the wisdom of God in a mystery, even the hidden wisdom, which God ordained before the world unto our glory* (1 Corinthians 2:7).

None of these mention time and in fact imply there was time before the 'world' began. It would be more accurate to interpret these as a belief that time did not have a beginning but is eternal – something we now know to be untrue.

This example illustrates both a failure to understand the passage quoted and ignorance of science. It states a 'scientific principle' that, well… just is not a scientific principle – that the dimensions of the universe were created.

> *For I am persuaded, that neither death, nor life, nor angels, nor principalities, nor powers, nor things present, nor things to come, Nor height, nor depth, nor any other creature, shall be able to separate us*

---

[17] (Deem, 2013)

The Fallacy of Holy Books

from the love of God, which is in Christ Jesus our Lord (Romans 8:38-39).

There is no scientific principle which says the dimensions of the Universe were created. This would be a frankly absurd claim for science to make, but this passage makes no such claim anyway. In fact, the 'dimensions' of the Universe are not a fixed quantity because space is increasing within the Universe. This is not only a false claim about science but a false claim about the holy book being presented as a source of scientific truth.

We have similar claims frequently made for passages in the Qur'an[18]. For example,

> *We created man from an extract of clay. Then We made him as a drop in a place of settlement, firmly fixed. Then We made the drop into an alaqah, then We made the alaqah into a mudghah* (Qur'an, 23:12-14)

The Arabic word, *alaqah,* can have three meanings: a leech, something suspended or a blood clot. The word *mudghah* means 'chewed substance'. Without looking it up, try to work out what science this verse is teaching mankind, according to Muslim apologists. (Answer at the bottom of the page[19])

.

Try the same exercise with this verse from the Qur'an:

> *Have you not seen how God makes the clouds move gently, then joins them together, then makes them into a stack, and then you see the rain come out of it....*(Qur'an 24:43)

Have you worked out what science this is about yet? (Answer at foot of page[20])

.

On evidence such as that, Muslim children in faith schools are being taught that they do not need to learn science because it is all in the Qur'an already. They just need to read the Qur'an where they will learn that people are made from clay and first become leeches and end up as a chewed substance!

---

[18] (A Brief Illustrated Guide to Understanding Islam)

[19] Muslim apologists claim this is an account of human embryology. Did you work it out?

[20] This is about meteorology. Apparently, scientists have only just worked out that rain comes from clouds. This was totally unknown to 7th Century BCE Arabs, allegedly.

Ten Reasons To Lose Faith

Faith in the holy books does not come from reading the holy books. Faith in the holy books is the reason for reading them. Faith is an expression of human arrogance and the delusion that knowledge can be acquired not through evidence but by choice.

Before moving on to examine what this faith in holy books can lead to, it is worth dispensing with one of the most idiotically fallacious arguments you will ever see but which is commonly used by religious apologists. It is known as the taxicab fallacy.

This was probably best expressed by an anonymous comment on one of my blogs a couple of years ago in an attempt to refute an article about an obvious error in the Bible:

> *In no sense is an argument a valid one if it is built upon the accuracy of what it is arguing is inaccurate. If the bible is false, then those entries are false, and cannot, therefore be used as part of your argument to show that the bible is false. You've created a loop. If those entries are true, then the bible is true, therefore your argument is false.*

This is called the taxicab fallacy by religious apologists because the analogy is with getting into a taxicab. Once in the cab you cannot then pretend you are not in it. If you 'hop into' the Bible and argue that it is wrong, you cannot demand Christians use the Bible to prove it is not wrong. I must admit the logic of that is lost on me somewhere. If we try to apply it to a real world situation it becomes clear just how absurd and even desperate is this attempt to avoid dealing with the errors in the Bible.

Imagine you are in court charged with a crime of which you are completely innocent and the prosecution has put up a statement by an eye-witness as evidence against you. The statement says the crime was committed on a Tuesday afternoon by a 6 feet tall, 220 lbs (15 stone 12 lbs or 100 Kg if you are not American) woman with red hair and one leg. Your defence has pointed out that you are a 5 feet 6 inch male with black hair and the full complement of legs, and that the crime was actually committed on a Friday morning.

"Ah!" says the prosecution, "but you cannot use the errors in the statement to prove the statement is false because in no sense is an argument a valid one if it is built upon the accuracy of what it is arguing is inaccurate. If the statement is

The Fallacy of Holy Books

false, then those entries are false, and cannot, therefore be used as part of your argument to show that the statement is false. Therefore you have no grounds for questioning the accuracy of the witness statement".

"Got a good point there!" says your defence lawyer, "Can't dispute that logic!"

I wonder if my anonymous contributor would put his hands up and admit he or she must be guilty in that case because the witness statement is obviously true, or whether he would fire his defence lawyer.

The fallacy in the reasoning is that you are not using the Bible as a whole to prove there are errors in the Bible; you are using the errors in it. To take the taxicab analogy at face value, if the taxicab had an engine problem, it would be a taxicab with an engine problem. The engine problem would not go away if you were in the taxicab.

Now let us see what this faith can lead to.

Some time ago the well-known journalist Mehdi Hassan got involved in a little public spat with Richard Dawkins when he said in a debate between the two of them that he believed completely that Muhammad had flown to Heaven on a flying horse. Now, no-one who has listened to Mehdi Hassan could regard him as unintelligent and certainly not an extremist. Mehdi Hassan is no more a Muslim extremist than is the Archbishop of Canterbury a Christian extremist, yet, like the latter, he believes in magic and when you believe a god can suspend the laws of physics you have no real reason to doubt anything.

The problem is that religious moderates can and do, albeit unwittingly, enable and permit religious extremism simply by giving a gloss of respectability to the idea that faith is a valid way to determine the truth and that belief in magic is perfectly sensible; that the contents of a holy book can logically be held to be true, not on evidence or deductive reasoning, and even despite contrary evidence and common sense, by faith alone. I am happy therefore to be seen as biased in this matter, if being objective can be considered biased.

I am certainly biased in favour of factual and logical evidence because I do not regard my intuition or wishful thinking – call it what you will – as overriding the evidence, and I certainly do not feel any obligation to hold evidence-free beliefs just because my parents pinned the label 'Anglican Christian' on me shortly after birth and got a priest to cast magic spells over me. If there is no evidential reason to believe something I see no reason to believe it. If I see evidential reasons not to believe something then I not only see no reason to believe it, I see reason not to believe it. It is that simple really. I have no difficulty following the evidence, no matter the conclusions to which it leads me. So in this respect I can see exactly where Richard Dawkins is coming from.

I admire Mehdi Hassan because I see him brilliantly arguing some political point or other by skilfully marshalling the facts and showing the logical deductions to be drawn from them – and 'facts' is the operative word here. Would anyone bother to read Mehdi or listen to him on BBC Question Time if he only ever argued that such-and-such must be true because he had faith in it, or because it was written down somewhere and he believed the author unswervingly and uncritically? I think he would long ago have been dismissed as just another swivel-eyed, sanctimonious fanatic. What makes him the journalist he is, is his mastery of the facts and devastating use of logic – together with his ability to communicate these with words, of course.

How then does he come to believe, apparently with complete certainty, and certainly without any hint of embarrassment, in flying horses? The answer of course is that Mehdi accepts without question that the Qur'an is unquestionable truth and that the god described in it is capable of performing miracles. So, not only is a flying horse possible because his god can produce one at will, but Mohammad would not have said he flew to Heaven on one if he did not. Therefore, the only permissible belief can be that it really happened.

To believe otherwise would call the entire Islamic faith into question because it would call Mohamed's reliability into question. It is not permitted to even think that Mohammad could have been hallucinating or worse. The idea that he mistakenly took a mythical Greek beast he had heard stories about as being real and used it in some sort of poetic metaphor to describe a transcendental 'experience' had whilst fasting has to be dismissed because he was guided by Allah, who would not have made that mistake.

But let's not forget that Islam is not the only religion that requires belief by faith in things for which there is no evidence and which logic tells us are absurd. Christianity also has its mythical creatures, including talking snakes, donkeys and plants. Christianity has the belief that a primitive blood sacrifice and the act of humans is required to satiate and empower an already omnipotent god; that killing an innocent person somehow absolves you of responsibility for something you did not do anyway. The only reason to believe these things is because they were written about in a book; other people in your culture believe them and most of all because your parents did. There is no evidence for them outside the book so they can only be believed by faith.

The frightening thing is what this ready, even proud, acceptance of the absurd by faith can lead to, especially when it is presented as a good, moral, even intellectually honest thing and something to be proud of and admired for. Admired for believing something absurd without any evidence? Really?

If one believes in flying horses, talking snakes, and the efficacy of human blood sacrifices, why not also believe that women should be subservient to their husbands, father and brothers, that apostates and atheists should be killed, that a raped woman has committed a crime, that clerics can mandate you to kill someone without trial for saying something they disagree with, and without the right of appeal?

And if you can believe in human blood sacrifice, talking snakes and a person surviving in the stomach of a fish for three days, why not carry out Jesus' instructions in Luke 19:27 and slay his enemies or that women should not teach, nor usurp authority over the man (1 Timothy 2:12) or that women should submit themselves to their husbands (Ephesians 5:22, Colossians 3:18)?

Moderates Muslims like Mehdi Hassan seem capable of compartmentalising and sanitising – of cherry-picking – their faith, so that harmless beliefs like that in flying horses and miracles can be held with conviction because they do not do anyone any harm. Yet they manage somehow to avoid following the same logic to its obvious conclusions when it would lead to behaviour not acceptable in a civilised society.

Just so with the many moderate Christians who can believe with conviction that a barbaric human blood sacrifice worked once and a mythical first couple did something wrong for which we all somehow bear individual responsibility, and yet not repress women, stone rape victims, naughty children, gays and people who eat shellfish, and slay Jesus's enemies like he ordered.

Even otherwise perfectly rational Christians who accept the evidence for human evolution and thus that there was never a first couple who could have committed 'original sin' nor any point at which humans ceased to be animals and became the special creation of a god, can believe they need to say the right magic spells on a Sunday to be forgiven for that 'sin', or that they have a close personal relationship with the magic creator of everything.

The problem is, the fundamentalists of all faiths do not seem capable of that degree of discrimination – of being able to discern shades of grey – and can point to the respectable, harmless and 'admirable' faith of the moderates to justify it, even accusing those same moderates of hypocrisy or worse. If you believe in flying horses why not believe unbelievers should be killed? Who are you to decide which of Allah's truths and instructions is right and which you can ignore? In their simplistic, black and white world of certainties, if you believe in original sin and talking snakes, why not slay Jesus' or Allah's enemies?

As the 9/11, 7/7 and Boston Marathon faith-based initiatives and the Sabra, Shatila[21] and Srebrenica[22] massacres show, there is nothing which humans are incapable of in terms of inhumanity to their fellow man, once they subscribe to the notion that truth and the will of a god can be determined by faith alone, that their actions are demanded, even mandated by that god and that death is not the end but the beginning – and life is a cage from which death liberates us!

The problem is the delusion that faith is a good thing. Faith, or rather the delusion that faith is a good thing, is probably the greatest crime against humanity, inflicted on us by the priesthoods. Religious faith has probably been responsible for more death, destruction and human misery, and has filled more psychiatric wards, than any other single human idea.

How do you tell a dispossessed, disillusioned young person who has gone to join ISIS in the belief that this is the way to put the world to rights or at least teach it a lesson, that it is perfectly okay to suspend disbelief and accept that Muhammad literally flew to Heaven on a flying horse, but that it is not okay to martyr yourself for a cause by blowing up innocent people? How do you

---

[21] (Wikipedia, 2016)
[22] (Wikipedia, 2016)

explain that it is not okay to decapitate non-believers even though it says in the Qur'an that this is their sacred duty and Allah requires it?

Once you have accepted one absurdity on the authority of a holy book alone, and once you have accepted the supreme moral authority of the Qur'an, on what basis do you claim the moral authority to tell someone else that **that** particular verse should be ignored because it is morally wrong?

An almost perfect illustration of how faith can be used to excuse atrocity can be seen in the apologetics of a well-known American fundamentalist evangelist.

But before I show how this works, first consider your reaction to someone who told you that invasion and genocide can be moral acts and that there is nothing wrong with infanticide; that infanticide can be a good thing. Something out of the most depraved rantings of a 1930s 'New Order' Nazi, maybe? Would you need to look in a holy book to see if you agree with him or whether his beliefs were morally repugnant?

What would you think if that same person told you that it is those who react instinctively with horror at those beliefs who have a 'disappointing' character defect?

The following is from a defence of the Canaanite genocide, supposedly ordered by God, by Dr. William Lane Craig, a widely respected (in Christian fundamentalist circles) American evangelical Christian apologist. I am including it here partly because this use of religious apologetics to defend something so repugnantly immoral deserves wider publicity:

> *According to the Pentateuch (the first five books of the Old Testament), when God called forth his people out of slavery in Egypt and back to the land of their forefathers, he directed them to kill all the Canaanite clans who were living in the land (Deut. 7.1-2; 20.16-18). The destruction was to be complete: every man, woman, and child was to be killed. The book of Joshua tells the story of Israel's* (sic) *carrying out God's command in city after city throughout Canaan...*
>
> *So then what is Yahweh doing in commanding Israel's* [sic] *armies to exterminate the Canaanite peoples? It is precisely because we have come*

to expect Yahweh to act justly and with compassion that we find these stories so difficult to understand. How can He command soldiers to slaughter children?...

I think that a good start at this problem is to enunciate our ethical theory that underlies our moral judgements. According to the version of divine command ethics which I've defended, our moral duties are constituted by the commands of a holy and loving God. Since God doesn't issue commands to Himself, He has no moral duties to fulfill. He is certainly not subject to the same moral obligations and prohibitions that we are. For example, I have no right to take an innocent life. For me to do so would be murder. But God has no such prohibition. He can give and take life as He chooses...

So the problem isn't that God ended the Canaanites' lives. The problem is that He commanded the Israeli [sic] soldiers to end them. Isn't that like commanding someone to commit murder? No, it's not. Rather, since our moral duties are determined by God's commands, it is commanding someone to do something which, in the absence of a divine command, would have been murder. The act was morally obligatory for the Israeli soldiers in virtue of God's command, even though, had they undertaken it on their on [sic] initiative, it would have been wrong.

On divine command theory, then, God has the right to command an act, which, in the absence of a divine command, would have been sin, but which is now morally obligatory in virtue of that command...

But why take the lives of innocent children?... if we believe, as I do, that God's grace is extended to those who die in infancy or as small children, the death of these children was actually their salvation. We are so wedded to an earthly, naturalistic perspective that we forget that those who die are happy to quit this earth for heaven's incomparable joy. Therefore, God does these children no wrong in taking their lives.

So whom [sic] does God wrong in commanding the destruction of the Canaanites? Not the Canaanite adults, for they were corrupt and deserving of judgement. Not the children, for they inherit eternal life. So who is wronged? Ironically, I think the most difficult part of this whole debate is the apparent wrong done to the Israeli [sic] soldiers themselves.

> *Can you imagine what it would be like to have to break into some house and kill a terrified woman and her children? The brutalizing effect on these Israeli [sic] soldiers is disturbing.* [23]

Note how Dr. Craig plucks a new theory – the Divine Command Theory (DCT) – out of nowhere to justify blaming God and ends up actually saying we should pity the murderers! All this is justified because Dr. Craig has faith in the Bible, with not the slightest piece of real evidence ever being produced. Nowhere does Dr. Craig explain why an omnipotent god was unable to correct its earlier mistake in creating the Canaanites by its own omnipotence had but needed the Israelites to do it for him. Presumably, that would have been all too easy and would not have tested the Israelites' faith and obedience sufficiently. The Canaanites had to be made to suffer at their hands to achieve that.

In a follow-up article, answering what looked suspiciously like a pre-arranged question from 'Peter' asking if he had seen the reactions to his apologetic, Dr. Craig actually attacked the moral character of those who react instinctively against this repugnant philosophy:

> *I've seen those kinds of responses, too, Peter, and find them disappointing because they fail to grapple intellectually with the difficult questions raised by such stories. Emotional outbursts take the place of rational discussion, leaving us with no deeper understanding of the issues than before we began. I find it ironic that atheists should often express such indignation at God's commands, since on naturalism there's no basis for thinking that objective moral values and duties exist at all and so no basis for regarding the Canaanite slaughter as wrong. As Doug Wilson has aptly said of the Canaanite slaughter from a naturalistic point of view, "The universe doesn't care." So at most the non-theist can be alleging that biblical theists have a sort of inconsistency in affirming both the goodness of God and the historicity of the conquest of Canaan.*

The smug self-satisfaction in that reply can barely be concealed. It is not those who think genocide and infanticide are wrong, but those who see it only in terms of what a holy book tells them to do; who have abdicated personal responsibility, using 'faith' as their excuse, who hold the moral high-ground in the view of a fundamentalist Bible literalist.

---

[23] (Lane Craig, Slaughter of the Canaanites)

It is worth reading Dan Barker's response[24] to this repugnant philosophy at this point:

> *This is despicable. There is no heaven— and Craig certainly does not know if such a place exists— but even if there were, how does it make killing right? (He actually shoots himself in the foot. Craig's reasoning is a good argument for abortion: kill the fetuses now so they can go to heaven without the risk of being raised in a godless family.) This idiocy of theodicy makes a mockery of morality. Under this kind of thinking, no action would be wrong. It puts the lie to the Christian claim of moral absolutes. Nothing that humans value dearly, including the lives of our beloved children, would count for squat. No human is capable of acting morally, which turns into a joke the Christian claim that our moral impulses were implanted by God. If you believe that God commanded you to do something that "in the absence of a divine command" would be obviously atrocious, then is such an act actually good? This is moral bankruptcy, but I know exactly where it comes from. It comes from the purpose-driven life whose goal is to bring glory to God. It comes from the toddler morality of pleasing Daddy. The father figure is always right, must be always right (he is the father, after all), and to challenge his goodness will hurt his feelings, offend his ego, undermine his authority, and get you in deep trouble. No matter what he does, Daddy is good— God is good, good, good, they have to keep telling themselves.*

As though Dr. Craig's spirited defence of all that decent people find repugnant was not bad enough, in a third article replying to a long detailed question[25] which basically dismantled the DCT by pointing out that people who join ISIS and behead infidels could also quote the DCT as moral justification, Dr. Craig discovered that there are now two forms of the DCT:

> *In answering such a question, we need to keep in mind that there are two types of divine command theory: voluntaristic and non-voluntaristic. On voluntaristic theories God's commands are based upon His free will alone. He arbitrarily chooses what values are good or bad and what our obligations and prohibitions are. It seems to me that the voluntarist has no choice but to bite the bullet, as you say, and affirm that had God so*

---

[24] (Barker, Life-Driven Purpose: How an Atheist Finds Meaning, 2015)
[25] (Lane Craig, If ISIS's God Were Real, Would I Be Obliged to Follow Him?)

> chosen, then we would be obligated to engage in rape, mass murder, and forced conversion.

These are of course the very people who would kill Canaanite and murder their children and think they should be pitied for the trauma they suffer in murdering women and children.

> Well, it seems to me that the objection is best framed by saying that we have modal intuitions that certain moral values and duties are broadly logically necessary and so could not be merely contingently valid, as voluntarism seems to imply. There are countermoves which the voluntarist might make here, but let us not pursue this rabbit trail, since I don't know of a single divine command theorist today who is a voluntarist.

Apart from people who carry out God's will by committing genocide, and those who defend them, of course.

> Most divine command theorists are non-voluntarists who hold that moral values are not grounded in God's will but in His nature. Moral duties are grounded in His will or commands; but moral values are prior to His will, since God's own nature is not something invented by God. Since His will is not independent of His nature but must express His nature, it is logically impossible for Him to issue certain sorts of commands. In order to do so, He would have to have a different nature, which is logically impossible.

So the decent ones are the ones who do not do what gods command but do what they think is right – the ones with a character defect...

> You ask, "What if, epistemically, I'd been mistaken and had the wrong God, what would the implications be of the DCT principle?" It is logically impossible that there be any other God. So if you were mistaken and believed in the wrong God, you would be a Muslim or a Hindu or a polytheist or what have you; but there wouldn't be another God. Remember: on perfect being theology, God is a maximally great being, a being which is worthy of worship. Lesser beings are not "Gods" at all. In fact, in my debates with Muslim theologians, this is one of the arguments I use against the Islamic conception of God: that Allah cannot be the

greatest conceivable being because he is not all-loving and therefore cannot be God.

So there you have it. You can easily tell if you have the right god; it is the one that agrees with Dr. William Lane Craig, and Dr. William Lane Craig would be only too pleased to tell you what it thinks. So the holy book has been no use at all in determining morality; its utility value is only that it confirms what Christian apologists want to be true to justify whatever morally repugnant act they need to have an excuse for.

"Don't blame me, Gov! It was God who told me to do it! You should thank me, actually!"

Note, incidentally, Dr. Craig's use of the word 'theory', in his Divine Command Theory. Creationists habitually claim it means a guess with no supporting evidence when used in scientific terms like the 'Theory of Evolution' so the theory can be waved aside and ignored as of no value. In fact the scientific meaning is almost the exact opposite, as I will explain in Chapter 6. Dr. Craig's use of it here in precisely the way creationists wrongly claim that science uses it; a notion with no supporting evidence. In fact, it is a utilitarian guess plucked from nowhere and inserted into the argument as an established fact without further ado.

The final example of how faith can completely take away reason and give permission not only to hold certain beliefs which run counter to the evidence, can be seen from the following excerpts from the 'Statement of Faith' on the Answers In Genesis website[26]. This website is owned and run by the evangelical Christian fundamentalist, Ken Ham. Its aim appears to be to providing creationists with disinformation as part of the campaign to undermine the influence of science and reason, primarily in America, in order to pull down Thomas Jefferson's 'Wall of Separation' between church and state, abolish the 'Establishment Clause' in the US Constitution, and establish a fundamentalist Christian theocracy.

At no point is any evidence offered to support these dogmas.

---

[26] (AnswersInGenesis, 2015)

Section 1: Priorities

- *The scientific aspects of creation are important but are secondary in importance to the proclamation of the gospel of Jesus Christ as Sovereign, Creator, Redeemer, and Judge.*
- *The doctrines of Creator and Creation cannot ultimately be divorced from the gospel of Jesus Christ.*

Section 2: Basics

- *The 66 books of the Bible are the written Word of God. The Bible is divinely inspired and inerrant throughout. Its assertions are factually true in all the original autographs. It is the supreme authority in everything it teaches. Its authority is not limited to spiritual, religious, or redemptive themes but includes its assertions in such fields as history and science.*
- *The final guide to the interpretation of Scripture is Scripture itself.*

So do not go looking elsewhere! If the Bible says the Bible is true, the Bible is true… because the Bible is true and Ken Ham has designated it as the literal, inerrant word of God.

- *The account of origins presented in Genesis is a simple but factual presentation of actual events and therefore provides a reliable framework for scientific research into the question of the origin and history of life, mankind, the earth, and the universe.*
- *The various original life forms (kinds), including mankind, were made by direct creative acts of God. The living descendants of any of the original kinds (apart from man) may represent more than one species today, reflecting the genetic potential within the original kind. Only limited biological changes (including mutational deterioration) have occurred naturally within each kind since creation.*
- *The great Flood of Genesis was an actual historic event, worldwide (global) in its extent and effect.*

- *The special creation of Adam (the first man) and Eve (the first woman), and their subsequent fall into sin, is the basis for the necessity of salvation for mankind.*
- *Death (both physical and spiritual) and bloodshed entered into this world subsequent to and as a direct consequence of man's sin.*

Section 3: Theology

- *The Godhead is triune: one God, three Persons—God the Father, God the Son, and God the Holy Spirit.*
- *All mankind are sinners, inherently from Adam and individually (by choice), and are therefore subject to God's wrath and condemnation.*
- *Freedom from the penalty and power of sin is available to man only through the sacrificial death and shed blood of Jesus Christ and His complete and bodily resurrection from the dead.*
- *The Holy Spirit enables the sinner to repent and believe in Jesus Christ.*
- *The Holy Spirit lives and works in each believer to produce the fruits of righteousness.*
- *Salvation is a gift received by faith alone in Christ alone and expressed in the individual's repentance, recognition of the death of Christ as full payment for sin, and acceptance of the risen Christ as Savior, Lord, and God.*
- *All things necessary for our salvation are expressly set down in Scripture.*
- *Jesus Christ was conceived by the Holy Spirit and born of the virgin [sic] Mary.*
- *Jesus Christ rose bodily from the dead, ascended to heaven, and is currently seated at the right hand of God the Father, and shall return in person to this earth as Judge of the living and the dead.*
- *Satan is the personal spiritual adversary of both God and mankind.*
- *Those who do not believe in Christ are subject to everlasting conscious punishment, but believers enjoy eternal life with God.*

The Fallacy of Holy Books

Note the threat there – believe or else…, never believe because…

Every other statement of dogma takes just a sentence or two, but when it comes to the Christian obsession with other peoples' sex life we have:

> • *The only legitimate marriage sanctioned by God is the joining of one naturally born man and one naturally born woman in a single, exclusive union, as delineated in Scripture. God intends sexual intimacy to only occur between a man and a woman who are married to each other, and has commanded that no intimate sexual activity be engaged in outside of a marriage between a man and a woman. Any form of sexual immorality, such as adultery, fornication, homosexuality, lesbianism, bisexual conduct, bestiality, incest, pornography, or any attempt to change one's gender, or disagreement with one's biological gender, is sinful and offensive to God.*

….

Section 4: General

The following are held by members of the Board of Answers in Genesis to be either consistent with Scripture or implied by Scripture:

> • *Scripture teaches a recent origin for man and the whole creation, spanning approximately 4,000 years from creation to Christ*
> • *The days in Genesis do not correspond to geologic ages, but are six [6] consecutive twenty-four [24] hour days of creation.*

It is not entirely obvious why the numbers were repeated in square brackets there.

> • *The Noachian [sic] Flood was a significant geological event and much (but not all) fossiliferous sediment originated at that time.*
> • *The gap theory has no basis in Scripture.*

Then we finally discover what this dogma had been leading up to – do not believe the evidence!

71

- *The view, commonly used to evade the implications or the authority of biblical teaching, that knowledge and/or truth may be divided into secular and religious, is rejected.*
- *By definition, no apparent, perceived or claimed evidence in any field, including history and chronology, can be valid if it contradicts the scriptural record. Of primary importance is the fact that evidence is always subject to interpretation by fallible people who do not possess all information.* [My emphasis]

This evidence, which can be cherry-picked and accepted or rejected at will, was supposedly created by the same god who inerrantly wrote the Bible, yet the evidence of this 'creation' is at best unreliable and at worst a deliberately misleading. But the 'evidence' of its other 'creation', the Bible, is inerrant… All on the authority of Ken Ham who has nothing but the Bible as his source.

Relate this now to the situation of the court case I mentioned earlier where you have the choice of accepting the scientific evidence, or the 'faith' of a prosecutor with a vested interest who asks you to dismiss the evidence and just take his word for it 'on faith'. On such fallacious, circular reasoning is the entire creation industry founded and the people behind it are made extremely rich by it.

This dogmatic view, based on nothing more than the personal authority of a very rich evangelical preacher, is considered enough to justify the demand that the USA changes its Constitution so that it becomes legal for this same dogma to be taught to vulnerable minds as scientific truth in schools funded by American tax-payers. Meanwhile, creationists attempt to get themselves onto school boards to circumvent and subvert the US Constitution by slipping creationism into the classroom unnoticed, and are even prepared to lie under oath in court, as was shown in the Kitzmiller vs Dover Area School District case.[27, 28]

---

[27]Kitzmiller vs Dover Area School District – Decision. Throughout the trial and in various submissions to the Court, Defendants vigorously argue that the reading of the statement is not 'teaching' ID but instead is merely 'making students aware of it.' In fact, one consistency among the Dover School Board members' testimony, which was marked by selective memories and outright lies under oath, as will be discussed in more detail below, is that they did not think they needed to be knowledgeable about ID because it was not being taught to the students. We disagree. ….. an educator reading the disclaimer is engaged in teaching, even if it is colossally bad teaching. …. Defendants' argument is a red herring because the Establishment Clause forbids not just 'teaching'

The Fallacy of Holy Books

Lying under oath in a court of law, supposedly to defend a religion which specifically forbids the bearing of false witness betrays a political agenda for which religion is merely providing an excuse.

Faith is the abandonment of reason and an abdication of personal responsibility.

As I am writing this, we are hearing of yet another atrocity in the name of religion at Bacha Khan University in Charsadda, Pakistan where twenty-one unarmed students were killed by the Pakistan Taliban in the name of Allah. We will have heard of many more such atrocities before this book goes to press.

[As this book is in its final stages, news is coming in of terrorist suicide attacks in Brussels, Belgium. These were almost certainly carried out by Islamic fundamentalists, convinced that Allah requires them to randomly kill people and that this is a good thing!]

This is just one of a growing list of apparently random mass murders throughout the world in the name of Islam by a militant sect based on Saudi Arabian Wahhabi Islam in the belief that their faith requires them to kill non-believers because Allah demands it.

It would be easy to fill the remaining pages of this book, and probably several more with accounts of similar massacres carried out in the name of various religions. The history of Europe, at least since the fall of the Roman Empire, has been one of religious warfare, persecutions, massacres, purges, genocides and repression of whatever religious minority happened to be at hand, often to suit a political agenda but frequently at the behest of religious leaders simply to increase or maintain their own power and influence.

Heresy, in other words, disagreement with official dogma, was normally punished by death, often by burning alive but rarely quickly and mercifully; the clear intention being to frighten and terrorise other people into compliance and acceptance of dogma. Rarely, if ever were matters of theology settled by dialogue and civilised, respectful debate.

---

religion, but any governmental action that endorses or has the primary purpose or effect of advancing religion. (footnote 7 on page 46)
[28] (Wikipedia, 2016)

The Thirty Years War which started out as a degeneration of the Catholic Holy Roman Empire into waring Protestant and Catholic states saw massive destruction and population reductions with some towns and cities losing up to half their populations.

Throughout the European Middle Ages, rightly called the Dark Ages between the Christianisation of the Roman Empire and the European Enlightenment, when Christianity reigned supreme, witch burnings and bouts of witch hysteria were common.

Both the Bible and the Qur'an fulminate against witches and sorcerers. The Bible is quite specific in one of the least ambiguous and shortest verses in it, "Thou shalt not suffer a witch to live." (Exodus 22:18). Witch hysteria reached a peak in Europe in the fourteenth and fifteenth centuries when 12,000 people, overwhelmingly women, are known to have been burned for witchcraft. Some estimates put the actual number of executions at between 40,000 and 100,000.

In 1484 Pope Innocent VIII issued his notorious Papal bull: *Summis Desiderates*. It was used as a preface to the book *Malleus Maleficarum* (The Hammer of Witches), published by two German Catholic Inquisitors in 1486. In it, it described in detail ritual satanic and sexual aberrations as practiced by witches – women in particular. Under the terms of *Summis Desiderates* there was almost no defence available against the charge of witchcraft since denial was a sign of guilt, something latched onto by the Witchfinder General, Matthew Hopkirk, who earned his living travelling around England seeking out likely victims for whom he was paid a reward.

In England in 1612, twelve people who lived in the area around Pendle Hill in Lancashire, were charged with the murders of ten people by the use of witchcraft and tried along with the Samlesbury witches and others, in a series of trials that have become known as the Lancashire witch trials. Of the eleven individuals who went to trial—nine women and two men—ten were found guilty and executed by hanging; one was found not guilty.

In 1645, in Springfield, Massachusetts Bay, then an English Colony, experienced America's first witchcraft trial when Hugh and Mary Parsons accused each other of witchcraft. Hugh was acquitted, while Mary was acquitted of witchcraft but sentenced to be hanged for the death of her child. She died in prison.

The Fallacy of Holy Books

About eighty people throughout England's Massachusetts Bay Colony were accused of practicing witchcraft, thirteen women and two men were executed in a witch-hunt that lasted throughout New England from 1645-1663. Probably the best known example of witch hysteria in America is the Salem Witch Trials held between February 1692 and May 1693.

The Salem Witch trials illustrate the confirmatory bias of believing the holy books by faith. No one now seriously believes the Salem Witches were guilty. The trials are regarded as a notorious miscarriage of justice and yet, unlike the stories in the Bible for which there is not a single piece of independent documentary eye-witness evidence, there are literally cartloads of documents and court records of sworn eye-witness accounts testifying to the guilt of the Salem witches. Many of these testimonies are from close relatives of those convicted. The evidence was presented to the court and was considered sufficient evidence on which to find the defendants guilty and for the judge to pass the death sentence.

Almost non-one now believes that evidence or believes that evil demons can possess people and give them magical powers enabling them to suspend the natural laws and bring about sickness or cause unnatural events to occur with a look, a touch or a few muttered words. And yet a substantial number of people believe the stories of miracles; of driving out evil demon that possess people and cause sickness or insanity; of the suspension of natural laws and of causing unnatural events with a look, a touch or a few muttered words, as related in the Bible – and for which there is no known evidence outside the Bible.

Why are Bible stories believed but the apparent tried and tested evidence of the guilt of the Salem Witches dismisses as absurd? The reason should be obvious. The Salem Witch 'evidence' is of something that could not be true, but the Bible confirms pre-existing bias so is accepted uncritically or after extraordinary mental gymnastics has been performed to make it fit. It is easier and more comforting to believe 'on faith' than to cope with the cognitive dissonance that would come from applying the same critical test to the Bible as is used for the Salem Witch evidence.

In fundamentalist Islamic Saudi Arabia the death penalty for sorcery is still in use. Fawza Falih Muhammad Ali was condemned to death for practicing witchcraft in 2006. In 2007 an Egyptian pharmacist working there was accused, convicted, and executed. Saudi authorities also pronounced the death penalty on a Lebanese television presenter, Ali Sabat, while he was performing the hajj (Islamic pilgrimage) in the country. In April 2009, a Saudi woman, Amina bint Abdulhalim Nassar, was arrested and later sentenced to death for practicing witchcraft and sorcery. She was beheaded in December 2011.

In the UK in 2012, the police were unable to bring charges again a Christian Pastor, Dieudonne Tukala, for accusing children of witchcraft and praying for children to die, because this is not illegal in England.

Today, in Nigeria and in other parts of Africa, Christian priests often participate in ritual abuse of children accused of witchcraft and they are not without support in America. Needless to say, Pentecostal preacher, Helen Ukpabio, draws thousands to her revival meetings. In August 2011, when she had herself consecrated Christendom's first "lady apostle", Nigerian politicians and Nollywood actors attended the ceremony. She has of course written books and produced DVDs which explain how Satan possesses children, and which she sells to those credulous enough to buy them.

Major features of European history were the frequent purges and pogroms against Jews often involving the massacre of the entire Jewish population of town such as Erfurt where a local Catholic clergy encouraged it. In 1298 a local Christian demagogue, the self-styled 'Lord Rindtfleisch' claimed he had been given a mandate from Heaven to exterminate the Jews. Starting at Röttingen on 20 April 1298 where his mob burned the Jewish population, he then destroyed the Jewish populations of Rothenburg ob der Tauber, Würzburg, Bamberg, Dinkelsbühl, Nördlingen, Forchheim and Nuremberg. He then moved into Bavaria and Austria where a further 5,000 Jews were massacred.

In 1543, Martin Luther, founder of the Protestant Reformation publish, *On The Jews And Their Lies,* a 65,000 word diatribe of anti-Semitic hate in which he urged, amongst other thigs, that people should shun Jews and throw dung at them. He formulated a seven-point plan for dealing with Jews:

1. to burn down Jewish synagogues and schools and warn people against them;
2. to refuse to let Jews own houses among Christians;
3. for Jewish religious writings to be taken away;
4. for rabbis to be forbidden to preach;

The Fallacy of Holy Books

5. to offer no protection to Jews on highways;
6. for usury to be prohibited, and for all silver and gold to be removed, put aside for safekeeping and given back to Jews who truly convert; and
7. to give young, strong Jews flail, axe, spade, spindle, and let them earn their bread in the sweat of their noses.

The anti-Semitic rhetoric which characterised the early Protestant Church, especially but by no means exclusively, in Germany, culminated in the Holocaust in which six million European Jews were systematically murdered on an industrial scale by the German state and by a people whose faith told them this was what God wanted. The Catholic Church meanwhile smiled on approvingly and announced that the Holocaust was God's punishment on the Jews for the sin of killing Jesus.

Europe and the Middle-East have not been the only places to suffer grotesque human rights abuses in the name of religion. On being partitioned into India and Pakistan and given independence from Britain, both countries quickly degenerated into inter-religious strife and genocides as Muslims and Hindus fought for local dominance by ethnic cleansing.

Ethnic cleansing as a term came into popular usage during the break-up of former Yugoslavia into waring states along religious lines as Catholic and Greek Orthodox states drove those with the wrong religion out of homes they had had for centuries and Orthodox Bosnia tried to assert dominance, culminating in the Srebrenica genocide in which Muslim men and boys were summarily executed by Bosnian troops supported by neo-fascist Orthodox volunteers from Greece egged on by Greek Orthodox priests.

And now, as Iraq and Syria degenerate into warring factions, self-appointed extremist Sunni Muslims are killing Shia Muslims and Christians in the name of Allah to try to recreate a brutal, misogynistic ignorant Iron Age desert despotism that faith tells them will be heaven on earth because all the truly faithful want to do is worship Allah all day – while self-appointed male clerics make all the decisions and have arbitrary powers of life and death over people, where daughters are given into sexual slavery for life and husbands can abuse and murder wives and daughters at will, all in the name of Allah because faith says so.

All this death and destruction; all this suffering and waste of human life and potential; all this denial of the right to others to live in peace and to enjoy the one opportunity that the great good fortune of having been born at all has given then, is done by people who have fallen for the fallacy of faith and who have been duped by those who told them faith is the only way to know the truth. By people to whom they have abdicated personal responsibility and under whose power and control they now operate like automatons.

Evolution has taken 3.5 billion years to evolve the human brain and religion has turned it into a guidance and delivery system for bombs. With religion, young men and women kill themselves believing by faith that this life is merely a cage from which death liberates them to go the a magical paradise.

Yet the very thing they want to be liberated from is the result of religion.

3. The Fallacy of Apologetics.

But surely, there are very good logical arguments for the existence of a god, are there not?

As we shall see, all apologetics are circular in that they presuppose the outcome. It is simply not possible to arrive at proof of the existence of anything for which there is no tangible evidence. Merely being able to accommodate an idea in an argument is not, in itself, evidence that the idea is right. Even if apologetics such as the argument from design could show that **only** conscious design can account for the appearance of design, this tells us nothing of the nature of the designer, nor of its intentions. As we will see though, the argument from design is merely the circular fallacy of gap-filling, which presupposes the god being promoted.

Religious apologetics is a strange thing. No other academic discipline has or needs anything like it. People who work in the fields such as history, sociology, psychology, science, literature, art, etc., need neither apologetics nor faith because they have evidence, logic and reason, and logic and reason follow naturally from evidence. Theology is the only discipline which takes an unquestioned, sacred, evidence-free dogma as its starting point.

Theology is regarded as a branch of philosophy. This is curious, because all other philosophies are concerned with interpretation and understanding of the real world, or natural phenomena such as human consciousness, morality, moral development, ethics, mathematics, logic, methodology of science, etc., etc. Only theology deals with an unproven, hypothetical abstraction such as the idea of a creator god, or a god which dispenses morals and gives humans a sense of right and wrong, apparently without feeling the need to show that this hypothetical entity actually exists. Imagine an entire, respected academic discipline devoted to the assumption that there are fairies at the bottom of the garden!

Only theology starts with the desired conclusion and works backwards to find excuses for believing it. Only theology invents arguments seemingly designed to appeal to ignorance and superstition and to satisfy the need for confirmation of bias. Only theology needs to find reasons to ignore or dismiss contrary evidence from the real world and adopts double standards according to the need to arrive at the foregone conclusion by arbitrarily weighting the evidence.

Only religions need apologetics. They need apologetics because faith really is not enough when you think about the subject, instead of just accepting dogmas without question or analytical thought. Religions would not need faith if they had evidence. They would not need apologetics if faith alone was enough.

Because they invariably start with the conclusion, the same apologetic used by different religions will always support that religion and only that religion. Apologists for Islam will invariably 'prove' Allah exists and dictated the Qur'an. Apologists for Christianity will invariably 'prove' that the Christian god exists and inspired the Bible. Apologists for Judaism will invariably 'prove' that Yahweh gave the Laws to Moses and that the Messiah will only come when the Temple has been rebuilt in Jerusalem. They will all use identical arguments!

The fact that the very same argument can lead to whatever conclusion is needed, depending on who is deploying it, should be a clue that apologetics, like faith, is not a reliable way to discover truth. To all apologetics, without exception, you can legitimately ask, 'Which god?' when the argument reaches its final and predictable 'conclusion'.

In this chapter I'll look at the main arguments used by religious apologists to show how they are either arguments from personal incredulity and/or ignorance, or are merely circular argument, designed to appeal to those who want to be convinced.

The Fallacy of Personal Experience.
Firstly, there is the crude and unsophisticated, but probably commonest, 'the evidence is all around you', argument. This argument basically says I have found reasons to believe in this particular god because I have chosen to assign this particular god as the cause of arbitrarily selected observations or experiences. There is no attempt to show a causal link or to demonstrate the existence of the particular god before it was designated as the cause.

The Fallacy of Apologetics

The fallacy of this argument can be readily understood by considering what it was that convinced people those ancient gods from earlier times, such as Zeus, Horus or Mithra existed. We can readily accept, because of course those old dead gods were not real, that they were merely invented to explain things people did not understand. It stood to reason that something made the wind blow and the rain fall, so there were gods for wind and rain.

Of course, to their believers, the evidence was all around that these gods existed because the wind blew and the rain fell. Belief in those old, imaginary gods, inspired people to build great monuments like the Pyramids at Giza, the Parthenon, Stonehenge and Silbury Hill, the temples at Karnak, Knossos, Angkor Wat and Nara, and thousands more all over the ancient world.

Silbury Hill in southern England, for example, took an estimated eighteen million man-hours to construct and probably twice as many man-hours simply growing and preparing the food to support the labour force. Judging by its scale and proximity to other religious structures, and judging by the organisation needed to build it, Silbury Hill is unlikely to have been anything other than a religious site of some significance. Yet we know nothing whatever of that religion.

We do not have the least idea what gods they had, what those gods were believed to do, how they had to be prayed to, what ceremonies were needed or what priests they had. We know nothing because there is no evidence for their gods' existence, and those gods died when their last believer died. The power of gods is directly proportional to the number of their believers. When the number of their believers reaches zero, gods disappear without trace.

Yet, for their believers, all the evidence they needed would have been 'all around'. They only had to look around themselves to see it. The personal experience of these dedicated and faithful believers would have been no less real than that of the most devout Muslim, Hindu or Christian today.

The Cosmological Fallacy.
Slightly more sophisticated is the argument from first cause, or first mover. This is, of course, a slightly more advanced form of the 'evidence is all around' argument. The evidence is all around because the existence of evidence itself

shows something must have caused it, just as the evidence of wind shows something must have caused it. This is perhaps best expressed in the Kalâm Cosmological Argument, devised by a medieval Islamic philosopher, Al Ghazali of the Kalâm tradition, but wheeled out and dusted off by, amongst others, the American Christian fundamentalist and professional apologist, Dr William Lane Craig.

As with all these apologetics, it is not considered necessary to show which god your apologetic is for. That step is left to the cultural assumptions and parochialism of the audience. There is only one god on offer, obviously, so the fact that Al Ghazali thought he was making an irrefutable argument for Allah is not seen as a problem. Only the Christian god exists, so the KCA can be used in America to 'prove' only the Christian god exists.

See the circularity there? It works for Ganesh or Khali too!

Briefly, the KCA as used by Dr Craig argues:

1. Everything that begins to exist has a cause.
2. The Universe began to exist.
3. Therefore the Universe had a cause.
4. (Therefore the cause was the Christian god).

But hold on! Where in that argument was it shown *a priori* that the god in the conclusion existed or that it was the actual cause, assuming for a moment that the rest of the assertions in the argument are correct? Does the logic change if we randomly select any other notional entity? Of course it does not! The only thing that changes is the notional entity in the conclusion.

The trick here is to play to your audience's cultural biases, like a snake-oil salesman or a confidence trickster hitting on his mark. They are already fully signed up to the belief that not only does the Christian god exist but that it is the only god and the only thing capable of creating a universe. In effect, they have already bought into the required conclusion so the actual argument is already redundant.

The argument is nothing more than an assertion that the Christian God exists and is the only god capable of creating a Universe – therefore the Christian god exists and created the Universe. I believe God exists, therefore God exists!

The Fallacy of Apologetics

In fact, the trick is rather subtle. It is in the assumption that there exists a set of things that began to exist, and a set of things that did not begin to exist. The membership of the latter set is then arbitrarily restricted to whatever god or other notion you want in your conclusion, and everything else is assigned to the other set.

But why restrict the set of all things that did not begin to exist to a single god? Why restrict it to just hypothetical gods or supernatural entities at all? How were all possible natural causes identified and then excluded? How were the qualities of the member(s) of that set determined? They were not of course. The argument is rigged. It is nothing more than a circular argument and a dishonest begged question, dressed up to look philosophical and designed to appeal to a preconditioned audience; a trick that would grace any snake-oil peddler.

But the KCA is factually wrong anyway, so not only does it fail on the false logic and dishonesty in the way the argument is framed to ensure the 'right' conclusion, but it fails in its specific claims.

The Big Bang, generally accepted as the best explanation for the beginning of the Universe, was a quantum-level event. It is known that quantum events do not always need a cause! Causality is a law of the relativity domain. This is experimentally well documented. The Big Bang did not necessarily need a cause.

To dismiss this established fact because it seems counter-intuitive is to substitute rational thought for personal incredulity. Uncaused quantum events are a well-established principle in quantum mechanics. This is not a fact that can be ignored for the convenience of the religious apologetic; it is an elementary error.

The KCA also presupposes that there was ever 'nothing' in the first place. Before the Big Bang however, there was no space and no time, so questions of what was 'before' the Big Bang are actually nonsensical. There was no 'before'. The very concept of nothing itself is nonsensical and is merely an assumption built into the KCA. Where has it been established that non-existence is the default state of existence?

How can nothing exist? If 'nothing' is non-existence, for 'nothing' to exist would mean that 'nothing' can exist and not exist at the same time. 'Nothing' cannot be defined or measured so nothing can be said about what it is or what qualities and capabilities it has. So the claim that everything must have come from something because nothing can come from nothing is a nonsensical and unproven assumption.

The final failure of the KCA is that it is just a form of special pleading. The required conclusion is arbitrarily allowed to be eternal and to not need a beginning to explain, but a much higher standard is demanded of everything else. Without that special pleading, even **if** all the other claims and assumptions in the argument were valid, the 'goddidit!' explanation simply begs the question, "What caused God?"

The argument that everything must have a cause, therefore there must be a 'prime mover', is so ludicrously self-falsifying that it immediately needs to grant an exemption to itself to make itself work. And yet, if this exemption can arbitrarily be granted to the 'prime mover', it can arbitrarily be granted to anything else, so rendering the entire logic of the argument immediately redundant.

Without special pleading as an escape hatch from the self-falsifying logic of the argument, we end up with an endless progression of higher and higher gods, all making lesser gods until the least of all gods creates the Universe. Yet there appears to be no reason why we should grant this assumed entity this special privilege. It is merely demanded by religious apologists because, without it, they would not have an argument.

This comes about, of course, because there is no evidence upon which to hang this argument. The entire thing is hanging from an imaginary sky hook.

Normally at this point, an apologist will shift the goalposts and demand science explains how everything came from nothing, in apparent violation of the Laws of Thermodynamics. The simple, honest answer is that we do not yet know precisely what happened in the first Plank unit of time. This time is the smallest unit of time possible – 10^{-43} seconds – but it still needs to be explained. Theoretical physics has various competing theories but the truth remains that, at the time of writing, the exact details remain uncertain.

The Fallacy of Apologetics

This goes for theology too. It is simply dishonesty and pretending to know something you do not know to argue that 'don't know' = 'God did it!' However, science does know that it can explain why there is so much available energy with which to make matter, apparently starting with zero or as close to it as a quantum fluctuation will allow. The total of all energy in the Universe is still zero!

The Universe appears to be made of four fundamental forms of energy which manifest as four basic forces:

1. The Strong Force – which can hold a nucleus together against the enormous forces of repulsion of the protons.
2. The Electromagnetic Force – manifests itself through the forces between electrical charges and the magnetic force. Fundamentally, both magnetic and electric forces are manifestations of an exchange force involving the exchange of photons.
3. The Weak Force – a force involving exchange of elementary particles in the atomic nucleus.
4. Gravity – an attractive force proportional to the mass of an object.

Both the strong and weak forces have a very short range, while the electromagnetic force and gravity have a theoretically infinite range. The important thing for understanding the fundamentals of where the Universe came from is that the first three in this list together total the force of gravity. Gravity is a negative force totalling the sum of the other three positive forces.

Gravity is actually a very weak force but it acts over a theoretically infinite distance. Consider Newton's apocryphal apple clinging to its tree by the nuclear forces holding the molecules of its slender stalk together, but still able to resist the entire gravitational force exerted by Earth. Yet everything that has mass has gravity so the sum total of the Universe is, massive.

An important principle of quantum mechanics is that there is no such thing as an absolute value. Even zero energy is not an absolute but fluctuates around zero. This can be proven by observing pairs of virtual particles arising spontaneously in a quantum vacuum. There is no theoretical limit to the magnitude of this fluctuation.

One explanation for what happened in the initial 10^{-43} seconds is that a quantum fluctuation was large enough for relatively weak gravity to become stripped away from the other three forces. 10^{-43} seconds was enough time for this to cause a hyperinflation in which almost unlimited positive and negative energy could be created, but always totalling zero. Plank Time is the minimum time that can exist, so the instant the Universe came into existence it was immediately 10^{-43} seconds old. Again, we have a counter-intuitive idea for which we have to allow the evidence to override any personal incredulity.

In energy content, the Universe is literally zero. Not something, but nothing has come from quantum zero!

To put it simply, this is a bit like borrowing from a bank. The Bank lends you $1000. You now have +$1000; the Bank has -$1000. You both have an asset which you can use (the Bank can actually sell your debt as an asset because it represents a bit of your future earning that the bank now owns, and you can use the $1000 for whatever you borrowed it for) and yet no wealth was created by that transaction. Anyone who tells you this is impossible doesn't understand basic finance.

So, the argument from first cause, and the argument from false physics can be dismissed as factually and logically false and with a hefty dose of dishonesty, especially in the KCA. And both are merely forms of 'the evidence is all around you' assertion.

Note how nowhere so far has the slightest piece of real, testable and definitive evidence featured in these arguments. Would that be so if there were any? Can you imagine a scientist trying to reason that something must exist despite there being no evidence for it, just because he or she would like it to exist or because his parents believed in it?

The Teleological Fallacy.

I'll look now at the so-called Teleological Argument or argument from design, also known as Paley's Watch argument. Basically, this relies on the assumption, and it is nothing more than an assumption, that anything that looks like it was designed must have been designed. Once again, the existence of whatever designer god the argument is being deployed in support of, is implied, and cultural biases are left to fill in the gaps.

This argument is best illustrated with the watch analogy proposed by William Paley, of whom Charles Darwin was an admirer in his youth. Paley argued that if you found a watch on a patch of heathland you would recognise immediately that there must be a watchmaker to make the watch. It could not have sprung spontaneously, fully formed and working, from its environment. Paley argued that exactly the same argument applied to living creatures.

Paley proposed his argument more than fifty years before Darwin and Wallace succeeded in explaining exactly how complex organisms could acquire the superficial appearance of design. Their explanation was an entirely logical, natural and inevitable process, once you have variation due to imperfect replication in a selective environment.

Of course, the argument from design is unarguable for a watch found on a heathland path, for the simple reason that there is no other mechanism which could explain the watch's production, nor how it came to be there. That explanation requires no supernatural mystery; there is nothing required which cannot be readily understood and certainly there is no need to include an unproven supernatural hypothesis in the explanation. The explanation that a watch was designed and made by a watchmaker is complete and the most parsimonious answer available.

With the state of our knowledge of biology and biological systems in 1802, there seemed to be no reason why this analogy did not apply to living animals as well. Living animals appear to be designed in that they have component parts which need to be arranged in the right way. Curiously though, there are no wheels in nature, so any movement has to rely on levers with lots of inefficient pushing and pulling, and acceleration and deceleration of parts, not the far more efficient rotary action of wheels (imagine a car with legs!) but that's by the by.

However, there is a fundamental flaw in the argument. Ask yourself how, handed a watch and a cat, you could tell which one is man-made and which one is living?

What purpose does a living animal have which is in any way comparable to the utility value of a watch? Living things exist ultimately only to produce other living things. Not so watches. Watches have a very specific purpose and that is to keep an accurate record of the passage of time for humans.

There is an even more fundamental way in which watches are not like living things. They are not self-replicating.

Watches do not need elaborate mechanisms for finding their own energy source and to avoid becoming some other devices energy source. They do not need circulatory and excretory systems to supply energy to their component parts and to carry away the waste. Most significantly, watches do not need mechanisms for finding mates and for producing and providing for their offspring.

Because they do not need any of these things they do not need sensory, reproductive and locomotory systems. Because they are not self-replicating, they need no mechanism for replicating information and passing it on to the next generation.

They do not need any of these things because they are designed and made by humans for humans and humans provide energy to them by winding them up or putting a battery in them. Without humans, watches have no purpose, no function, and no existence. Watches are merely human artefacts. Living creatures existed before humans and would undoubtedly exist without us. For the most part, living creatures are self-reliant and self-replicating because they have no designers and have no purpose other than existing for their own sake.

Moreover, if we look inside the watch we would not find any redundancy in the design. There would be no cogs spinning purposelessly away, no springs holding back levers for no reason at all, no overly elaborate mechanisms using several cogs and levers where one or two would do. There would be no mistakes having to be compensated for by hugely inefficient work-arounds and no evidence of bits of earlier designs still included but having no current function at all.

The watch would be efficiently and accurately designed with obvious intelligence by someone who had a complete over-view of the purpose of his design and who knew how to make it as simply, therefore as efficiently and accurately, as possible. Additionally, if you were to look in different models of watch made by this watchmaker you would certainly see the same solutions used to overcome the same engineering problems. You would see the same springs, cogs, levers and bearings being used in the same way. You might even see exactly the same mechanism, just in a different case.

Unlike watches, living things have masses of inbuilt redundancy. The DNA of most living things is vastly more than is needed. There is DNA which does nothing other than produce copies of itself, for example. There are vestigial organs to be found in most species, like evidence of legs in whales and the human appendix.

There is evidence of work-arounds for earlier mistakes such as a complicated neural function to compensate for the blind spot in the mammalian eye because the wiring of the retina is backwards. And of course there is the ludicrous path taken by the recurrent laryngeal nerve in mammals, especially in the giraffe where it travels all the way down the neck into the thoracic cavity, under the aortic arch and back up the neck to the larynx.

There is evidence of repeated new 'designs' of structures like wings and eyes, not the re-use of earlier solutions such as a watchmaker would use. No intelligent watchmaker would think to redesign springs and cogs each time he decided to make a new watch.

In short, living things show evidence of design, but not of intelligent design.

So, does that apparent design itself point to a god but just not a very intelligent one perhaps? Maybe one with a fixation with beetles, of which there are some 500,000 different 'designs' alone?

Paley, and those who were convinced by his argument, did not know about a great deal of this redundancy, of course, because so much of it is at a microscopic level. Nor did they appreciate that watches have an obvious purpose which is not paralleled by living things, because the accepted religious dogma of the time was that God had created living things for humans. Because of this, they failed to appreciate that design does not necessarily indicate either a designer, or intelligence.

This argument was never more than an argument from personal incredulity – I cannot understand it therefore it must have been a god – and of course the locally popular god. They failed to appreciate this not because they were stupid or dishonest; they could only work with the state of knowledge of the times. They failed to appreciate it because they lacked one essential piece of knowledge, because science had not discovered it then.

What they failed to appreciate was that, unlike a watch which is made fully-formed, living things did not spring fully formed into existence just as they are now. This again was an assumption conditioned by the religious dogma of the day. Living things were made by an entirely natural process over a very long time. That natural process, natural selection of inherited variations by a selective environment, can explain all these things. Just like the explanation for Paley's Watch, the explanation does not require an unexplained supernatural mystery for which no hypothesis can account, nor does it require magic.

All the components of this system can be seen and understood, just like all of the components of the system for making watches can be seen and understood. Natural selection is the most parsimonious explanation both for the appearance of design and for the appearance of a stupid designer. Living things look exactly as you would expect them to look if designed by a utilitarian, mindless, purposeless design process, given direction only by the environment in which it operates.

Now that we can stand on the shoulders of giants like Darwin and Wallace, we can see further than other men. We can now see further then the Bronze Age goat-herder who thought up the creation myth; who could not even see over the horizon and thought the earth was flat.

We can see now that there is nothing supernatural required and nothing supernatural involved.

The Ontological Fallacy.
This apologetic is perhaps one of the more surprising ones, yet you will still see it deployed by serious theologians. In essence, it is nothing more than the

The Fallacy of Apologetics

argument that because we can define a god and make claims of its qualities, it must exist.

It was devised by St Anselm, then Archbishop of Canterbury, in a 1087 work he called *Proslogion.* In this, he defined God as "that than which nothing greater can be conceived". He then argued that this god must exist in the mind, even in the mind of non-believers. He argued that, if the greatest possible being exists in the mind, it must also exist in reality. If it only exists in the mind, then an even greater being must be possible – one which exists both in the mind and in reality. Therefore, this greatest possible being must exist in reality.

But, as Anselm's contemporary, Gaunilo of Marmoutiers, pointed out, you can use this argument to 'prove' the existence of anything. He used the analogy of a perfect island. Believe me! I have tried this with a swimming pool in my back garden. No matter how perfect I define this imaginary swimming pool to be, it never appears.

David Hume refuted the argument by denying that existence can be a necessity and Emmanuel Kant rejected it on the grounds that it is a false premise to argue that existence can be a predicate. Kant also argued that the mere fact of existence does not add perfection and thus it is equally valid to define a perfect being as a non-existent one. (More on that in a moment...)

Earlier, Thomas Aquinas had argued that, since it is beyond the ability of humans to conceive of God's perfection, the argument was fallacious in its premise. Note though that just as Anselm's argument is based on assumed prior knowledge and is thus circular, so is Aquinas's counter argument.

But of course, just as the test of the validity of the Cosmological Argument is exposed by applying the same 'logic' to other gods or imaginary notions such as fairies or perfect teapots orbiting Mars, and noting that it works equally well for them, so we can do the same with the Anselm's Ontological Argument.

There is another more basic objection that I touched on earlier – that non-existence could be regarded as perfection in just the same way that perfection is. C. D. Broad pointed out that some definitions of perfection conflict with others. For example, in classical theism, God is both omnipotent and omniscient, which means an omnipotent god should be able to create beings

91

with free will, yet an omniscient god must know the eventual choice of these beings in advance, so rendering them without free will. Hence God cannot be both omnipotent and omniscient, so cannot be perfect.

Simpler tests than this which show the limited power and hence lack of omnipotence of a god can be seen by asking, "Can God make an object so heavy he cannot lift it?", "Can God change the value of pi?", "Can God make a Euclidean triangle with other than three sides and whose internal angles do not add up to 180°?"

Of course, no god could do these things; the first because whatever answer is given, the god is rendered limited in its powers and the other two because these values are defined by mathematical laws.

Muslims claim that Allah is the most just and most merciful, so any definition of perfection for Allah must include maximally just and maximally merciful, yet, as Dan Barker has pointed out:

> *Justice means that punishment is administered with the exact amount of severity that is deserved for the crime that is committed. We don't put children in prison for stealing cookies, and we don't merely fine a murderer $50. Mercy, on the other hand, means that punishment is administered with less severity than deserved. When the police officer lets you off with a warning instead of a ticket for breaking the speed limit, that is mercy. If God is infinitely merciful, he can never be just. If God is ever just (not to mention infinitely just), then he cannot be infinitely merciful. A God who is both infinitely merciful and just not only does not exist, he cannot exist. This is one of the positive arguments for the nonexistence of God based on incompatible properties (or incoherency). If God is defined as a married bachelor, we don't need to discuss evidence or argument; we can simply claim a logical impossibility.*

Here are two mutually exclusive, maximally great theoretical qualities, one of which must be less than maximal for the other to be maximal. So, Anselm's definition of a maximally great god cannot be met in practice, yet we **can** conceive of it. It is very easy to think of pairs of opposites – large/small, thin/fat, heavy/light – where any maximally great god should be both, yet being one precludes the other, hence the concept of maximally great is itself flawed. There are also simple paradoxes like God's honesty. If God cannot lie then his powers are limited; if he can lie, then he is not maximally honest or maximally good.

A non-existent god suffers from none of these irreconcilable paradoxes of course, so can be argued to be more perfect, and much closer to maximally perfect, that an existent one.

In his book, *The Problem with "God": Classical Theism under the Spotlight*, Johnathan Pearce succinctly sums up these problems for the ontological argument:

> ... any such argument [of ontological perfection] for or against God does not really get off the ground since it is contingent upon the idea of perfection being logically coherent as an intrinsic value and characteristic. This, I am afraid, is wrong. One cannot make this assumption because perfection, as a stand-alone conceptual characteristic to ascribe to anything, is nonsensical.
>
> I can only understand perfect as a goal-directed adjective such that A is perfect for B, or this catapult is perfect for getting this stone over the wall in such and such a manner. Now, one could say that God is perfect at being God, but this implies an infinite regress or circularity. What does it really mean to say that God is perfect? Is he perfect at getting a stone over the wall? Perfect at being loving, merciful and just; at being perfect, designing and moral?
>
> Even establishing what a perfect painting is, is an entirely subjective process, depending upon personal tastes. And this applies to all sorts of things such that perfection becomes either subjective or incoherent. Being perfectly powerful and knowledgeable are admittedly simpler proficiencies to hold, conceptually.
>
> The other problem is that perfection of a being involves multiple aspects such that, as the classic problem goes, God cannot be perfectly just AND perfectly merciful since to be perfectly just assumes punishing justly for a misdemeanour, and to be perfectly merciful assumes some kind of leniency.

> *With all of these characteristics which conflict, the theist retreats to maximal perfection, a sort of optimal scenario given all of the nuances and variables. But this becomes arbitrary and subjective. One more ounce of mercy and one less ounce of justice might be perfect for a God wanting to achieve A, but vice versa might be better for wanting to achieve B.*
>
> *Therefore we need to establish, without circularity or incoherence, what God is to be perfect FOR, before establishing whether God is or can be perfect. To have a timeless God sitting there and label it as perfect is, to me, meaningless (as a stand-alone descriptor).*
>
> *Therefore, and given the subjective nature of appraisals of perfection, I see any argument using the term perfection as incoherent or wholly under-developed.*[29]

With even the idea of perfection being incoherent and essentially arbitrary, Anselm's Ontological Argument was never anything more than an attempt to define his god into existence. It was little better than asserting that God must exist because he thought it existed. "I believe in God, therefore God exists and because I say God is perfect, God is perfect."

Why would anyone need to perform these mental gymnastics if they had the smallest scrap of definitive evidence?

The Transcendental Fallacy

Briefly, the Transcendental Argument for God[30] (Which God?) runs as follows:

There are three logical absolutes:

1. Law of Identity: Something is what it is and is not what it is not. Something that exists has a specific nature. For example, an apple is that apple, and a rock is that rock. In other words, whatever is, **is**.
2. Law of Non-contradiction: Two opposing statements cannot both be true. For example, "this is an apple" and "this is a rock" cannot both

---

[29] (Pearce, 2015)
[30] (Slick, 2011)

be true if the object in both statements is referring to the same thing. In other words, nothing can both be and not be.
3. Law of Excluded Middle: A statement cannot be both true and false at the same time in the same sense. For example, the statement "this is an apple" is either true or false; an object being an apple cannot be both true and false at the same time. In other words, everything must either be or not be.[31]

The Transcendental Argument for God builds on these premises to construct the following argument:

1. Logical absolutes exist.
2. These laws of logic are conceptual in nature, not physical. They do not exist anywhere in the physical world.
3. Because these absolutes are conceptual, they must have been conceived in a mind.
4. However, these laws are perfect and absolute. Human minds are not perfect or absolute.
5. Logical absolutes are true everywhere and are not dependent on human minds.
6. Therefore, these laws of logic must exist in a perfect, absolute, transcendental mind.
7. That mind is called God. [Which God?][32]

In essence, the argument depends on the idea that logical arguments must be a product of a mind.

This is a fallacy of equivocation. The logic breaks down at the second step. Although it needs a mind to formulate the logic and put it into words, the description of the logic is not where the logic resides, nor is the mental concept. The description, like the description of all scientific laws, is not the law itself. It is simply a description of reality.

An apple is an apple and not a rock, not because a mind conceptualised it to be so but because it **is** so. The concept follows from the fact, not *vice versa*, and the facts most certainly exist in the physical world. The three logical

---
[31] (Navabi, 2014)
[32] (Navabi, 2014) (Kindle Locations 928-935).

absolutely are wholly materialist in nature. There is nothing transcendental about them.

For example, a photograph of a mountain is not the mountain itself. You cannot look at a photograph of a mountain and assume that it is the mountain itself, no matter how good the photographer was, how accurate the colours are or how good a concept of the mountain it might be. If the description of a mountain (the photograph) and the real thing were the same, a mountain would be two-dimensional. You could print it out and hold it in your hand and wave it around, or even post it on the Internet.

This mistake comes from the same failure to appreciate the descriptive nature of these laws of nature and to distinguish them from the proscriptive nature of man-made laws. I will cover this in more depth in Chapter 6, Hypotheses, Experiments, Theories and Laws.

An uncharitable person might conclude that this apologetic, like so many other religious apologetics, was invented to confuse those for whom logical thought presents a challenge, but maybe it was just devised by those suffering from that disability themselves.

Pascal's Wager.
Also known as Pascal's Gambit, this fallacy was first enunciated by the French mathematician, Blaise Pascal (19 June 1623 – 19 August 1662). He argued that, because neither the existence nor the non-existence of God can be proved by pure reason, a believer has everything to gain by believing in God, while a non-believer has everything to lose.

In its crudest form, this is the 'What if you're wrong?' argument levelled against atheism.

Apart from its abject and disgraceful abandonment of pure reason, in the implicit assumption that reality can be determined by wager, where else does Pascal's Wager fail? The first and most important assumption is that there are only two possibilities from which to choose.

As many people have pointed out, and as many apologists for other gods have shown, Pascal's Wager can be just as easily used for **any** deity, whether actually believed by anyone or merely hypothetical. All this deity needs is its supporters to claim it promises eternal life to believers and eternal suffering for non-believers.

Using Pascal's Wager alone, should people believe in the Christian god, the Jewish god, the Muslim god, the Shinto gods, the Hindu gods, the Aztec god Quetzalcoatl? The very obvious counter to the question, 'What if you're wrong?' is, 'What if **you** are?' Has a Christian or a Muslim placed a safer bet than an atheist if there turns out to be a god, but that god is Ganesh or Zeus? If Pascal's premise that neither existence nor non-existence of gods can be proved by reason alone, then this holds true for **any** notional god, not just the Christian god.

Given that there is an infinite number of possible hypothetical gods, a bet placed on any one god becomes indistinguishable from placing no bet at all. My personal favourite response is to ask, 'What if when you die you find Satan waving the Bible/Quran at you and laughing?'

But apart from that damaging error, there are several unstated and fatal assumptions in Pascal's Wager which show that it only 'works' if you assume *a priori* the following:

1. There is an after-life – requiring a priori belief in the existence of a god and a soul.
2. The Abrahamic belief in Heaven and Hell is valid – requiring a priori belief in the existence of the Abrahamic god.
3. That the Abrahamic god is the only god, requiring *a priori* belief in the existence of the Abrahamic god.

What if we exclude these assumptions?

1. The wager fails since there is no difference in outcome no matter which we opt to bet on.
2. The wager fails because what happens, even if there is an after-life, may not depend on which option you bet on.
3. The wager fails because you will have almost certainly lost everything by opting to believe in the wrong god. With an infinite array of all possible gods being bet against just one, the bet to believe becomes indistinguishable from the bet not to believe.

So, without these *a priori* assumptions, where does that leave Pascal's Wager? It leaves it as a gamble in which you opt either to sacrifice your intellectual integrity, independence of thought and action, and responsibility for your own beliefs and actions, against a lifetime of freedom, personal integrity, self-reliance and personal responsibility. You surrender freedom and self-respect in favour of abject, cringing, voluntary slavery.

What benign, benevolent, truth and honesty-loving god could respect a person who did that?

And this is the final nail in the coffin of Pascal's Wager: as any god with an IQ above that of a cucumber should be able to work out; it assumes the god it purports to promote is too stupid to notice that its 'believers' do not have any real reason to believe in it but are merely pretending to believe in it just in case it is true.

In fact, Pascal's Wager, far from being the trump card apologists like to keep up their sleeve for when they look like losing, actually shows what poor, tenuous things religious faiths are. The Abrahamic faiths in particular seem especially feeble, in that they need to depend on such weak and hypocritical fallacies, and implied threats to maintain themselves.

Pascal's Wager is nothing more than an attempt to fool an omniscient god, and it is based on nothing more substantial than a morbid fear that a story used to frighten children into obedient compliance might actually be true.

Would any maximally good god want its believers to believe by fear?

The God of the Gaps and Arguments from Ignorance.

Although not strictly a formal religious apologetic, the 'God of the Gaps' fallacy absolutely suffuses religious argument, often appearing under cover in formal apologetics. It is a special case of the False Dichotomy Fallacy which we will meet again in Chapter 4 as an example of a spectacular failure of logical thinking.

The entire premise of this fallacy is that if there is something that science cannot explain, or more often has not yet explained, then the only possible explanation is that the god in question must have done it.

It turns up in the Cosmological Argument in that this argument is an attempt to show that the cause of the Universe cannot be explained because it requires something to pre-exist it. Leaving aside the scientific validity of that claim, even if true it merely creates a gap in which to place the required god.

It turns up in the Argument from Objective Morality where a gap is supposedly revealed in our understanding of where humans get their 'objective' morals from. It turns up again in science's supposed inability to explain consciousness or the origin of 'life'. The God of the Gaps can be found sitting in the gaps in the fossil record and when another gap is filled by science, more often than not a gap either side of it is found.

A considerable amount of commercial creationist propaganda consists of trying to create imaginary gaps in the minds of customers by misrepresentation of science or often straightforward lying. The scientific Theory of Evolution, for example, is routinely presented as something that no evolutionary biologist would recognise as the real thing. Science is then 'challenged' to provide 'proof' of this or that parody and failure to do so is presented as a gap which can only be filled by Allah or the god of the Bible.

The only place a God of the Gaps is never found is where science examines the gap and discovers how to close it. Not a single scientific mystery has even been filled with a god and not a single scientific advance was ever made by a scientist contentedly sitting back and declaring with smug self-satisfaction that 'God did it!'

The God of the Gaps argument is not only fallacious, in that the existence of the god should have been formally established before it can be inserted into the argument, it must be shown to be the **only** explanation on offer otherwise it becomes a false dichotomy too.

The God of Personal Necessity.

The God of Personal Necessity is probably the second most popular religious fallacy and, like the God of the Gaps fallacy, is accepted by very many otherwise intelligent people. Like the God of the Gaps fallacy it too is so ludicrous when spelled out it is quite astonishing that it is even attempted, yet it crops up time and again in discussion with believers of all creeds.

It takes several forms but essentially the argument is always, there must be a god otherwise the consequences would be [something undesirable, unpleasant or otherwise unacceptable].

Some examples are:

- There must be a god otherwise there would be no morality;
- There must be a god otherwise there would be no purpose to my life;
- There must be a god otherwise I would have nowhere to go when I die;
- There must be a god otherwise I would not be so special that the universe was created for me;
- There must be a god otherwise the explanation for everything would be too hard for me to understand;
- There must be a god otherwise I would be just another animal and I am too important for that;
- There must be a god otherwise my invisible friend would not be real;
- There must be a god otherwise I would just be talking to myself when I pray;
- There must be a god otherwise my belief in it would be wrong. (This is often referred to as 'faith' – I believe it, therefore it must be true.)

There is always the unspoken subtext that this god is the locally popular god, or at the very least, the god I was told to believe in when I was a child. There is never any question that it might be a different one, even one no one has heard of. Nor is there ever any consideration that things may indeed not be as the believer would like them to be. The idea that the universe may not be compliant and cosy is never considered.

There is absolutely nothing at all in this argument unless it can be shown that somehow, personal necessity creates gods; that somehow gods are obliged to exist if and when believers require them to and these gods have exactly the right characteristics required by personal necessity.

The surprising thing is that this delusion often persists into adulthood and so allows believers to be duped by charlatans who earn a living by reassuring them that their god is indeed everything they need it to be. It is probably the nice warm glow of self-affirmation which makes this such a persistent and attractive fallacy for both religious exploiters and their victims alike.

It is also one of the hardest fallacies to explain to a believer because so much of their persona is invested in this delusion. That their god fills their personal requirements so perfectly and completely is often the reason they subscribe to the 'faith' in the first place. To consider for one moment that their god might not conform to their requirements is to attack their entire reason to be deluded in the first place.

The 'God Is Pure Energy' Fallacy.

An argument which is commonly found in 'spiritual' and even some mainstream religions, and is even advanced by people who like to think 'there is something out there', is the idea that God is a synonym for pure energy. In a 2007 article, Brendan McPhillips attempted to argue that Einstein had proved God exists with his $e=mc^2$ formula showing that energy and mass are interchangeable.[33] Sadly, the vacuity of his argument in which he merely showed how you can build assertion on assertion with never a piece of solid evidence or logical connection, serves to illustrate the vacuity of the 'God is Pure Energy' fallacy itself. For example:

> *It takes a tremendous amount of energy to create mass. So what would we call the energy that would be large enough, powerful enough and pervasive enough to create the solar system, the planets, the stars, the sun, you, me and everything on earth…come on…that's right…say it with me…**GOD! God is Energy.***

That claim can be dismissed as easily as it is made. Come on… that's right… say it with me… **No! It is not! It does not work that way!**

We already have a perfectly good working definition of energy which gains nothing from assigning to it the qualities of a god, even the particular Christian god that McPhillips was promoting. There is nothing to suggest that energy has any sentience; that it can plan and operate at will to make things happen; that it can be benevolent and 'love' its creations or be vengeful and punishing or a source of morals.

---

[33] (McPhillips, 2007)

There is not even anything to suggest that the energy in the Universe has always existed. Indeed, to assume that energy has always existed (in another case of special pleading) removes any need to explain where anything came from in the first place, so removes any need to postulate a god.

Try the 'Which God?' test.

C. S. Lewis's Christian Apologetics.

Clive Staples Lewis (29 November 1898 – 22 November 1963) was an Oxford academic, novelist, Christian apologist and broadcaster. He claimed to have been an atheist in his youth but in all his writings about his 'new-found' faith nowhere does he explore the different possible gods and religions.

Having become convinced that some phenomena must have a supernatural origin, he seems to have concluded without further questioning that this must be the Christian god of the Bible and that the Anglican Church into which he had been baptised as a child must be the True Faith. It is therefore highly likely that, rather than being an atheist in the sense of accepting that there is no evidential reason to be otherwise, and that the only reason for belief is evidence, he was simply a non-practising believer. As a positive atheist he would have known that merely not knowing or not understanding how something works or why something is as it appears, is itself no reason to believe a god did it, let alone which particular god.

His reasoning is therefore often little more than a verbose and self-satisfied God of the Gaps or an Argument from Ignorance fallacy which he keeps well hidden beneath his homely fireside chat style. This was often adapted from his radio broadcasts which were intended to be just that. He was also obviously filling a war-time propaganda function in helping to keep the morale of the population high, secure in their belief that they had the one true faith and therefore God could be guaranteed to be on their side.

Running through all his writing is an ingrained English upper-class snobbery and freedom from the encumbrance of self-doubt. This may have been influenced by his Belfast Protestant childhood. It often leads him to not explain the reasoning behind many of his assumptions and it underpins his condescending and patronising style.

He was writing for a deferential, class-ridden audience which could be expected to accept what Lewis was saying and be in thrall that a 'brilliant Oxford academic' was confirming what they already knew. The English had the right culture, the right church, the right religion and the right god; a god who was, of course, as English as roast beef and the smack of leather on willow on a sunny Surrey Sunday afternoon in summer. God was in his heaven and all was right with the world!

The Argument from Desire.

Briefly, Lewis's argument from desire is:

> *Every desire is necessarily a desire for something, and every natural desire must have some object that will satisfy it. Since humans desire the joy and experience of God, therefore there must be a God that will satisfy our desires.*

This is little different from St. Anselm's Ontological Argument in practice. Somehow, simply desiring something makes it pop into existence, just as being able to conceive of it does.

In a sermon preached at St Mary the Virgin Church in Oxford in 1941, later published in *Theology*, he explained it thus:

> *A man's physical hunger does not prove that man will get any bread; he may die of starvation on a raft in the Atlantic. But surely a man's hunger does prove that he comes of a race which repairs its body by eating and inhabits a world where eatable substances exist. In the same way, though I do not believe (I wish I did) that my desire for Paradise proves that I shall enjoy it, I think it a pretty good indication that such a thing exists and that some men will. A man may love a woman and not win her; but it would be very odd if the phenomenon called "falling in love" occurred in a sexless world.*[34]

This seems to be more an example of Lewis's arrogance in assuming that there is something out there organising the Universe so it conforms to his desires. Like Anselm's Ontological Argument is can easily be refuted just by applying

---

[34] (Lewis, 1942)

it to anything other than Lewis's god or his notion of Heaven. If a Hindu desires 'the joy and experience' of Brahma or a Muslim desires 'the joy and experience' of Allah' they also exist, just as the Norse and Greek gods once existed, presumably. So, with lots of different people from lots of different religions all desiring 'the joy and experience' of their particular god, they all become the one true god!

Why is this restricted to gods or abstract notions like Heaven? Lewis himself seems to think it applies to mundane things like bread, so try desiring a heated swimming pool or a brand new car, for example. Try desiring world peace and freedom from hunger and want.

This argument put me in mind of the thousands of creationists who swarm the Internet to tell us what they think the Theory of Evolution is (and how it is all wrong) even though it is manifestly obvious they have never tried to learn any of the science. They just know what it is, and it is so. No-one is going to tell them otherwise. If the theory is not what they want the theory to be, how can they attack it? Like Lewis's god, it has to be that way because that is what they want.

Lewis's Argument from Desire is nothing more than a God of Personal Necessity fallacy, dressed up to look deep and intellectual.

The Argument from Objective Morality.

In essence, Lewis's Argument from Objective Morality goes as follows:

1. Objective morals can only come from God.
2. Objective morals exist.
3. Therefore God exists.

The first premise is really nothing more than an assertion; a God of the Gaps and an argument from ignorance fallacy. Does Lewis imagine that people who follow different gods or no gods at all have no morals? This is a common claim made by fundamentalists of all religions but it is simply not borne out by the evidence. The evidence from Europe where religion has been in headlong decline for the last sixty years or so, is that people do not become less moral as they become less religious – quite the opposite in fact.

The Fallacy of Apologetics

This argument was never more than a smug, and more than a little arrogantly condescending, assertion that a Christian such as C. S. Lewis is the only person with real morals because they come from the Christian god. Yet when we look for the evidence of these objective morals in the Bible, what do we find?

We find slavery condoned. We find women relegated to an inferior status and treated as goods that can be bought, sold or bartered. We find brutality in place of justice. We find rape condoned and rape victims blamed and forced to marry their rapist. We find autocracy taken for granted. We find disability stigmatised as an abomination and we find homosexual love condemned as a capital crime.

We find people being killed for collecting firewood on the Sabbath, not as an example of an act of arbitrary brutality but as a virtuous obedience to God. We find transgressions of food taboos and dress codes deserving the same punishment as murder – but only if the murder victim is a Hebrew. We find daughters being sold as sex slaves by their fathers and children being given a monetary value with girls commanding only half the price of boys.

We find not a single mention of democracy, of freedom of conscience, of free speech, of the right to choose our own leaders and remove them when they fail us. We find nothing about child abuse, though we are told disobedient children should be killed. We see not a single word spoken in condemnation of slavery; of racism; of sexism or disability discrimination yet we find that genocide and land theft are encouraged and have the blessing of this 'god of objective morals'.

In fact, we find in the Bible a moral code so repugnant that we have had to outlaw much of it throughout the civilised world and which, if followed, would, and should, result in a prison sentence for the perpetrator in order to protect decent people from his or her psychopathy.

In the Bible we find the morality of the protection racketeer. We find a creator who, as Christopher Hitchens said, creates us sick and commands us to be well. We find an allegedly omniscient creator who knows we will go to Hellfire before he creates us, yet creates us anyway. This is the equivalent in human terms of a grotesque sadist who breeds kittens intending to douse them in petrol and set them on fire. Is this really a role model for moral behaviour for our children to admire and to sing songs in praise of?

So where are non-Christian, Humanist morals to be found?

They are to be found in our **rejection** of the Old Testament morals and a great deal of the New Testament morals. They are to be found in the way decent folk recoil in horror at the Bible-based apologetic for infanticide as excused by William Lane Craig and others like him. They are to be found in our rejection of the faith-based condemnation and dehumanisation of homosexuals and transgender individuals. And they are to be found in our acceptance of the few scraps of decent humanism plagiarised by the authors of the Bible and presented as Christian.

We know the Good Samaritan was good, not because the Bible says so but because what he did was innately good. We know a woman taken in adultery should not be stoned and that those who judge others deserve to be so judged. We know it is right to feed the hungry, care for the sick and give a helping hand to those down on their luck. We know it is right to forgive and to understand and to respect the other, to value them as human beings and not take life needlessly, not because the Bible says so but because we are kind, decent people.

We know when the holy books are right and wrong, not because the holy books tell us but because we judge the holy books as decent human beings. When the Bible is right it is right because **we** say so, not because the Bible says so.

Is it wrong to kill because God says so, or does God say it is wrong because it is wrong? Christians tie themselves in knots over this question yet Humanists have no problem at all understanding that those who wrote down what they thought a good God would say, knew it was wrong; that a moral god would say so.

If you really believe you get your morals from the Bible, ask yourself what you would think if Jesus had told you to be unkind to old ladies and to hurt babies? With William Lane Craig's 'Divine Command Theory', he would undoubtedly say we would then have a duty to be unkind to old ladies and to hurt babies – it would be immoral not to do so.

If you cannot see what is wrong with that then you need psychiatric help.

The Fallacy of Apologetics

We know these things because decent people have empathy and can put themselves in the mind of another person and understand how they would feel. We do to others what we would have them do to us because we are decent people and want to live in a good, safe, society; a society which works.

So how did we get these morals?

Humans are evolved social animals. Just as our physical bodies are the result of evolution, so are our cultures. We know cultures evolved the way we know species evolved, because they share basics in common but differ in the details.

Let us go back to the plains of East Africa to the early childhood of mankind; to a time when our ancestors had left the trees and were surviving as best they could on the grasslands.

Here we were, a puny ape, walking upright and able to throw sticks and stones, maybe even sticks with stone points tied to them as simple spears. We were surrounded by predators like lions, hyenas, cheetahs, leopards, crocodiles, pythons and poisonous snakes. Out there in the grasslands was food a-plenty on the hoof, if only we were big enough to catch and kill it and not get caught and killed by something else out looking for dinner. If not, we would have to depend on foraging for insects, lizards, roots and berries in season; more gatherers than hunters.

We were not then the top predator, at the top of the food chain, but some way down it. We were never going to succeed as a species unless we worked together as a team and we were never going to work together as a team unless we all understood the first rule of teamwork – trust.

Trust means you can depend on other team members to play their part and they can depend on you. Betrayal of trust would have meant exclusion and almost certain death. To be in the team you had to do your bit. That might have meant simply being a look-out for predators looking to catch their dinner. It might have meant being a beater who drove the gazelle towards the spear-throwers. It might even have meant being the one who made the spear tips and tied them on the sticks. Or it could have been the ones who stayed behind and looked after the children.

Trust meant you got your share of the kill because you had played your part. Trust meant that the handful of people who actually made the kill did not make off with it and keep it all for themselves. We are still the only ape which gathers food and takes it back to the group to share it!

A successful group would have been the group which understood the basic rule of treating other people the way you would want them to treat you, and the most successful groups, by definition, would be the groups which left the most descendants. The most successful groups would have been the ones whose members understood that you succeed by doing least harm and that generosity pays off in the long run. The most successful groups would have been composed of individuals who cared for one another and gave a helping hand when one was needed.

The most successful groups would have been the ones with altruistic members because altruism produces more survivors who carry the genes for, or the cultural idea of, altruism.

In short, the most successful groups would have been the groups with shared morals and ethics. They would have taken the land formerly occupied by those without morals and ethics or the vacant land that needed cooperation to survive in. Groups with shared morals would have been the survivors. The survivors were the ones who cared for one another.

Then we evolved religion and created gods. In our primitive understanding of the world, in which the unexplained was explained by magic, and magical forces were reified and given human characteristic, those things which caused bad things to happen were bad spirits. They were the ones who you did not want in the team. The ones who caused good things to happen were the good ones. They were the ones you would want in the team and so they must have had good team skills. They must cause good because they care about us!

But, they were powerful gods, were they not? They were gods who could cause magic and control a world in ways far beyond the capabilities of mere humans. How could they possibly have got these morals from humans? Obviously, they must have given them to us! How could it be otherwise?

That mistake set us up for the sucker punch.

That set us up to fall for the notion that 'good' must have come from a god; that somehow 'good' was whatever a god said was good. And who told us what the gods said? The priesthood, of course!

So we abdicated responsibility for our own morals and handed them over to the priesthood. It seemed so right at the time and so much easier too! All we had to do was gather together to be told what was right and what was wrong; what was good and what was bad. And the priesthood used our naive gullibility for their own ends and took control of our society and set kings and rulers over us to help in that control, in an unholy alliance designed to control the people. Our caring and sharing cultures had succumbed to a parasitic class, facilitated by the memetic parasite of religion; a parasite of our own naive creation.

We believed them when they told us to kill the Canaanites to take their land, to enslave the Africans and take their countries to teach them 'morality', to slaughter foreigners by the tens of thousands with machine guns for a few yards of territory. We believed them when they told us to kill the Jews because God did not like them, to destroy the Pacific Fleet at Pearl Harbour for the God-Emperor, to drop atom bombs on the Japanese to teach them civilised ways. We believed them when they said to fly planes full of people into buildings full of people to show them how great Allah is and to strike a mighty blow against Satan.

And we told ourselves we were being good because God said so, or so the priesthood and the theologians told us...

But we have grown up now. In the civilised, educated world we no longer see a world controlled by magic spirits. Science has shown us that there is never a need for a god to explain anything. It has shown us that including a god in any explanation simply adds unnecessary complexity whilst adding nothing useful to it. Science has shown us how human psychology, primitive ignorance and magical thinking in the childhood of our species has combined to produce the naive reification of gods.

We now have the knowledge and understanding to take back our morality and to develop it with us as we progress. We no longer need to allow it to be used to control us and to hold us back in some imaginary world of magic spirits and all-powerful deities, who dispense morality to us through the priesthood and whom the priesthood has declared immune from enquiry.

We are now capable of looking back at our history and conclude that, if religion told us that was right, religion was wrong.

No wonder then that the political right employ right-wing religious apologists to bamboozle the ignorant, the credulous and the intellectual indolent into continuing to abdicate moral responsibility and allowing the priesthood to keep it.

No wonder then that self-serving charlatans are advocating a creed of greed and selfishness, division and discrimination – the very antithesis of what our morals first evolved to give us and which made us succeed against the odds in a hostile environment. A society which is based on caring, compassion, teamwork, cooperation and a willingness to lend a helping hand to those down on their luck or suffering misfortune. A society which values all of its members and not just a small, powerful elite who require us to be primitive in our understanding in order for them to get away with it and make off with the results of the kill and keep it for themselves.

Religion is not a source of morality but an abdication of moral responsibility and an abandonment of our humanity.

Perhaps we can forgive C. S. Lewis for not knowing about cultural memes and how these replicators are subject to the same evolutionary process as genes, just as we can forgive William Paley for his ignorance of evolution. Maybe we can forgive Lewis for his ignorant assumption that only Christians have morals and all other people are lacking. After all, he only ever left Britain once in his life briefly as a soldier in the First World War before being wounded and sent back home. Maybe he really **did** think the non-Christian world was lawless and amoral, no matter how unlikely that is.

But what we should not forgive Lewis for was for his smug failure to consider other possibilities with which to fill the gap in his knowledge and understanding. Arbitrarily filling this gap with his favourite god and presenting this as a conclusive argument was unforgivable in someone who purported to be an intellectual and an Oxford academic whose only goal was truth.

C. S. Lewis, like all Christians, got his entire 'knowledge' of God ultimately from the Bible, whether related by theologians and preachers or from reading it himself. This included his idea of objective morals – the yardstick by which he measured right and wrong. But, since he also believed in Satan and saw the world in terms of an eternal struggle between God and Satan, there is one important consideration neither he, nor those like him, ever addressed: how did he know that Satan did not write the Bible?

By insisting that the Bible is the ultimate source of his knowledge of right and wrong he excluded the possibility of using it as an objective measure of its own morality. He had no external measure by which to judge, yet he could not use the Bible to validate itself, either logically or because Satan could have written whatever he cited, in order to fool him.

By abdicating his moral responsibility to determine right and wrong for himself, he was forever in a moral quagmire with no map and no possibility of escape. He could, for all he knew, be Satan's agent when he told us to believe in the god of the Bible. Unless those like C. S. Lewis, who wave their Bibles around as though they have higher morals than the rest of us, can prove Satan could not have written the Bible, or whatever holy book they are waving, they are morally bankrupt since they have not even bothered to consider that they could be leading us straight to the damnation they purport to be leading us from.

The Trilemma.

Of all Lewis's apologetics, this is perhaps the most transparently fallacious but is also one of the most frequently deployed. I have heard is presented by an Anglican Bishop no less, on the BBC Radio 4's *Thought For Today* in which people from various religions spend five minutes every weekday morning talking down to the British people. Basically the trilemma is that Jesus can only have been:

1. A lunatic
2. A liar, or
3. Lord

It would be doing Lewis an injustice to blame him for thinking up this appallingly dishonest argument all by himself because it was used at least as far back as the middle of the nineteenth century by preachers like Mark

Hopkins, John Duncan, Reuben Archer Torrey and others. Lewis merely plagiarised it and claimed it for himself. But his or not, Lewis found it to be a nice little earner, and got a BBC Radio series and a book, *Mere Christianity*, out of it.

It has been described as, "The most important argument in Christian Apologetics", by other Christian apologists like Peter Kreeft. No! Seriously!

All Lewis is doing here is producing an extended version of the false dichotomy fallacy. This fallacy is where the proponent of an otherwise unsupportable idea tries to present it as a choice between that and something completely absurd, or as the only reasonable choice. You see this used all too often when creationists attack science expecting you to believe that if science is wrong about something, the only alternative is to believe their favourite locally popular god must have been responsible. This only works if you fall for the idea that: a) science is wrong and; b) there is no other possible explanation, like a different scientific explanation, a different god, etc.

All the 'Trilemma' does is present a third option, a false trichotomy, in the hope that you won't think of a fourth, fifth or sixth, or more. For example, there are several more which could (should?) be added:

4. Made Up.
5. Legendary.
6. Mistaken.
7. Misinterpreted.
8. Misreported.

Reading the Bible, which is after all the primary (indeed, only) source of any information about Jesus, and seeing the several confused and often contradictory accounts of his life and teaching in it, the most vicarious explanation is one of these five, not one of the three Lewis presents as the only choices.

This is also borne out by biblical historians, few of whom would argue that: a) the Gospels were written by four different eye-witnesses to the accounts they describe; or b) that they were written contemporaneously with those events. There is very clear evidence of a developing of a legend, either based on a real figure or on one derived from several Jewish activists and teachers. Onto this seems to have been grafted the idea that he was a manifestation of the Jewish god Yahweh, using old prophecies, mistranslated where necessary, to give it credence.

Lewis must have been aware of these possibilities yet chose to ignore them and present us with a narrow choice. The first two of these choices were almost unthinkable in those days – and indeed I know of no atheist arguments that propose Jesus was mad and/or a liar.

In effect, Lewis was arguing that Jesus must be God or you must be stupid. Only stupid people do not agree with Clive Staples Lewis!

The Argument from Childish Thinking.

The following is an argument for the Christian god which Lewis put forward in all seriousness and which, if they are to be believed, at least some Christians find convincing. It is taken from his 1952 book *Mere Christianity* and seems designed to appeal to those who want to believe his self-proclaimed 'former atheism' was delusional:

> *My argument against God was that the universe seemed so cruel and unjust. But how had I got this idea of just and unjust? A man does not call a line crooked unless he has some idea of a straight line. What was I comparing this universe with when I called it unjust? If the whole show was bad and senseless from A to Z, so to speak, why did I, who was supposed to be part of the show, find myself in such violent reaction against it? A man feels wet when he falls into water, because man is not a water animal: a fish would not feel wet. Of course I could have given up my idea of justice by saying it was nothing but a private idea of my own. But if I did that, then my argument against God collapsed too—for the argument depended on saying that the world was really unjust, not simply that it did not happen to please my fancies. Thus in the very act of trying to prove that God did not exist—in other words, that the whole of reality was senseless—I found I was forced to assume that one part of reality—namely my idea of justice—was full of sense. Consequently atheism turns out to be too simple. If the whole universe has no meaning, we should never have found out that it has no meaning: just as, if there*

> *were no light in the universe and therefore no creatures with eyes, we should never know it was dark. Dark would be a word without meaning.*

So, having realised that his childhood belief was childish, and based on his own false expectations, Lewis concludes that the only possible explanation is that the Christian god must exist.

Typically for Lewis, how he gets from the realisation that his expectations for the universe were naïve and the startling realisation that he could not define these notions, to the conclusion that therefore the locally popular god from his culture exists, is never explained. All that is required is for Lewis to discredit his supposed earlier childish beliefs and the rest just follows, apparently.

But, if we examine his reasoning and break it into its component parts we get:

1. The universe should conform to my preconception because a god would ensure it does.
2. The universe does not conform to my preconception therefore this god does not exist.
3. I do not know what my preconception is so I do not know if 2 is right or wrong.
4. Therefore 2 is wrong.
5. Therefore this god must exist.

But, there is a world of difference between realising that you do not know if your preconception is right or wrong and the apparently arbitrary conclusion that it is wrong. Why not conclude with equal confidence that it was right?

Given his initial premise, Lewis has no option but to reach that conclusion because otherwise his ultimate conclusion would be wrong. Where is the logic behind the assumption that his preferred god should be ensuring the universe conforms to his preconception in the first place?

All he has proved is that the initial preconception was wrong. There is no requirement at all for the universe to conform to Lewis's preconception. There is no reason at all to assume that, because Lewis realised he did not know what his preconception was, that it was therefore wrong.

The Fallacy of Apologetics

Still not convinced? Okay... If Lewis's logic holds we should be able to apply it to other arguments with equal validity. Let us change the initial premise slightly and see what we can prove with the same 'logic':

1. The universe should be unjust because the Christian god does not exist.
2. The universe is just; therefore the Christian god must exist.
3. I do not know what justice is therefore I do not know if 2 is right or wrong.
4. Therefore 2 is wrong.
5. Therefore the Christian god does not exist.

Exactly the same 'logic' can be used to 'prove' exactly the opposite, if only we change the initial unproven premise. This is the classic apologetic tactic of starting with the required answer and working backward.

We can also show the basic fallacy and circular reasoning here by applying the 'Which god?' test because nowhere in all this has Lewis presented any reason to conclude that the only god on offer is the locally popular one. Even if his dots had joined up, they could be used with equal validity for any god, or indeed a Celestial Peanut-butter Sandwich, if that was what you were trying to prove runs the universe.

This is why it can be used equally to 'prove' there is no god. It is nothing more than an intellectually dishonest circular argument designed to hide the fact that the initial premise is merely an assumption inserted to beg the question and rig the logic so the outcome is the required one. This is a Christian apologetic designed to make Christians feel secure in their beliefs. It is not designed to make converts or win over the doubters.

There is no proof of anything in this argument but it does highlight the following problem for Christian theology. If the universe is run by an omni-benevolent god, why does it still look just as you would expect it to if such a god is entirely absent? Perhaps it was his subconscious awareness of this fundamental problem which motivated him to abandon his intellectual integrity in order to try to dismiss it. Cognitive dissonance and years of practice at coping with it, often seems to explain much of religious apologetics.

The Argument from Reason.

The last of these Christian apologetics was also Lewis's last, probably because it was his most careless and was invented when he felt over-confident in his intellectual abilities. He published it in *The Case for Christianity*:

> *Supposing there was no intelligence behind the universe, no creative mind. In that case, nobody designed my brain for the purpose of thinking. It is merely that when the atoms inside my skull happen, for physical or chemical reasons, to arrange themselves in a certain way, this gives me, as a by-product, the sensation I call thought. But, if so, how can I trust my own thinking to be true? It's like upsetting a milk jug and hoping that the way it splashes itself will give you a map of London. But if I can't trust my own thinking, of course I can't trust the arguments leading to Atheism, and therefore have no reason to be an Atheist, or anything else. Unless I believe in God, I cannot believe in thought: so I can never use thought to disbelieve in God.*

It is hard to believe he thought this through but perhaps he had just got carried away with his early success and was taking his target audience too much for granted and getting careless.

Of course, even if we share Lewis's genuine ignorance of neurophysiology and physics and his feigned ignorance of evolution (which was a well-established science by the time Lewis was writing his apologetics), and accept for the sake of argument that thinking is a random process, it is unavoidable to any honest thinking person that the same logic applies equally to his argument leading to belief in a god as to arguments leading to atheism.

Lewis has opened up another gap in his understanding and without further ado, had plonked his favourite god down in the middle of it. It is quite remarkable how neatly gods exactly fit these gaps in the ignorance of their believers. They seem to expand so as to fit the ignorance available to them. In Lewis's case, this intellectual laziness is dressed up to look intellectual and presented as a virtue.

Lewis has too obviously betrayed his double standards and ability to compartmentalise his thinking, using one standard for arguments against atheism and a much lower standard for arguments leading to belief in gods.

The Fallacy of Apologetics

Deservedly so, this argument was systematically dismantled by Elizabeth Anscome, an Oxford Philosophy don in a debate at the Socratic Society. Although this has been disputed by others, according to George Sayer, Lewis's friend and biographer, Lewis regarded the debate as a defeat, and felt humiliated by it:

> *He told me that he had been proved wrong, and that his argument for the existence of God had been demolished. ...The debate had been a humiliating experience, but perhaps it was ultimately good for him. In the past, he had been too proud of his logical ability. Now he was humbled .... 'I can never write another book of that sort' he said to me of Miracles. And he never did. He also never wrote another theological book.*[35]

---

[35] (Root, 2010), Footnote to P. 152

4. Failures of Logic.

But are there not still good, logical reason to believe in a god or gods?

If there were, philosophers and theologians would not be constantly arguing about the arguments themselves. Just as with the logical reasons to think Earth orbits the sun, scientists would have something to test, because a logical argument is a scientific hypothesis.

In fact, it is much easier to show logically that gods do not exist, at least gods as they are represented by the different religions. Faith is merely the failure to bring logical thought to bear on the subject.

We have looked at 'faith' alone as a reason to believe in gods and found that what is normally presented as a reason, is actually nothing more than an attempt to rationalise a pre-existing belief received from others and for which there is nothing that would qualify as evidence.

We have seen too how faith is useless as a means for determining truth and how it can lead to little more than random guesses that, if ever they are right, are right by accident.

We have seen how believing by faith is an abandonment of reason and an abdication of personal responsibility, how this can lead to grotesque abuses in the name of faith such as mass murders, genocidal massacres and destruction, and how it divides humanity into warring factions.

We have seen how faith cannot be obtained from holy books without pre-existing belief and why this can lead different people with different pre-existing beliefs to conclude that only their particular holy book was written or inspired by their particular god or is the eye-witness testimony of the events described.

We have seen how religious apologetics is essentially circular reasoning, designed not to determine the truth but to help confirm the existing bias of believers, often for no other reason than to make them feel smugly self-satisfied with their evidence-free beliefs. And we have seen how all of it is fallacious for the simple reason that the conclusion is always predetermined and depends on dishonest false logic deliberately designed to hide the flaws in the argument.

I will move on now to look at logical reason **not** to have faith; firstly the omni-claims where gods are assumed to have infinite abilities. Infinity is often used as a sort of get-out-of-jail-free tactic by theists rather like their 'ineffable god' argument because it seems to excuse everything. However for a theist, infinity is far from a constant friend, as we shall see.

Omniscience.
Gods are supposed to know everything; to have infinite knowledge, but who, even if they are a god, could possibly be certain that they know everything?

To know that you know everything, you would have to be certain there is nothing you do not know, but how is it logically possible to know what you do not know? How could even a god know what it does not know?

Assuming for a moment that gods exist, it is perfectly possible for a god to think it knows everything but to be unaware that this belief was placed there by another god and that almost all knowledge has been placed beyond its reach. How could the god in question be aware of this?

An omniscient god should be capable of working out that possibility – it is not exactly rocket science – so why claim omniscience in the first place, unless it is to deceive, and why would an omniscient god want to deceive people?

Given then that a claim of omniscience could not have come from an omni-benevolent god, where did this come from? It can only have been invented by people who never thought things through properly, or at least who knew they could depend on people believing what they were told by faith.

But any claim to have infinite knowledge, even notwithstanding the impossibility of knowing that you know everything, is irrational anyway because knowledge is not a fixed quantity. Even allowing that an omniscient god would know the future so would be aware of knowledge new to humans, its own knowledge would never cease to accumulate. Have you ever played that game which goes, "I know you know!", I know you know I know!", "I know you know I know you know I know!". How quickly did you get bored?

But a god would always be one step behind its own knowledge because it cannot know it knows something before it knows it. Therefore it will always be playing catch-up in its knowledge that it knows everything – and then it will know just one thing more than it knew a moment ago.

Now, let us explore what knowledge is exactly and how a god would know everything. Knowledge is holding a conceptual model of reality in one's mind. But this omniscient god needs to hold a **perfect** conceptual model in its mind. This brings me to the impossibility of infinite gods.

Theists who believe in an infinitely omniscient deity, believe in a god which must hold in its mind a conceptual model of the entire universe in absolute detail. If there are other universes, it must hold a conceptual model of those as well. This model will need to be constantly updated even to the exact position of every elementary particle and every vibration of every super-string. If any information is lost, the god ceases to be omniscient.

Have you ever done that thing with a mirror where you hold it up to another mirror and see a tunnel of diminishing mirrors disappearing into the distance, usually round a bend, unless you are holding the mirror exactly parallel to the other one? This looks like an infinite number of mirrors, but there is actually a lower limit to the size of the image of the mirror you are holding which can be reflected back to you, even if your eyesight is perfect. This is directly related to the wavelength of light. Below that distance, using visible light, two objects will appear as one.

Near Beaconsfield in Buckinghamshire, England, just a short ride down the M40 from London, is the model village of Bekonscot; reputedly the world's oldest model village. It is as accurate as its creator could make it in 1929. It includes a model of the model village, in which there is a model of the model of the model village... and so on, until it becomes a shapeless blob, because, with the best of intentions, no one could create accurate buildings, streets, roadside furniture, etc. to sufficient detail to be seen by human eyes below a certain size.

In a truly omniscient god's conceptual model will be a model of itself, complete with its conceptual model, which will also need to be constantly updated in real time, as will the conceptual model of itself within that conceptual model of itself, and every other infinitely diminishing model within it.

Of course, being omniscient, there can be no limit imposed by something like the wavelength of light or even the Plank length. Because it knows all things, our god cannot allow itself the luxury of diminishing models. It cannot reduce its conceptual model to a mere blob or stop at the lower limits of resolution because, being omniscient, it has no such lower limits, otherwise it will not be all knowing. Making a model smaller than the real thing invariably involves a degradation of the information therefore there would be a limit to its knowledge, so each model must be perfect with all information intact.

It is a bit like fractals, only where fractals repeat at a lower level of magnification, an omniscient god's conceptual models will all have to be full-sized.

So, to be omniscient, any god must have an infinite number of conceptual models of the Universe, including itself, all of which are accurate in absolute detail and all of which are being simultaneously and instantly updated. The transfer of information cannot be limited by the velocity of light but must be instantaneous; otherwise there would be a period during which the god does not know something.

In fact, because this supposed god is omniscient, its conceptual model will be indistinguishable from the real thing, as will all the infinity of full-sized models within that conceptual model, and so will be all the gods in those models. Each of those gods will also have infinitely many conceptual models all having to be instantaneously updated. Of course the god itself must monitor this infinitely complex conceptual model to keep itself omniscient, as must all the infinite number of gods.

Because they are indistinguishable from the real thing, they will no longer be models. They will be real things, just as a full-size, accurate in every detail model of a steam engine, house or village would be a real steam engine, house or village.

Failures of Logic

So, if any god is omniscient, there must be an infinite number of them in an infinite number of identical universes, each of which contains an infinite number of identical gods in identical full-sized universes... and so ad infinitum. A single god cannot be an omniscient god.

Believers in this (these) god(s) have to explain how this infinite complexity arose out of nothing...

Omnipotence.

Gods these days are supposed to be maximally powerful. This means there is literally nothing they cannot do.

But, we can show this cannot be true by a few simple mind experiments, some of which we met earlier.

Can a god make an object so heavy it cannot lift it? If yes, then there is a limitation imposed on its strength; if no, there is a limitation imposed on its ability to create. Since this paradox cannot be resolved, clearly a god cannot be maximally powerful.

Can a god change the value of pi? Pi is a mathematical constant which expresses the ratio of the length of the circumference of a circle to its radius. As the length of the radius of a circle varies, so the length of the circumference varies, but the ratio of these two values is always and invariably the same. The value of pi using the decimal system is an indeterminate value because the sequence of digits following the decimal never repeats, but they will always be the same no matter what the radius is.

It follows therefore that even a god has no control over the value of pi, nor of the sequence of the digits used to express that value using the decimal system of notation. A god's powers to vary the value of a universal constant such as pi is therefore limited by the laws of geometry.

In fact, people have often claimed to have found secret coded messages in the sequence of these digits but to encode a message in the value of pi, a god would need to be able to select them at will, yet there is only one unchangeable sequence, so no voluntarily arranged sequence is possible.

123

Similarly, a god could not vary the number of sides in a triangle nor change the internal angles for given lengths of sides. Nor could it change the sum of those angles. This of course goes for any other geometric shape, and the squared value of the hypotenuse of a right-angle triangle will always and invariably be the sum of the squared value of the other two sides.

Omni-benevolence.

The Christian, Jewish and Muslim view of their god is that it is an anthropophilic god who went to all the trouble of creating a Universe just so there was somewhere to put its special creation, mankind. They all believe it created Earth and everything in it for the convenience of mankind and it is a maximally good god, therefore the source of morality and the arbiter of right and wrong.

Omni-benevolence is another of those infinite characteristics of gods which believers feel covers everything but which, like omnipotence and omniscience, is irrational and actually impossible.

First we need a definition of 'good' before we can decide whether any particular god can be described as maximally good, and yet theists define 'good' as what their god says is good. Their god defines goodness, so we do not have any meaningful way to decide how well or badly gods measure up in any given aspect of goodness. This is a bit like defining a painting as perfect in every way, then asking, "Perfect for what?" Obviously a painting is not any good as a satellite navigation system, a telephone or a screwdriver, so it cannot be perfect in every way. It can only be perfect as a painting.

So, are gods only maximally good at being gods?

But, if maximal goodness is defined as being like gods, then gods cannot be anything but maximally good. Maximally good gods cannot be less than maximally good and so cannot be omnipotent, yet if they are not omnipotent, how can they ensure maximal goodness?

Goodness is irretrievably bound up with ideas of objective morality. However, when we try to fit, for example, Dr. William Lane Craig's definition of 'objective morality' we find he struggles with the idea. He resorts to arbitrarily designating his god as defining morality, so his morality is whatever he thinks God wants. You may recall Dr. Craig's definition of objective morality includes genocide and infanticide if God demands it.

> *To say that something is objective is to say that it is independent of what people think or perceive...*
>
> *... To say that there are objective moral values is to say that something is good or evil independently of whether any human being believes it to be so. Similarly to say that we have objective moral duties is to say that certain actions are right or wrong for us independently of whether any human being believes them to be so.*[36]

As Susan B Anthony astutely observed, "I distrust those people who know so well what God wants them to do because I notice how it always coincides with their own desires." This is more than a witty observation of how the pious behave; it captures the fact that many pious individuals interpret their own desires as coming from their god. You only need to read a page or two of *Mein Kampf* to see what 'morality' that delusion can lead to. Given that, to claim these morals are objective is little more than a claim that you yourself can define objective morality.

As Jonathan Pearce points out:

> *The problem that Craig seems to fall into in his writing is not really establishing the value system of this 'objective morality' other than by asserting that it comes from (finds its locus in) God. In other words, he claims that theism is the only pathway towards an objective morality without establishing a value code for said morality. There seems to be no explanation as to how one can value separate actions and compare them to each other and yet there is an implicit understanding that acts can be more or less good or bad than other acts. For example, is raping a small child more morally reprehensible than stealing a loaf of bread, or not giving a beggar some money, or kicking the beggar? All of these actions, for one who adheres to objective morality, must surely have different moral worth, different moral value? Craig provides no method of*

---

[36] William Lane Craig, quoted in (Pearce, 2015)

comparing, no formula with which to calculate moral worth or value of any given action.[37]

I would suggest then that the reason religious apologists can slip so easily into defining something that most people find morally reprehensible is because they are trying to redefine morality as something other than what humans culturally and instinctively acquire through empathy and a need to affiliate. They are trying to make it fit with a brutal Bronze Age tribal morality. A morality designed to control through fear, and to justify retrospectively, grotesque abuses motivated primarily by greed, with racism, misogyny and cultural arrogance.

As Professor Robin Dunbar of Durham University, UK pointed out in a debate on race, religion and inheritance:

Humans are very intensely social ... and our ability to act cooperatively in groups has been fundamental to our evolution (certainly our recent evolution), and we have managed to do this in very large social groupings – well, large by primate standards....I mean a few hundred as opposed to a few tens of individuals. But even at this scale, the freerider problem looms very large, and we seem to have evolved a whole suite of mechanisms for keeping freeriders at bay.

And one of these mechanisms, I suggest, has been religion. If you loo [sic] at the forms of religion (and especially the rituals) that you find in traditional societies, it is very much built around social bonding. Tradition religion typically has a shamanic form, associated with trance states and spirit journeys into the parallel spirit world. In the classic case of Bushman trance dances, they are very much designed to bond everybody to the common project of the group. They are very experiential, of the person. There is no grand theology – it's very much a religion of "doing" and "being". And it's this ecstatic element that I think cues us in to what's going on, because something seems to happen when you engage in these ecstatic activities that makes you feel more part of the community. It gets everyone signed up to the group project once again, especially if relationships within the community have become rather tense and fractured. I put it all down to endorphins myself, but

---

[37] (Pearce, 2015)

you can argue a case there are other neuro-endocrines such as oxytocins. The rituals of religion seem to be especially good at triggering a cascade of neuro-endocrines, and it is these that are responsible for that "kapow" effect we get in ecstatic experiences. But in my view, what's really underpinning it in the end is the endorphins. It seems to be the endorphins that create this sense of communal belonging, of being a member of the group, when you engage in these activities with others.

Endorphins, which are triggered by any kind of stressful activity like dancing, singing, holding awkward postures like standing or kneeling for long periods, or repetitive activities like counting rosary beads, anything rhythmic, create this sense of bonhomie, that the world, and particularly the people you do these things with, are all wonderful. Those of you who have ever rowed in an eight will probably know what I mean -- that sense of community that come out of co-ordinated effort, when everybody is stroke perfect – that surge that gives you the sense of belonging and bonding. In my view, this has played an extremely important role in the process of human evolution, by allowing us to create the kinds of integrated communities that work together.

So, seen from this perspective, religion is very much a small scale issue, a mechanism for bonding small scale communities. And in a sense, herein lies its problem. It is such a powerful mechanism for social bonding that it has been easy to exploit these very powerful psychological mechanisms in the contexts of large social groups once we developed our settled, urban way of life. Once church and state got together, it seems to be possible to mobilise very large groups of people in ways that are not normally possible – and for purposes that can easily become very destructive. Religion evolved to bond communities, and inevitably that means to create in-group/out-group boundaries, them versus us. In small communities, that's probably fairly innocuous, but on the large scale of nation states able to call up serious military power it's a recipe for trouble.[38]

So what might have seemed like objective morals for small human groups, and which may well have included threats of imaginary punishment because these were easier to enforce than actual threats and real punishments, are now

---

[38] (Dunbar, 2006)

ceasing to have their utility value and are becoming counter-productive. Rather than adding to the sum total of human happiness and group cohesion, they are dividing mankind into essentially arbitrary rival groups with a motive for killing one another.

How this can be regarded as objectively moral is nonsensical. It is only possible by the abandonment reason and abdication of personal responsibility theists call 'faith'.

The notion of omni-benevolence fails abysmally under even the most cursory glance at nature and the natural world theists like to present as the creation of their particular god. A maximally benevolent god could not allow evil and yet, if we define 'evil' as anything reducing the level of happiness or tending to cause suffering, we see a natural world full of unhappiness and suffering. We see it in the victims of religious strife; in the victims of famine and greed. We see it in the suffering of prey as predators hunt and kill them and we see it in the host victims of parasites such as parasitic worms, protozoans, bacteria and viruses.

There are very few pleasant ways to die, yet all things die. Very rarely does even a sentient animal simply die peacefully in its sleep. Almost everything is either killed by something else, often because it is too weak and infirm to defend itself through disease or infection, or it dies of thirst or starvation, no longer able to feed itself though age or infirmity. Suffering, often grotesque, is almost invariably the end of life.

That there is 'evil' in the world is really indisputable despite fundamentalist claims that this is somehow for our ultimate good because it punishes us for disobedience. What loving father would continue to randomly select some of his children for pain and suffering to teach the others a lesson? To even contemplate such a thing is an act of pure evil – but then what God does is defined as good, so good can also be something which causes suffering and good and evil become indistinguishable!

Remember, we are almost invariably dealing with a god who is not only claimed to be omni-benevolent but also omniscient and omnipotent.

As Epicurus pointed out, for suffering to exist, a god must be deficient in at least one of the above. At least one of the following must be true. God is:

1. Unable to prevent it, so it is not omnipotent.
2. Unaware of it, so it is not omniscient.
3. Unconcerned about it, so it is not omni-benevolent.

David Hume in *Dialogues Concerning Natural Religion* expressed very much the same with:

> *And is it possible... that after all these reflections, and infinitely more, which might be suggested, you can still persevere in your Anthropomorphism, and assert the moral attributes of the Deity, his justice, benevolence, mercy, and rectitude, to be of the same nature with these virtues in human creatures? His power we allow is infinite: whatever he wills is executed: but neither man nor any other animal is happy: therefore he does not will their happiness. His wisdom is infinite: He is never mistaken in choosing the means to any end: But the course of Nature tends not to human or animal felicity: therefore it is not established for that purpose. Through the whole compass of human knowledge, there are no inferences more certain and infallible than these. In what respect, then, do his benevolence and mercy resemble the benevolence and mercy of men?*
>
> *EPICURUS's old questions are yet unanswered. Is he willing to prevent evil, but not able? then is he impotent. Is he able, but not willing? then is he malevolent. Is he both able and willing? whence then is evil?*[39]

There have been various attempts by (mainly) Christian apologists to explain away the problem of evil, none of them successfully and most of them involving considerable mental gymnastics, resorting to quotes from holy books and flying in the face of reason. The following summary by Lee Strobel of Peter Kreeft's attempt for example:

a) God may use short-term evils for long-range goods,
b) God created the possibility of evil, but not the evil itself, and that free will was necessary for the highest good of real love. Kreeft says that being all-powerful does not mean being able to do what is logically contradictory, e.g., giving freedom with no potentiality for sin,

---

[39] (Hume, 1776) (Kindle Locations 1016-1023).

- c) God's own suffering and death on the cross brought about his supreme triumph over the devil,
- d) God uses suffering to bring about moral character, quoting apostle Paul in Romans 5,
- e) Suffering can bring people closer to God, and
- f) The ultimate "answer" to suffering is Jesus himself, who, more than any explanation, is our real need.

The simple answer to these points is:

- a) Why would a maximally benevolent, omnipotent god need to use evil for sort-term gain unless it is either not omnipotent or does not care?
- b) Why create the possibility of evil if the intention was not to allow evil? This claim also runs counter to the specific claim in the Bible that "I form the light, and create darkness: I make peace, and create evil: I the LORD do all these things" (Isaiah 45:7). Kreeft's assertion that omnipotence does not include being able to do things which are logically contradictory, yet this would mean gods are subject to the rules of logic – which then raises all sorts of problems with miracles which necessarily mean suspension of natural rules.
- c) Irrelevant, given that God supposedly created evil and the demonstrable fact that evil in the form of suffering and unhappiness still exists.
- d) Why would an omnipotent, maximally good god need to use suffering to help us build moral character?
- e) So could happiness. Why would a maximally good god choose suffering?
- f) If we have the ultimate answer, why do we still have suffering? In fact, this is just another get-out-of-jail-free assertion that we have suffering because we aren't faithful enough. It also assumes that only humans can suffer. How does this address the suffering of a zebra dying slowly in extreme pain as a lion disembowels it and eats its liver, or the suffering of a frog being eaten alive by an epomis beetle lava? This also leads to such hideous abuses as denying people in extreme pain from cancer the relief of the pain-killing drugs they need because it somehow helps them appreciate Jesus.

So, given the problem of suffering, we can confidently say that even if gods exist, none of them are omni-benevolent. This does not itself prove that gods do not exist, of course, merely that those who claim they do and who claim they were told so by those gods, are either mistaken or were misinformed.

The Eternal God Fallacy.

I'll turn now to another infinite claim routinely made of gods, usually to get around the logic of the first cause argument either being self-refuting or involving an infinite regress of ever greater gods. This is the convenient claim that gods exist outside time and space and are therefore eternal.

Without a scrap of evidence that everything else except for the locally popular god must have had a beginning in time, the required god is simply granted an exemption in an audacious example of double-think that would have graced the pages of George Orwell's *1984*.

Given what we know of the age of the Universe and the age of Earth, it is reasonable to ask, if it was God's plan to create Earth for humans, why he took so long? Not only did he, apparently, wait about 9.3 billion years between creating the Universe and creating the solar system complete with Earth, he then took another 4.3 billion years before he got round to creating modern humans.

But, this god has supposedly not just been around for the 13.8 billion years that the Universe has been around for; he has been around for an infinitely long time before that. And yet, if he is omniscient, he would have known too for infinite time that he was going to create humans on Earth in a planetary system around a star in a galaxy in the Universe. If he is omnipotent, he had the power to do it.

Why then did he wait for so long? Why, even when he had finally got going with his plan, did he take a break for 9.3 billion years and another for more than 4 billion? Was there a problem with the suppliers or the finances, maybe?

Well, what there certainly was, was a problem with the probabilities of him doing anything at all, given that he has existed for all eternity.

It is quite easy given a known duration of time to calculate the probability of any event occurring in any one moment, but first we have to agree a definition of a 'moment'. Given what we already know – that time is digital, not analogue, in that there is a smallest unit of time – the Planck Time (10^{-43} seconds) this would appear to be the most sensible definition of a 'moment'. It really does not matter how you define a moment since the maths is the same, just so long as you have the concept of units of time.

So, there are a discrete number of moments in any given length of time – a very large number for any reasonable duration but nevertheless a discrete number. All else being equal then, to calculate the probability of any event occurring in any one moment all we need do is divide 1 by this number and we have a probability of the event occurring. Probability is always expressed as a number between 0 (impossible) and 1 (certain) so if we know an event occurred, all the probabilities must add up to 1, hence our simple sum.

However, what happens if we have infinite time? The problem here is that we have an infinite number of moments too, so our probability calculation becomes 1 divided by infinity.

But, 1 divided by infinity is zero and a probability of zero means the event was impossible!

Given an eternal god existing for infinite time, it would have been impossible for it to create anything, or to do anything for that matter. Just as we saw with the omnipotent omniscience claim, the inescapable logic is that a god which has existed for infinite time could not have created the Universe.

It then becomes perfectly legitimate to ask of believers, who or what created your hypothetical god and out of what did it make it before there was anything out of which to make it? And then of course, who or what made that creator…and so on, *ad infinitum, ad nauseum*. The notion of a god creating the Universe is not only illogical but profoundly unsatisfactory. It never actually answers the 'first cause' question but simply keeps moving it back and putting off an answer – like a creationist who has been asked a direct question.

Failures of Logic

Impossible Prophesies.
Prophesies present a special problem for all the world's major religions because not a single one has a god revealing himself to the mass of the people. Instead, they all claim that god chose to reveal himself through one or more specially chosen people or prophets, who proved their credentials by telling us about something that had not yet happened but was going to happen.

Admittedly, this is taken to absurd lengths in, for example, the tale of Jonah, where the fact that the prophecy did not happen, is supposed to be evidence that it would have done if something else had not happened.

The problem stems from an even more basic conflict in religions such as the Abrahamic religions, where two mutually exclusive things have to be believed simultaneously. Believers must believe absolutely that the god has a plan and that everything is part of this god's plan. They also have to believe that humans have free will and are not merely automatons and passive players in their god's perfect plan for them but can chose their own futures.

Holding to both these views simultaneously means believers can blame themselves (or much more usually, others) when things do not turn out the way you would expect an omni-benevolent god to plan them, but they can also be fulsome in their praises when something good happens because it was part of a divine plan specially for them.

Starving babies in Africa or microcephalic babies due to the Zika virus currently in the news? Well, that's all the fault of humans who have chosen to disobey God (not those who have submitted to the will of Allah or who have let Jesus into their lives, obviously). But praying that your house will be the only one not to burn down in that forest fire, or the fact that one person survived a plane crash? Well, God had a plan, praise the Lord! The same god who burned down the other house and crashed the plane because of sin…

So religions stagger along despite these contradictions.

But, for an accurate prophecy to work, the future must be known at the time the prophecy was made and, at least from that point on, the future must be fixed and unchangeable and the free will of people must be controlled and constrained so as not to prevent that particular future happening.

It follows then that a Universe in which prophecies are possible is a Universe without free will. In such a universe there can be no concept of sin, let alone an original one, and no need for forgiveness and redemption; no need to submit to the will of Allah because Allah is already controlling you. No need to accept Jesus or to ask for forgiveness and no need even to exercise any moral judgement because we are all mere automatons with no more accountability than the computer I am using is accountable for the words I am typing.

The Numbers Fallacy.

Probably one of my favourite fallacies, and one that is frequently offered by even mature adults, is the numbers fallacy. Basically, the numbers fallacy is that x billion Catholics or y million Baptists, or z billion Muslims cannot be wrong.

Of course it ignores the indisputable fact that no single religion in the known history of the world has ever commanded the support of a majority of the world's population. The argument depends for its success on a parochial view, so, in the local culture, almost everyone seems to be a believer in the same religion.

This is nothing more than a manifestation of the fact that religions are inherited, not arrived at by logical thought, detailed examinations of the options and weighed up probabilities. Most people to whom religion is important will claim to have thought about it and arrived independently at their beliefs. If that were true it would be an astonishing coincidence that the religions they almost invariably decide is the one true one, is the one that they happened to have pinned on them as a baby by their parents. The facts of course suggests otherwise. Religions are largely inherited.

If the numbers fallacy were valid, given that more people do not believe in any one religion than do, the obvious conclusion is that **none** of them are right. But the numbers fallacy is not right, as a moment's thought will show.

If facts were dependent on the numbers of people who believe them and somehow become more right as the number of believer increased, this would mean that there are degrees of rightness. Yet the truth is that gods either exist or they do not.

Failures of Logic

Taken to its logical conclusion, the belief, if such a belief actually exists and the numbers fallacy is not just a claim made without thought, would mean that on the foundation of any new religion every other religion was more right than the new one. It would mean the founder of the new religion, whether Jesus, Moses, Muhammad, Guru Nanak or Gautama Siddhartha were completely wrong.

And of course it means in those countries where atheists are now in the majority, atheism is the most right.

The Argument from Incredulity.

The argument from incredulity is one of the commonest 'arguments' against science and history, and for gods. It is not based on rational discussion, or a dispassionate assessment of the evidence, but on intuition and usually ignorance and an intellectually dishonest attempt to shoehorn the Universe into a preferred view of it and force it to conform to requirements.

A person who has never read any science or history or paid any attention in school, nevertheless feels competent to dismiss it as wrong. Scientists or historians must be mad because it is hard to believe humans are biologically members of the Great Ape family, or that there really was nothing before the beginning of space and time, or that the Exodus story might well have been made up.

- That's just stupid!
- It cannot be true!
- I just do not believe it!
- I just happen to believe…!
- If that's what scientists say, they must be mad!

It operates like confirmation bias in reverse. With confirmation bias, the 'fact' is accepted and used to confirm a pre-existing belief, not because of the evidence but because it supports a desired conclusion. With personal incredulity, the facts are dismissed with barely a cursory glance because they conflict with a pre-exiting belief. Science books, magazine articles, even peer-reviewed scientific publications will be ignored if there is a risk that what they say will conflict with the pre-conceived, sacred notion.

Both confirmation bias and personal incredulity are manifestations of the same intellectually dishonest arrogance and yet they absolutely suffuse religious apologetics and anti-science arguments. You only need spend a few minutes on the social media when a swarm of creationists are calling other people names for not agreeing with them. You will see people who could not tell a test tube from a Bunsen burner or an amoeba from a cabbage, yet feel qualified to inform the world that the science they are using to send the message to the world has got it all wrong. They do not believe it, so magic done by a particular invisible magician is the best explanation for everything.

The argument from incredulity is of course just another form of the God of the Gaps fallacy which argues that, because I cannot think of any way this can be explained it must have been done by [insert preferred god]. It is found in the Cosmological Argument and the Teleological Argument, including its modern pseudo-scientific versions, Intelligent Design, Irreducible Complexity and Fine-tuned Universe arguments.

From the Wikipedia entry on The Argument From Incredulity:

> **Personal Incredulity.** *Another form, the argument from personal incredulity, takes the form "I can't believe P, therefore not-P." Merely because one cannot believe that, for example, homeopathy is no more than a placebo does not magically make such treatment effective. Clinical trials are deliberately designed in such a way that an individual personal experience is not important compared to data in aggregate. Human beings have extremely advanced pattern recognition skills, to the extent that they are objectively poor judges of probability.*
>
> **General incredulity.** *Sometimes argument from incredulity is applied to epistemological statements, taking the form "One can't imagine how one could know whether P or not-P, therefore it is unknowable whether P or not-P." This is employed by some (though not all) strong agnostics who say it is unknowable whether gods exist. The argument in this case is, "No one has thought of a way to determine whether there are gods, so there is no way." The implied major premise, "If there were such a way, someone would have thought of it," is disputable.*[40]

---

[40] (RationalWiki.org)

The psychological process going on here is our old friend, coping with cognitive dissonance. A sacred conclusion has to be protected – in Peter Boghossian's terms, the believer is doxastically closed. Whatever is being waved aside and dismissed is inconsistent with a pre-existing and preferred world view, so believing it would have set up a dissonance or conflict.

The simplest way to resolve the conflict is to dismiss it as stupid or the opinion of someone who is mistaken, stupid or insane, or even evil. Voilà! Conflict resolved! No need to assimilate that new knowledge or change your conclusion! You get a nice warm glow of self-satisfaction that your careful ignorance gives you a deeper kind of wisdom, a superior form of knowledge and the moral right to tell others what is right and wrong. A preferred view is preserved, undamaged by real-world facts and without much concern about its truth.

Preserved along with it is a sense of superiority to those who 'waste their time' learning all that 'nonsense' when superstition, intuition and believing what mummy and daddy, or that preacher at Bible/Qur'an class, said is obviously the best way to understand things.

The False Dichotomy Fallacy.
A false dichotomy, also called a false dilemma, false binary, black and white thinking, bifurcation, etc., is an almost universal component of religious apologetics and theology. The argument is presented as though there is only a choice between two alternatives, usually something patently absurd, and the answer being argued for.

It is a central component in, for example, the Cosmological Argument, where the choice is presented as a straight choice between no answer at all, or the god being promoted. No allowance is made for the answer being something perfectly natural and explainable by science, but which just has just not been discovered yet. This is why you can substitute any god you wish, or something patently absurd like a peanut butter sandwich, and the logic of the argument still holds. All you need do is grant to the preferred answer the same qualities and powers that religious apologists grant to their god to get it through objections such as the demand that it too must have its beginning explained.

The God of the Gaps argument relies entirely on the false dichotomy fallacy in that, like the Cosmological Argument, the choice presented is between no explanations at all and God, conveniently forgetting that 'no explanations yet' is not the same thing as 'no explanation possible'. It also ignores the evidence from the history of science which is entirely the history of one after another gap being examined, closed, and no sign of a god ever having been found.

No scientific explanation of any phenomenon has ever been found to require any supernatural component yet we are expected to believe the next gap will have a god in it. No scientific explanation has ever been abandoned in favour of a supernatural one and no scientific advance has ever been made by declaring a problem solved by 'goddidit!'

To be fair, most of these arguments will be made by people who are ignorant of the basic principles of logic and science, or who are too parochial to know that other options are available. These are 'accidental' false dichotomies rather than deliberate attempts to misrepresent the available choices. However, that defence is not available to those professional apologists and creationist disinformation websites and books. Their false dichotomies are the stuff of life and the means by which they earn their (usually very comfortable if not positively luxurious) living. For these, the entire thrust of their argument appears to be based on the notion that if they can prove science wrong, the only alternative on offer is a literal interpretation of the Bible.

Just a few moments rational thought will show that you do not prove **any** alternative hypothesis correct by falsifying a rival. Even **if** Darwinian Evolution or Big Bang cosmology could be falsified, this would go not an inch towards establishing that the origin myth of a Middle Eastern Bronze Age tribe was a scientifically accurate account of how the Universe came to be the way it is. That notion still needs to produce a coherent, testable and falsifiable hypothesis. Until it does so, there is no more reason to take it seriously than to take seriously the origin myths of any other peoples.

I should say here that there are other good reasons to take it seriously, just not in the scientific sense. We should take very seriously the fact that fundamentalists are insisting on the right to teach it as fact to impressionable children and seeking to impose their superstitions on us in the form of legislative prohibitions on, for example, a woman's right to choose not to continue with an unwanted pregnancy.

An example of the False Dichotomy Fallacy, and the weakness of gambling on the ludicrously pessimistic view that science will not close **this particular** gap unlike all the others, was the argument that amino acids are too complex to have formed naturally in the conditions found on Earth, therefore 'goddidit!' Amino acids are the building blocks of proteins. In fact, of course, there is nothing in the laws of chemistry and physics which precludes the formation of amino acids from simpler precursors, so the argument was weak and based on ignorance already. However, it imploded spectacularly when amino acids were detected in interstellar space and then in the Murchison Meteorite, showing that they can form in the harsh conditions in deep space and were probably available on the nascent Earth in abundance. No magic was required.

The Straw Man Fallacy.

This fallacy is so childish in its basic concept that it is perhaps surprising to see it deployed at all, yet it crops up constantly and repeatedly. Some apologists and anti-science propagandists seem to be so wedded to it as a debating tactic that they continue to use it even after being told they are attacking a parody.

Essentially, the straw man tactic is to construct a parody of the thing being attacked. This can be science, especially biological or climate sciences or anything to do with origins and evolution, atheism, other religions – preferably a parody that a person would need to be an imbecile or a complete ignoramus to believe. The parody is then attacked as though it were the real thing. Often the straw man is included in a begged question so that, to answer it, one is expected to accept the straw man parody as valid in order to answer the question. "If humans came from monkeys why are there still monkeys?"

But it is not just in the under-educated and scientifically illiterate community that we see the straw man being use. Nor is it just in the creationist sites established to make money by misinforming the scientifically illiterate and supplying them with a pseudo-scientific credence for their bias. We see them in the tactics of even the more sophisticated religious apologists such as Francis Collins, a devout Christian and former director of Human Genome Project (HGP) and now Director of the National Institutes of Health in Bethesda, Maryland. In his Old Earth Creationist apologetic, *The Language of God*, Collins comes up with these blatant straw man arguments:

139

Some have divided atheism into "strong" and "weak" forms. Weak atheism is the absence of belief in the existence of a God or gods, whereas strong atheism is the firm conviction that no such deities exist. In everyday conversation, strong atheism is generally the assumed position of someone who takes this point of view, and so I will consider that perspective here.[41]

In many years of debating atheism online across multiple social network sites, I have never seen atheism defined in those terms. Atheists are forever pointing out that atheism is nothing more than passive, sometimes even reluctant, acceptance of the fact that evidence is the only acceptable basis for belief and that there is no evidence for any god. With no evidence, there is no evidential reason to be anything other than atheist. Atheism is merely a default and the only honest, position in the absence of evidence, just as any good scientist should remain sceptical of a claim made with no evidence. Atheists do not employ any special definitions other than that used by people who do not believe in fairies or other peoples' gods.

The Existence of Nothing.

The problem with explaining how something came from nothing is that it could not have done; not because it is impossible but because it is impossible for there to be nothing. The problem is not with science; the problem is with human psychology and how it has evolved to help us survive on Earth where answers to questions like "What is nothing?" and, "What is outside the universe?", or even, "What is north of the North Pole?", do not really help us catch lunch, find a mate or rear children, or avoid being something else's lunch or food for their children, or food for a prospective mate.

In fact, the notion that the default state of existence is non-existence is just that – a notion. It is merely a product of human psychology. There is of course no reason; no fundamental law; no rule which says 'nothing' should be assumed and not 'something'.

You only need consider what the question implies. "What caused something to come from nothing?", or, "How did something arise?" All imply not nothing

---

[41] (Collins, 2007) Chapter 7

Failures of Logic

but something caused whatever it was. This is true whether you do what theists and religious apologists do and assume there was something and define this as a god or some force, or even a set of rules of some kind which 'caused' something to exist, or if you do what theoretical physics does and try to explain how matter arose in a quantum vacuum, which is about as close to defining 'nothing' as science can get.

Clearly, none of those things are 'nothing', not even a quantum vacuum, so they are not 'explaining' how something came from nothing but how something came from something else; and they are no closer to explaining where this something else came from than they were to explaining where something came from in the first place.

To avoid the absurd logical regress of invoking an assumed something to explain another something, the logical thing to do is to turn the question on its head and ask why we are assuming a 'nothing' in the first place. Where did 'nothing' come from and in what sense can 'nothing' exist?

The hypocrisy of religious apologetics in demanding science explain how something came from nothing, when they are hopelessly devoid of an answer to the same question and have to define their something as nothing to try to get round it, is too obvious. They are still unable to explain how magic created everything from nothing. There is absolutely no reason to assume the default state of existence is non-existence. This intuitive assumption is probably a result of our limited human psychology which has evolved fit for purpose, but not the purpose which we are now expecting of it.

The basic problem is with trying to use human intuition to arrive at answers to these questions which are outside our experience and not what our intuition evolved for. Human intuition is a very poor measuring device for the very small, the very large, and the very strange – and quantum events are nothing if not very strange. It takes humility to accept that the answer might not be what seems intuitively obvious and this is where science as a methodology scores against religion. Science demands that you explain things in terms of what can be shown to be so, and not in terms of what seems right to you. Personal incredulity is not a scientific argument.

One of the ways in which apologetics gets away with this question is that they aim their 'arguments' at those who do not have and do not want the humility to think their intuition is not the best available measure of reality. This is basically the same reason why these same people lack the humility to believe science no matter how compelling the evidence, and have no hesitation in condemning it based on nothing more substantial than personal incredulity.

Slicing gods, and magic, and absurdly infinite regresses away with Occam's trusty razor leaves us with the most parsimonious answer – nothing came from nothing because there never was nothing in the first place. There is absolutely no reason to assume there ever was, intuitive though that may seem. Your personal incredulity really is not the ultimate measure of reality.

The challenge of science is to explain what that was – which is another gap for intellectually dishonest religious apologists to declare unanswerable by science and to sit the preferred, evidence free god in.

The Impossibility of Miracles.

The problem with miracles is that, by definition, there can be no scientific evidence for them, so they cannot be proven. First, a definition from the Catholic Encyclopaedia, which, given the Catholic Church's heavy dependence on alleged miracles is probably the best working definition:

> *(Latin miraculum, from mirari, "to wonder").*
>
> *In general, a wonderful thing, the word being so used in classical Latin; in a specific sense, the Latin Vulgate designates by miracula wonders of a peculiar kind, expressed more clearly in the Greek text by the terms terata, dynameis, semeia, i.e., wonders performed by supernatural power as signs of some special mission or gift and explicitly ascribed to God...*
>
> *The wonder of the miracle is due to the fact that its cause is hidden, and an effect is expected other than what actually takes place. Hence, by comparison with the ordinary course of things, the miracle is called extraordinary. In analyzing the difference between the extraordinary character of the miracle and the ordinary course of nature, the Fathers of the Church and theologians employ the terms above, contrary to, and outside nature. These terms express the manner in which the miracle is extraordinary.*

Failures of Logic

A miracle is said to be above nature when the effect produced is above the native powers and forces in creatures of which the known laws of nature are the expression, as raising a dead man to life, e.g., Lazarus (John 11), the widow's son (1 Kings 17). A miracle is said to be outside, or beside, nature when natural forces may have the power to produce the effect, at least in part, but could not of themselves alone have produced it in the way it was actually brought about. Thus the effect in abundance far exceeds the power of natural forces, or it takes place instantaneously without the means or processes which nature employs. In illustration we have the multiplication of loaves by Jesus (John 6), the changing of water into wine at Cana (John 2) — for the moisture of the air by natural and artificial processes is changed into wine — or the sudden healing of a large extent of diseased tissue by a draught of water. A miracle is said to be contrary to nature when the effect produced is contrary to the natural course of things.

The term miracle here implies the direct opposition of the effect actually produced to the natural causes at work, and its imperfect understanding has given rise to much confusion in modern thought. Thus Spinoza calls a miracle a violation of the order of nature (proeverti, "Tract. Theol. Polit.", vi). Hume says it is a "violation" or an "infraction", and many writers — e.g., Martensen, Hodge, Baden-Powell, Theodore Parker — use the term for miracles as a whole. But every miracle is not of necessity contrary to nature, for there are miracles above or outside nature.

Both Spinoza and Hume had pointed out that miracles are, by definition, unnatural or 'super-natural' and are thus a violation of natural laws. To argue, as this last sentence above seems to, that a 'miracle' which is 'above or outside nature' is not contrary to nature is absurd, if one accepts the normal definition of 'nature' as everything about the material Universe.

There is very little real doubt that 'miracles' as generally understood are violations of natural laws, otherwise they are simply natural events, whether or not we yet have an explanation for them. Spinoza argued that the natural laws cannot be violated therefor 'miracles' must simply be unexplained natural events. Note here the difference between unexplained and unexplainable. Religious apologists will normally make the jump from unexplained to

143

unexplainable by deft footwork but, just as with the God of the Gaps, being unexplained does not mean a god did it.

Because there can be no scientific evidence for miracles, there is never anything more than someone else's claim that a miracle happened. Additionally, because miracles are unnatural, the likelihood of them occurring spontaneously is zero – otherwise they could have a natural explanation. Even if we are charitable and allow that they are not actually impossible (how can something that happened be impossible?) but are just so highly unlikely that a natural cause can be excluded, or at least given a lower probability than a supernatural or 'divine' intervention, we are left with a highly unlikely event.

We are, in effect, being required to take someone's word for it that a highly unlikely, even impossible, event actually happened, without them supplying any evidence. Why on earth would any rational person do that?

How many people would you believe if they told you, without the slightest scrap of evidence, that, for example, they had just seen the Virgin Mary appear out of thin air in Central Park, New York, or a man fly to Heaven and back on a winged horse from Hyde Park, London? How about if they claimed to have just witnessed a man satisfy the hunger of thousands of people with a few loaves of bread and a bit of fish in Montreal, Canada?

What other explanations would you consider first? Which other perfectly natural causes could there be for that person telling you such a thing? Note: 'because it is true' is only one possibility amongst many. Why would you consider explanations other than it being true to be more satisfactory or more believable than that they were telling you the truth?

Would you really believe them without wanting to see just a little evidence? I suggest that you would not believe a word of it. And yet when religious people read about or are told about miracles they believe what they are told, yet nowhere in all that was there ever more than one person telling another something that you would never have believed had they told you first hand. The story has been given a spurious gloss of credibility by being repeated by authority figures – authority figures who had no more basis for belief than you did.

Failures of Logic

This is how the church uses its 'authority' to persuade people to believe the unbelievable. Believing everything the church teaches by faith simply means the church has not yet found your lower limit of credulity.

A great many of the Catholic miracles involve claims of visions of the Virgin Mary, almost invariably manifesting herself to young girls, and often young girls with a troubled background. One 2001 study[42] found that of 8000 children aged 9-11, two-thirds had had a psychotic-like experience (PLE) that was more than a childhood fantasy.

One of the arguments for, for example, Bernadette Soubirous of Lourdes and Lúcia Santos of Fatima, experiencing more than a simple childhood fantasy was the tenacity with which they stuck to their stories when questioned, (although Bernadette Soubirous' memory of the event seems to improve with age). So, could these children have had a PLE?

The same case can be made for the Medjugorje 'miracle' of 1981 in Bosnia-Herzegovina in what looks remarkably like a re-run of Fatima, where the main instigators were a sixteen year-old girl, Mirjana Dragicevic and fifteen year-old Ivanka Ivanković. Once again, the Catholic Church had a very strong political motive for wanting a 'miracle' to keep control. The political situation was deteriorating as former Yugoslavia degenerated into inter-religious civil war, anarchy and eventually disintegration, following the death of Tito a year earlier.

In all these cases these 'visions' were then elevated to the status of miracles by first the local Catholic Church, then when it realised the potential, the Vatican itself, and in all cases with a clear political motive and now a financial one. What we probably have is essentially a childhood PLE, nothing more and nothing less.

Other supposed 'miracles' usually associated with the appearance of figures, normally Mary, to children, usually young girls, several of whom appear to have had a troubled childhood, include:

- Rue du Bac, Paris, France. Mary appeared to Catherine Labouré, in the chapel of the Daughters of Charity of St. Vincent de Paul, at Rue du Bac in Paris, three times in 1830. She showed her the design of the

---

[42] (Laurens, J., Sunderland, Green, & Mould, 2012)

medal of the Immaculate Conception, the "Miraculous Medal." This medal, when propagated, helped to renew devotion to Our Lady, both in France and eventually around the world. [Catherine Labouré was twenty-four at the time but had a history of claiming to have had visions.]
- La Salette, France. Mary appeared to two children, Maximin Giraud, aged eleven and Mélanie Calvat, aged fourteen, in 1846, one afternoon while they were looking after the animals high up on the mountain. She appealed for penance and an end to Sabbath breaking and blasphemy in the region. This apparition is credited with a major revival of Catholicism in the area.
- Pontmain, France. Mary appeared in the sky over the small town of Pontmain in north-western France to a group of young children for about three hours in January 1871, as the Franco-Prussian war was threatening the area. Her message appeared on a banner under her feet, and encouraged prayer while emphasising Jesus' love and concern. The village was spared invasion.
- Beauraing, Belgium. Mary appeared thirty-three times to a group of children in the winter of 1932-33 at Beauraing in Belgium, in a convent garden near a hawthorn tree. She described herself as "the Immaculate Virgin" and "Mother of God, Queen of Heaven," while calling for prayer for the conversion of sinners.
- Banneux, Belgium. Mary appeared eight times to Mariette Beco, aged eleven, outside the family home at Banneux, a small village, in Belgium. She described herself as the "Virgin of the Poor," and promised to intercede for the poor, the sick and the suffering. [43]

What is particularly noticeable in these alleged miracles is how they invariably happen in remote places or in private and only a very few, or more usually just one, person witnesses them. There is not, and for reasons given above, there cannot be, any evidence other than the claim of the witness, that anything at all happened. There is nothing at all to distinguish them from a psychotic event, a hallucination or simply a childish fantasy. Some of the girls actually have a history of bizarre claims that look for all the world like pleas for attention.

---

[43] (Theotokos Catholic Books)

It is also noticeable how, as human understanding of how the world works has improved, the supply of miracles, like prophets, has diminished.

The Supernatural Fallacy.

Many if not most religious people seem to have a dual belief in the nature of gods. On the one hand, they believe gods interfere with the Universe and can suspend the natural laws at will to produce miracles, to ensure a divine plan comes to fruition, to answer prayers and generally listen to praise. On the other hand, they exist outside the Universe in some supernatural realm apart from nature and so are undetectable and unknowable.

These views cannot both be true.

Why can we say this?

One of the things science teaches us is humility. We cannot really begin to understand things unless we are prepared to put aside our ego and resist the temptation to dismiss things just because they do not 'seem' right, or we find them hard to believe. This is the classic mistake Creationists make with Evolution, or often, with nearly all science – "You can't tell me... blah... blah... blah!" For some reason they seem to believe the universe must be easily understandable so anything which is hard to understand cannot be right.

Relativity is not hard to understand; it is hard to believe. It just does not seem right that no matter how fast you are moving, the velocity of a beam of light coming towards you is the same as the velocity of light going away from you, and yet every measurement ever made confirms that this is true and that it is time which changes when you go faster or slower.

The reason Einstein was able to conceptualise this idea was because he was able to ignore intuition and trusted the maths. Einstein allowed the evidence to lead him instead of assuming a right of veto over reality. Very many people, especially religious people, find it difficult or impossible to be that humble. That does not seem right to me so it cannot be true; I do not know how to explain it so my guess must be right; that conflicts with my belief so the fact must be wrong.

We know the Universe is expanding because we can measure how quickly the bodies within it are moving apart – the rate of recession – but the universe is not like a balloon being inflated. A balloon is being inflated into something. Not so the universe. The universe is expanding into itself because all time and space are inside the universe.

When the universe expands, it is the amount of space inside it which increases. There is no outside because there is no time and/or space for an outside to exist in 'outside' the universe, so the universe has nothing to expand into. This is the reason the rate of recession is the same wherever you measure it. A better analogy with an expanding balloon is to imagine space not as the space inside the balloon but the surface of the balloon itself. Dots and patterns drawn on that surface will all move apart from one another and the further apart any two points are, the faster they will appear to be moving apart – just so with bodies within the expanding Universe.

Because there is no spacetime 'outside' the Universe, this means there **is** no outside. The universe does not have an 'edge' or a boundary. In other words, the universe is finite but unbounded. It also means that, if you could somehow stand outside the universe, the universe would not exist for you. It could not exist because there is nowhere outside the universe for it to exist in and no time for it to exist. Physical existence only has any meaning in terms of occupying space and time. Nothing can exist without space and time.

This is the reason we could not detect other universes. They do not exist in our Universe's spacetime so, as far as this Universe is concerned, they do not exist at all. The universe only 'exists' inside itself. Asking what is outside the universe is as daft as asking what is north of the North Pole. A bit like an ant walking endlessly round a wheel, wondering when it is going to get to the end.

The implication of this for notions of a supernatural realm outside the Universe is that there is not such a place. Without a supernatural realm there can be no supernatural being. The inescapable conclusion for theology then is that a god that can communicate with mankind and with whom mankind can communicate; a god that can interact with the Universe in any way, must be an integral part of the Universe. The only way it can interact with the Universe is by exerting an effect on matter, whether that be on elementary particles, planets, entire galaxies, the electrons in our neurones or whatever, to cause them to be deflected from their paths.

Failures of Logic

At its simplest level, science detects the effect of something by measuring or observing its effect on something else. For example:

- We know how much electricity is flowing through a conductor because of the effect it has on a voltmeter.
- We know about gravity by measuring how objects move in a gravity field.
- We know about photons by measuring the effect they have on photo-sensitive chemicals or photo-electric plates.
- We know how hot water is by measuring how much the heat expands a column of mercury, a metal bar, how it changes resistance of an electrical conductor, etc.
- We know about wind-speed by measuring how quickly it rotates a wind-speed detector or anemometer.

Try this for yourself. Can you think of anything science can detect which does not depend on detecting its effect on something else? Even just observing something is actually measuring the effect photons have on the cells in the retina of your eyes.

In other words, to be detectable by science, something must exert an effect, and to exert an effect on something means that that effect can be measured. Therefore, anything which cannot be detected cannot possibly be influencing or changing anything in any way, otherwise we could measure it.

And yet no-one has demonstrated any force or interference or influence which is not explainable by reference to something natural. No supernatural influence has ever been detected because, by definition, anything that is detectable is not supernatural.

It follows then that an undetectable god is an impotent god, entirely indistinguishable from a non-existent god.

But surely gods answer prayers, do they not? Well, no, they do not, at least in any way that has ever been demonstrated in controlled experiments. Apologists will often claim to have first-hand knowledge of their particular god answering prayers. It will invariably 'answer' prayers in one of three ways:

1. Yes – the prayed for thing happens or the prayed against thing does not happen.
2. No – nothing changes.
3. Wait – it might change at some unspecified time in the future.

But it would be perfectly valid to make that same claim of a bottle of milk, or a brick or Zeus, or anything else you can think of. The simple fact is that those are the only possible outcomes because they are the outcomes from not doing anything at all.

There is a tree in my back garden right now. Is it going to fall down?

1. Yes – it falls down.
2. No – it does not fall down
3. Wait – it might fall down at some point sometime in the future.

No-one would conclude that I have some magical ability to make trees fall down or forecast the future, except in anything other than the most trivial detail, would they?

The only way out of this paradox for believers is to assume that their god makes everything look just as it would look if it had done nothing. In that case their 'god' is simply the operation of nature; of physical and mathematical laws and we have a 'god' in the sense of Einstein's and Spinoza's god or at best a deist god who is completely disinterested, even dead. A god, in fact, that is indistinguishable from a non-existent one and which, for all practical purposes, does not exist.

5. Absence of Evidence.

But does faith need evidence anyway? Is not the fact that there is no evidence for gods, merely evidence that gods want us to discover them without evidence, so looking for it is disloyal?

It is difficult to formulate that question in such a way as to not make it seem absurd or contrived, yet the argument comes up time and again in discussion, even with the most moderate and open-minded of theists. The notion that somehow the absence of evidence is not a problem for those making a fact claim and can even be evidence for that fact, is so absurd that this chapter will be a short one. It is a measure of the mental gymnastics and intellectual dishonesty required by faith that this is even considered to be a valid argument.

As comedian and actor Ricky Gervais has pointed out: imagine for a moment that only one person believed in a god. We would probably regard that person as more than a little strange, yet, as we saw in the Numbers Fallacy above, the number of believers has no bearing on the validity of that belief. If it is strange for one person to have a whole edifice of beliefs based on no evidence whatsoever, then it is strange for billions of people to have the same strange beliefs.

The primary and perhaps the only real reason to not have faith in gods is of course the fact that there is not a single piece of authenticated definitive evidence for any god. Estimates vary about how many gods have ever been believed in. We have no way of knowing since we do not know what religions or how many gods were believed in by our early modern ancestors or even our pre-*Homo sapiens* ancestors, let alone cousin species such as Neanderthals and Denisovans.

A nominal figure of about three thousand known gods is often quoted but the actual number is not particularly important; just the fact that there have been very many. More importantly, not a single one of these ever provided a single scrap of evidence that would be accepted by anyone other than a believer. This is as true of today's clutch of gods as it was of the ancient ones.

All of the believers in these god believed they were real and none of the believers in other gods, or at least pantheons of gods, believed they were. Notwithstanding that in polytheistic societies people could and did believe in many gods; they just did not believe in other people's gods. Every believer has only ever had the one true god or pantheon of gods. Not those other folk! They have all been fooled and believe nonsense!

The standard fall-back position regarding the absence of evidence for any particular god, even if that is reluctantly conceded by apologists, is the maxim, 'absence of evidence is not evidence of absence'. This is often misattributed to the late cosmologist, Carl Sagan; it was actually coined by the cosmologist Martin Rees.

Who in their right mind crosses a road by faith instead of checking to see that there are no cars close enough to be a danger? The absence of evidence for cars is perfectly adequate to bet your life on and no sane person would question that. Yet absence of evidence is evidence of absence for gods no less than for cars in an empty street, for the simple reason that if there were gods and they intervened in any way in the affairs of the Universe, this interference should be detectable.

In formal logic, absence of evidence is not **proof** of absence but it is certainly evidence. In situations where evidence should be clear-cut and expected, it can be regarded as proof with a fair degree of certainty. Consider a situation where a court of law is presented with no evidence against the accused. Would that not be considered reasonable grounds for acquittal? Of course it would. In English Law, offering no evidence is a reason for a judge to dismiss the case without further ado. It is a device to signal that the prosecution are withdrawing the charges. It would not even go to a jury. And yet you will regularly see religious apologists acting as though absence of evidence is actually evidence of presence with the 'You cannot prove me wrong!', argument.

To illustrate this, I'll use an analogy of the claim that gods exist but are undetectable, so would not be expected to provide evidence that science can detect.

Supposing that, in some deranged, delusional moment, like Ricky Gervais' only one person believing in God, I again made the claim I introduced in

Absence of Evidence

Chapter 1 – that there are undetectable hippopotamuses living in my loft and I know this because I have faith.

Given that 'undetectable' is an essential part of the undetectable hippo claim, how could you formally prove that I do not have any such thing in my loft? You cannot use evidence because none would be expected, so absence of evidence is not proof of absence of loft hippos.

So would I be correct in telling you that your inability to prove there are **not** undetectable hippos in my loft entitles me to claim I have proved they exist, or that there is even a slight chance of my claim being true?

Of course not! You would probably be less inclined to believe me on the basis of no evidence than you would have been because I claim to have faith in loft hippos. You might be tempted to suppose that at least I must have had **some** hint of evidence to believe by faith in the first place – that I am not totally away with the fairies.

The problem here is that the burden of proof has been shifted. It should not be for you to disprove my claim; it should be for me to prove it. Your position should be sceptical until I have substantiated my claim. My claim does not impose any obligation on you. I have to substantiate my claim by providing you with evidence; otherwise it is just an assertion.

Based on factors such as likelihood and how it compares to what we know of the Universe, you would be right to dismiss it. It would not be right for me to claim to have proved my hippo claim; but you would be right to question my sanity.

If we allow that any daft notion can be true unless proven otherwise, we can believe in anything. We can believe that something is making us imagine the evidence all around us that the Universe actually exists. In other words, if assertions can be regarded as true without any evidence then nothing can be regarded as true because the assertion that it is false also becomes true. As the late Carl Sagan said, "Extraordinary claims require extraordinary evidence", and as Christopher Hitchens said, "A claim made without evidence can be dismissed without evidence."

But how is a claim to have undetectable hippos in my loft any different to a claim to have undetectable gods about the place? It is not, of course. Just as the likelihood of there being undetectable hippos in my loft is absurd enough to raise concerns about my mental welfare if it were made in all seriousness, so the likelihood of there being undetectable magic beings about the place is absurd. It would require extraordinary evidence to prove it and it can be dismissed as easily as the claim was made.

The final point to make here is that if religions **were** based on evidence, there would only be one just as there is only one science. In fact, religion based on evidence would be a branch of science. We would not call it 'religion' or 'faith' but 'knowledge'.

So shrill and frequent are the absurd claims of believers to have proof of god that you could be forgiven for thinking there must be masses of the stuff. Yet you can bet your life on the fact that, if ever a single piece of definitive evidence for any god were to be found, we would never hear the last of it. The finder would instantly become one of the most famous people ever to have existed. Sainthood would be guaranteed. Pious parents and faith schools would bus their children to see this wondrous thing that would be the major tourist attraction for the world. Special measures would have to be made to prepare for the billions of pilgrims to the shrine wherein this wondrous artefact were housed.

None of that ever happens because, when examined, the 'proof' always turns out to be nothing of the sort. It could not even pass the 'Which god?' test.

We can say with a fair degree of confidence that none of the unknown gods from ancient civilisations ever left a piece of evidence upon which those religions were founded because there is nothing to form the basis for recreating those religions or rediscovering those gods.

A few miles south of Heraklion in the Greek island of Crete there are the remains of a vast city and palace/temple complex built by the Minoan civilisation. It is undoubtedly the work of an advanced culture. They had a unique style of writing but we know nothing of their language or how it relates to other Mediterranean world languages, if at all and their writing has never been deciphered.

Absence of Evidence

We can make a few deductions about what their gods looked like because they have left images and figures which are assumed to be those of a goddess of some sort holding snakes. The bull seems to have featured in their culture, maybe as some sort of male initiation ceremony although we do not know for sure and there is evidence of human sacrifice.

Whatever it was that these gods were assumed to do, belief in them was sufficient to inspire the building and decoration of this temple complex and seems to have been the glue which held an advanced civilisation together.

Yet when the entire culture was wiped out when the volcano Thera blew up in a massive super eruption those gods died with it. There is nothing in the archaeology because there never was anything. The entire religion was founded on no evidence.

We can make precisely the same point about many other civilisations which left no decipherable written records; civilisations that built Silbury Hill and Stonehenge in southern Britain; the people who built the huge stone brochs of Western Scotland or the Orcadian village of Skara Brea; or the wonderfully painted caves in southwestern France. All over the inhabited parts of Earth there are ancient remains and artefacts highly suggestive of religions and rituals of some sort and evidence of a belief in an afterlife, and yet we know almost nothing of their gods or the details of their religions.

We have no idea, though we can make some guesses, about why certain colours may have been important; why certain plants featured in some ceremonies or why graves contained particular goods or had a particular shape. We know a lot about the Egyptian religions because we have written records, but we do not have any idea why the temples at Karnak had that particular design nor why the columns were modelled on a lotus shoot with either closed or open lotus flower buds at the top. It may be that the later Egyptians themselves did not know the reason for this form

We can see stylistic changes over time in the carvings on Egyptian tombs that suggest some of the original purpose for them may have been lost to later generations of artisans. For example, a depiction of a pharaoh or important person carved in stone was meant to represent the 'essence' of that person, including, most importantly, their immortality, not their physical likeness.

Since hard stone is long-lasting and the deeper a figure is carved the longer it will last, the intention was that it would last forever. The importance of the person was not represented in their physical, earthly representation but by the depth of the carving. By the Greco-Roman period however, depictions of important people became more 'life-like', indicating a shift in the basic understanding of the importance of immortality and the purpose for carving them in the first place.

Compare this to the situation where an ancient civilisation had made some major scientific or mathematical discoveries but these had then been lost in a natural disaster. It is difficult to imagine how important scientific discoveries would gradually be lost without a catastrophic disaster killing everyone with a scientific education. However they were lost though, it would just be a matter of time before these were rediscovered because they will have been founded on evidence.

For this reason, science always converges on a single answer, no matter the starting point or the cultural biases of the scientists. Scientists from Japan, India, Europe, Africa or America, no matter the religion of their parents, will, and do, work together to solve the same problems using the same methodology and starting from the same base of what is known. It will not matter whether they believe in one god, multiple gods or no gods at all because they are working with established, evidence-based facts and discovering new facts based on new evidence.

Significantly, to be sure their discoveries are real, not matter what their personal beliefs, scientists need to put aside any faith they might have and behave like atheists.

We can even say with complete confidence that the science as understood by alien beings on another planet in another galaxy will be the same science that we have. The names would be different and the mathematical base for expressing values might be different, but the values would be the same: the same elementary particles; the same chemical elements; the same laws of physics and universal constants like the velocity of light in a vacuum; the same principles of levers and gears, etc.

We can be equally confident that religions never converge and even the same religion tends to diverge. We can be certain that if they have religions on another planet they will not be the same as ours. We can be sure of this because there is no evidential basis for religion and no firm foundations on which to build one. Religions are built on nothing more substantial than the shifting sands of speculation and guesswork.

Ten Reasons To Lose Faith

6. Knowledge, Science and Uncertainty.

But is faith not a good thing if it gives people certainty and freedom from doubt? Is it not better to be certain than to be full of self-doubts and constantly having to change your mind?

It often seems to puzzle theists, genuinely or otherwise, and especially fundamentalists that science does not have an answer to every question. Unlike religion, which supplies an answer to every question, science seems to be forever discovering something else it does not know. Even worse, it changes its mind more often than a dithery thing on the planet Dither. What is the use of text books that have to be rewritten every few years?

The reason for this is very simple; the answers that religion supplies are always the same basic one – a variation of 'God did it!' No evidence is ever supplied that the particular god actually exists or that it in fact did it. It is a dogma; faith without evidence and the real truth is the first casualty in the search for an easy answer.

Science, on the other hand, is about real truth; about the weight of evidence and how strongly that evidence supports a hypothesis. Nothing is ever known with absolute certainty by science. In fact certainty is the antithesis of scientific objectivity because a certain mind is a closed mind and science demands an open mind. It is only by acknowledging what we do not know; by recognising that we might be wrong, and by accepting that all knowledge is approximate and provisional, that we are spurred on to discover something new and to correct past mistakes.

Science text books are always in need of revision because science works; not because it fails. Today's knowledge on average, will always be better and closer to the ultimate truth than yesterday's knowledge because it is based on a more complete or a better understood evidence.

It seems almost trite to point out that no scientific advance was ever made by a scientist simply memorising what other scientists had written about; least of all by sitting back in self-satisfaction and concluding the a god must have done it.

As Isaac Newton said in a letter to Robert Hook, 'If I have seen further, it is by standing on the shoulders of giants!'

This metaphor was probably a snide swipe at Hook, Newton's professional and personal enemy and rival as the nation's greatest scientist, because Hook was a very short man, but it still holds true as a metaphor for how science progresses from the known to the unknown. It follows then that the textbooks can never be better than the current state of scientific knowledge.

Gravity and the Laws of Motion

Newton's 'discovery' of gravity is a case in point here. I have enclosed 'discovery' in quotes because of course we knew about gravity; we knew that if you throw a stone up in the air it will fall down again and we knew that apples fell from trees down to the ground. What we did not know, and what Newton believed he had supplied, was a description of it as a natural force. Newton worked out the mathematical laws that appear to govern the motion of bodies in space, all stemming from the three laws of motion:

1. Every body continues in its state of rest, or of uniform motion straight ahead, unless it be compelled to change that state by forces impressed upon it.
2. The change of motion is proportional to the motive force impressed, and it takes place along the right line in which the force is impressed.
3. To an action there is always a contrary and equal reaction; or, the mutual actions of two bodies upon each other are always directed to contrary parts.

So far as the Law of Universal Gravity is concerned, what Newton realised was that bodies exert a force on other bodies which is directly proportional to their mass, so what gives an object weight on a planet like Earth, is the gravitational pull of the larger body on the smaller one. The same object on the Moon or Mars, would weigh less than on Earth because those bodies are less massive than Earth.

These laws enabled people to understand how to predict the movement of bodies and to make calculations that were perfectly good for practical, every day use, but they were not perfect. They assume the body in question is a single point. Even planets have to be regarded as single points as though they were point particles.

These laws however were a vast improvement on superstitions which had to postulate angels pushing planets around. Since this relied on magic and the belief that the natural laws can be suspended or altered at will, any absurdity became possible. It was possible, even seemingly logical, to argue at Galileo's trial that even though it looked like the planets orbited the sun, the angels were moving them in such a way as to make it look that way for reasons we could not comprehend. The Bible said the sun, moon and stars orbited Earth and that Earth is fixed and immobile, so that was that. (1 Chronicles 16:30, Psalm 93:1, Psalm 96:10, Isaiah 45:18).

Within the thinking of the time, observations such as those made by Kepler on which Galileo based his heliocentric view were incidental to the 'known' facts. The accepted scientific view of the time was that Earth was the centre of the Universe.

But Newton's Laws of Motion were not the final word because a body is not a single point. So, some fifty years after Newton formulated his Laws, the Swiss mathematician, Leonhard Euler, succeeded in modifying them by treating a body not as a single point but as a collection of points. The difference is small, but science had progressed a little closer to the truth.

Ultra-purists, especially those with simplistic, black and white thinking, would say Newton was wrong. He was not wrong, of course, he just was not perfectly right. But then neither was Euler, although Euler was more right than Newton. In 1915 Albert Einstein succeeded in adapting his 1905 Special Theory of Relativity to include acceleration and produced the General Theory of Relativity. He showed that neither Euler nor Newton were entirely right.

He also showed that gravity, rather than being a force pulling or pushing on a body, is the effect of a deformity in spacetime itself. The path of a moving object does not curve due to being pulled or pushed but travels in a straight line through curved space. In a gravity well, such as that produced by a large body like the sun, or a planet, that curve can be an ellipse, so a planet or satellite following that curve will be in an elliptical orbit around the larger body.

Again, Newton and Euler were not wrong, but they were not as right as Einstein. It is always possible that someone will come up with something better than Einstein's General and Special Theories of Relativity which will be more right still. For practical purposes though, and within the technological development at the time, all three had provided a scientific understanding of motion which has been perfectly adequate and fit for purpose.

The lesson here is that none of these advances would have been possible without doubt and uncertainty; without knowledge of our own ignorance. Without doubt and uncertainty and a humble acceptance of ignorance, we would still believe Earth is the centre of the Universe, with the Sun, Moon, stars and planets orbiting around it. We would still believe they are pushed by angels who deliberately fake it so the planets look like they go round the Sun in elliptical orbits, for reasons that will forever remain a mystery, unknowable by mere humans.

We arrived at our present approximation of the truth because Galileo stood on Kepler's shoulders; Newton knew Galileo's arguments and had Kepler's figures, Euler had Newton's mathematics and Einstein understood Euler's Laws. To get from the biblical superstition to our present understanding would have needed four or five major rewrites of the physics books, but each rewrite would have brought us up to date with current knowledge and a little closer to the truth.

Meanwhile the fixed and unchangeable 'truth' in the Bible has a Late Iron Age view of the Universe which has never been revised.

Phlogiston.
The value of uncertainty and doubt in the search for genuine truth, as opposed to a comforting delusion, is nicely illustrated by the 'Phlogiston Theory'. The term 'phlogiston' comes from the Greek for 'burning up'. The theory was an early attempt to explain how combustion and rusting worked in the days before oxygen had been discovered.

The theory has its origins in an earlier belief, held since Classical times, that everything was composed of four 'elements', earth, air, fire and water. In 1667, Johann Joachim Becher published a theory in *Physica subterranean*, in which he removed fire, water, and air from the classical model and replaced them with three forms of earth: *terra lapidea, terra fluida,* and *terra pinguis*. *Terra pinguis* was the element that imparted oily, sulphurous, or combustible properties. Becher believed that *terra pinguis* was released during combustion. This theory was later refined in 1703 by Georg Ernst Stahl, a professor of medicine and chemistry at Halle. He proposed a variant of the theory in which he renamed *terra pinguis* to *phlogiston*.

The phlogiston theory was refined to:

> *In general, substances that burned in air were said to be rich in phlogiston; the fact that combustion soon ceased in an enclosed space was taken as clear-cut evidence that air had the capacity to absorb only a finite amount of phlogiston. When air had become completely phlogisticated it would no longer serve to support combustion of any material, nor would a metal heated in it yield a calx; nor could phlogisticated air support life. Breathing was thought to take phlogiston out of the body.*[44]

The point about this theory from a scientific perspective is that it explained the then known facts and even helped explain later discoveries. When Daniel Rutherford discovered nitrogen in 1772, the result was explained in terms of phlogiston. It was the residue of air left after burning. All the phlogiston had been taken out, so the resulting mixture of carbon dioxide and nitrogen was referred to as dephlogisticated air.

But, complete though this theory seemed to be, eventually quantitative experiments using more accurate technology, began to reveal problems for the theory. Metals were found to gain weight as they corroded yet a theory which required them to lose a substance should have resulted in a loss of weight. This was explained by assuming phlogiston had negative weight. What did they know of the relationship between mass and gravity?

As more evidence accumulated that phlogiston was not a substance in the conventional sense, people were still reluctant to discard it as a principle. Joseph Priestly, for example, who is generally credited with having discovered oxygen, referred to it as a principle. In trying to explain the action of steam on

---

[44] (Conant, 1950), p 14.

iron to form iron oxide and hydrogen, he concluded that iron had given up the 'combustion principle' (hydrogen). Later, when Lavoisier explained that oxygen was the 'oxidising principle' (referring to its role in the formation of acids) Priestly referred to hydrogen as the 'alkaline principle'.

Eventually Lavoisier showed by using closed vessels, that combustion required a gas that had mass. In fact, the process of combustion was almost the reverse of the phlogiston theory: combustion involves taking a gas with positive mass out of the air, not releasing a gas with negative mass into it. The phlogistonists had not got it entirely wrong, they had just got it backwards; but in doing so, they had produced a better approximation to the truth than the earlier one where everything was made of earth, air, fire and water. In every case, progress was made because people had doubt and uncertainty and accepted that current theories could be inadequate or even completely wrong.

Interestingly too, is the reluctance of people to give up on a theory which seems to explain the observable facts until there are enough observable facts to make clinging to an outmoded theory untenable. This ensures that all arguments are tested with counter-arguments in what amounts to a Darwinian evolution of ideas in a selective environment. The selective environment is the body of scientific opinion which is biased in favour of a more accurate or more complete explanation of the evidence. By allowing for doubt, and allowing for new ideas and new information, science has created variation on which the natural selection of informed opinion can operate. Therefore we have an evolutionary process.

Unlike genetic evolution however, science evolution is goal-orientated Its goal is the ultimate description of reality, so science evolves and converges on single truths. This is the opposite to faiths which can have no objective test in reality, so faiths diverge and are never better than evidence-free opinion. If you doubt this, you need to explain why there are some 38,000 Protestant Christian sects alone, all claiming to be the one true faith. Just about every serious physicist now accepts Einstein's Relativity theories and the Big Bang, and only a handful of idiosyncratic biologists seriously doubt the basic principles of neo-Darwinian evolution. None of those ever publish the data on which they base their doubts in peer-reviewed publications.

Miasmas and Germ Theory

No-one seriously doubts now that infectious diseases are caused by 'germs'. We know what causes malaria, cholera, chlamydia, influenza, the common cold, measles, mumps, etc., etc., etc. We know that to treat a disease caused by these 'germs', we have to treat the symptoms but more importantly we have to attack the causative organism. Most importantly though, we know we need to prevent infection to prevent getting the disease in the first place.

Biologically, we know that 'germs' are parasites which have evolved opportunistically to exploit the niche offered by our bodies. We also now know that 'germs' can be divided into bacteria of different types, species and varieties; viruses of different types and varieties with different modes of operation; fungi; protozoans such as amoebae, and parasitic worms. It is a matter of semantics whether we classify some ectoparasites or endoparasites as germs or not.

But this was not always so.

The first person to try to explain diseases such as malaria, cholera, chlamydia, Black Death, etc., and in particular why they appeared to move in waves across the country, was Galen, the first century Greek physician. He proposed that a 'miasma' of noxious or bad air caused these diseases as it passed across the country. A miasma was a mist of particles of decomposed matter which arose from rotting organic matter. These could arise due to environmental factors such as bad water, poor hygiene and foul air. Individuals caught these diseases not by catching them from other people but by living where these miasmas were being produced. A miasma could be identified by its foul smell.

Given the state of knowledge in first century Greece this seemed a complete and satisfactory explanation of the observable facts. It even contained a testable prediction: move people away from the source of the miasma and they should not get the disease. In fact, it proved such a good description that it remained the predominant theory of disease until the nineteenth century, even though an Italian physician, Girolamo Fracastoro, had proposed a primitive germ theory in 1546. He suggested 'seed-like' organisms transmitted diseases by direct or indirect contact even over long distances.

However, it was not unto Anton van Leeuwenhoek actually saw microorganisms in the 1670s, when lenses were of sufficient quality to give enough magnification and resolution, that Francastoro's 'seed-like' organisms were actually shown to exist.

The first conclusive demonstration of a disease caused by an organism was that of a disease in silkworms known as calcinaccio, which the Italian, Agostino Bassi, showed was caused by a 'vegetable parasite' which has since been shown to be a fungus pathogenic to insects, now named in his honour, *Beauveria bassiana*.

But the final clincher for the germ theory was the famous case of the Broad Street cholera outbreak of 1854 in Soho, London, in which 12.8 percent of the population died. A local physician, John Snow, was skeptical of the miasma theory and showed that the likely cause was a water pump in Broad Street, the source of drinking water for the area. He persuaded the local council to remove the pump handle to prevent it from being used and the cholera outbreak ceased, although it may have been declining by then anyway.

Snow later showed by use of dot maps known as Voronoi diagrams and by statistical techniques, that there was a close correlation between cholera outbreaks and the source of drinking water. This study is often held up as the founding event of modern epidemiology and established with little doubt that organisms cause some diseases.

In Snow's own words:

> *On proceeding to the spot, I found that nearly all the deaths had taken place within a short distance of the pump. There were only ten deaths in houses situated decidedly nearer to another street-pump. In five of these cases the families of the deceased persons informed me that they always sent to the pump in Broad Street, as they preferred the water to that of the pumps which were nearer. In three other cases, the deceased were children who went to school near the pump in Broad Street...*
>
> *With regard to the deaths occurring in the locality belonging to the pump, there were 61 instances in which I was informed that the deceased persons used to drink the pump water from Broad Street, either constantly or occasionally...*

> *The result of the inquiry, then, is, that there has been no particular outbreak or prevalence of cholera in this part of London except among the persons who were in the habit of drinking the water of the above-mentioned pump well.*
>
> *I had an interview with the Board of Guardians of St James's parish, on the evening of the 7th inst., and represented the above circumstances to them. In consequence of what I said, the handle of the pump was removed on the following day.*[45]

It later transpired that this well had been dug only three feet from a leaking cesspit. Contamination had occurred when nappies from a baby who had contracted cholera elsewhere had been washed into this cesspit.

However, it is one thing to know that microorganisms cause infectious diseases; it is another thing to know which microorganisms cause which diseases. This required more research only known to be necessary because we now had the science of Germ Theory.

A major contributor to this was Robert Koch whose understanding of the problem grew out of his work with anthrax using cultures of organisms that had been taken from diseased animals. Koch developed a set of principles known as Koch's Postulates:

1. The microorganism must be isolated from a diseased organism and grown in pure culture.
2. The cultured microorganism should cause disease when introduced into a healthy organism.
3. The microorganism must be re-isolated from the inoculated, diseased experimental host and identified as being identical to the original specific causative agent.

The original postulates were four in number, and included a first postulate which Koch later abandoned:

> The microorganism must be found in abundance in all organisms suffering from the disease, but should not be found in healthy organisms.

---

[45] (Snow, 1854)

It soon became clear to Koch that this first postulate was not universally true, when he learned of asymptomatic carriers of cholera and typhoid. Clinically healthy carriers are now known to be major features of epidemiology especially those caused by viruses. They present a special challenge in control of epidemics. Despite this, Koch's remaining three postulates form the basis for proving the link between specific diseases and specific organisms.

In keeping with good scientific practice, Koch himself realised that his original understanding was wrong because the evidence did not support him. He changed his mind and came up with a more accurate set of postulates, now not suffering from a lack of coincidence with observable reality.

Koch also had to use the term 'should' rather than 'must' in the second of the final three postulates in recognition of the fact that some organisms, for example tuberculosis, only causes disease in subjects already in poor health or in people who seem to be susceptible to them.

Without this new knowledge of the cause of infectious diseases, we would not understand the need for good food and personal hygiene, of good sewerage disposal, of the need for safe water supplies and antisepsis in surgery, nor the use of antibiotics to treat these diseases. Nor would we know about the need for immunisation and vaccination. In all probability child mortality rates would be as high as they were before the advent of modern medicines, when the commonest funerals were those of children, not of the elderly.

None of this would have happened if people had simply accepted the received wisdom of the day by faith, believing that we knew the complete truth. It was only by doubt, scepticism and uncertainty and with the humility to accept our own ignorance that people found out the truth.

Despite the retrospective claims of Bible and Quranic literalists to have discerned evidence that God had put knowledge of germ theory into these books for us to discover, no one seemed to notice these messages until we knew about germ theory and had shown it to be true.

Bible literalists and fundamentalists will still insist that diseases are God's way of showing he loves us and wants to teach us a lesson because someone disobeyed him thousands of years ago. I can only assume they are using a private definition of 'love', not one normally recognised by decent people.

It is easy to see how Bronze Age Middle-Eastern peoples would have assumed a magical cause of illness and would have ascribed it to their default explanation – the displeasure of an aloof, patriarchal god, closely resembling a tribal warlord of the times. Had we retained that primitive attempt to explain illness with the same misplaced confident certainty that Bible literalists have, we would now be trying magic spells and incantations to control diseases. We would also need to invent increasingly Byzantine rationalisations to explain why the results appear to have an outcome indistinguishable from a purely random outcome.

Atomic Theory.

Atomic theory is an example of how science can progress from the abstract reasoning of philosophers to the evidence-based scientific theory which enables us to make accurate and testable hypotheses. In its original form, and from where it gets its name, an 'atom' was the logically smallest part you could cut a substance into which would still be that substance. It was *atomos* or 'uncuttable' in Ancient Greek.

This, like so many Ancient Greek ideas, was treated almost with reverence until it proved inadequate to explain the growing body of scientific evidence in the eighteenth and nineteenth centuries. In particular, it could not satisfactorily explain two laws which emerged from the work of Anton Lavoisier and Joseph Louis Proust.

In 1879, Lavoisier formulated the Law of Conservation of Mass in which he showed that the total mass of chemicals involved in a reaction remain constant. In other words, the products of a reaction weigh the same as the starting chemicals. In 1899 Proust formulated the Law of Definite Proportions, in which he showed that chemicals always react together in definite, whole-number ratios. When a substance is broken down into its constituent parts, these will invariably be in the same proportion, regardless of the quantity or source of the original substance.

Clearly, there was more to these hypothetical 'atoms' than simply being uncuttable small units of substance.

To solve this problem, John Dalton devised the Law of Multiple Proportions in which he showed that, when two chemicals react together in two different ways, the proportions of the second substance which react with the first substance will always have a small, whole number relationship. We will meet this again later in this chapter as an example of scientific Laws.

For example, Proust had found that the masses of the two oxides of tin were either 88.1% tin and 11.9% oxygen or 78.7% tin and 21.3% oxygen – tin oxide and tin dioxide respectively. Dalton noticed that 100g of tin will combine either with 13.5g or 27g of oxygen; and that these are in the exact whole-number ratio, 1:2. It was clear to Dalton that an atomic theory of matter accounted for this pattern in chemistry. In the example of tin oxides, one tin atom will combine with either one or two oxygen atoms.

Dalton concluded that chemicals were composed of atoms of small, unique types that, although they cannot be destroyed, can combine with atoms of other substances to form 'compounds'. This was the first scientific, evidence-based, theory of chemistry and still the basis of quantitative chemistry.

But Dalton was not entirely right in all cases. For example, he did not know that many substances such as oxygen (O), hydrogen (H) and nitrogen (N) do not normally exist as monatomic particles but as molecules, each of two atoms (O_2, H_2 and N_2 respectively).

Dalton's theory was later corrected by Amedo Avogadro who showed that equal volumes of any gas, at constant temperature and pressure, contain equal numbers of molecules. Using this he showed that 2 litres of hydrogen will react with 1 litre of oxygen to produce 2 litres of water vapour. This meant that a single molecule of oxygen must split in two to form a single molecule of water (H_2O), so molecules of oxygen must be composed of two atoms of oxygen.

At this stage, although science had useful models of how matter is composed of atoms and in what ratios these react together to form compounds, there was no satisfactory explanation of just how these atoms joined together nor why they did so in these fixed ratios. In fact, atoms continued to be thought of as the smallest possible units of matter until, in 1897, Sir Joseph John (J. J.) Thomson discovered electrons by using a primitive cathode ray tube. He showed that a cathode ray, rather than being light, was composed of negatively charged 'corpuscles' which had only 1 1800th the mass of hydrogen. Atoms were clearly divisible and contained these 'electrons' as they later came to be called.

In 1908, Ernest Rutherford discovered that the vast mass of an atom is concentrated in a very small space. By firing a stream of electrons at thin sheets of metal and measuring their deflection on a florescent screen, Rutherford's team showed that very small proportions were heavily deflected. They concluded that this was caused by striking the positively charged nucleus of the atoms of metal. This led Rutherford to propose the planetary orbital model for atoms in which electrons orbit around the nucleus.

To understand just how much of an atom is empty space, think of the nucleus of a hydrogen atom as the size of a football and on the centre-spot at Wembley Stadium. For non-Brits, that is the English National Football Team's home stadium in the West London suburb of Wembley. On that scale, the single electron which Rutherford saw as orbiting the hydrogen nucleus, would pass through Durban in South Africa. Everything in between is empty space.

Rutherford's model suffers from one major drawback, however. An accelerating electron should emit electromagnetic energy, so an electron would rapidly lose energy and collapse into the nucleus within a few microseconds. Nevertheless, this model is still taught to children as the basis of chemistry because it is easy to understand and explains almost all of the chemistry needed up to an intermediate level of understanding. Later on, these children have to unlearn this model in favour of a quantum-based theory.

The quantum theory of atomic structure was proposed in 1913 by Niels Bohr, incorporating Albert Einstein's and Max Planck's work showing how light is absorbed and emitted in discrete 'quanta' of energy. He proposed that electrons occupy discrete orbitals with fixed angular momentum. This means that an electron cannot lose energy continually; instead it can only make 'quantum leaps' from one energy level to another. Contrary to popular opinion, a quantum leap is not a large jump but a very small, discrete jump.

In 1924, Louis de Broglie proposed that all moving particles exhibit characteristics of waves and in 1926 Erwin Schrödinger, developed the equation named after him that describes electrons not as discrete particles but as waves.

This wave function has now been shown to be not the electron itself but the probability of it being in any one location. Quantum theory says, counterintuitively, that a particle will be in all possible locations simultaneously, so this probability distribution model successfully integrated quantum mechanics into the theory of atomic structure.

The science of Atomic Theory has thus progressed from an abstract concept, through a number of different models. Each of these was based on new or better information and each of them gave science a more useful model with which to explain the nature of matter and chemical interactions, culminating in the current theory which successfully integrates chemistry with particle physics and quantum theory. At no stage could the current model be described as 'wrong' although it was subsequently replaced or refined.

Incidentally, with Einstein's Special Theory of Relativity which with $e = mc^2$, shows how energy and mass are interchangeable, we now know that Lavoisier's Law of Conservation of Mass was not quite right. Chemical reactions always involve changes in the energy content of the products. Reactions which give off energy as heat (exothermic reactions) lose a small but calculable mass; those that take heat from the surroundings (endothermic reactions) gain a small but calculable mass. For normal everyday chemistry, however, the small changes are irrelevant.

This is another case of an experiment being 'right' but not completely right. It was enough to overthrow Lavoisier's Law of Conservation of Mass however, which has now been replaced by the Law of Conservation of Energy; an example of how even a scientific Law can be revised with new information. We will explore this idea more later on in this chapter.

The four examples above, gravity and the Laws of Motion, phlogiston, miasmas and germ theory, and atomic theory, are examples of how science generally progresses from the known to the unknown and accommodates and adjusts to new or better information. Despite the common claim that scientists are forced to conform to established doctrines by powerful senior scientists with a vested interest in their pet theories, the truth is quite the opposite.

You will have noticed in the above examples that reputations are made in science not by slavishly confirming established theories but by improving them or better still by overthrowing them. Even **if** some powerful autocrat in one scientific institution could wield enough power to prevent juniors from publishing anything he or she did not want published, these juniors would be unlikely to stay around for long. There would still be enormous prestige for the head of another institution for his or her team to have made a major new discovery.

In some ways, although it is generally conducted in polite, respectful debate and in objective terms free from personalities at least in public, there is a Darwinian culture in science which encourages healthy competition. Few budding scientists ever went into pure research wanting to remain an obscure, backroom functionary with no significant publications to his or her name. Competition between rival universities is even more intense with top performers and prize-winners frequently poached and offered prestigious positions. Universities with the best reputations for original research and innovation will attract the brightest students.

Small Changes, Big Differences.

The examples above also illustrate something else which sometimes goes unrecognised in science. We have seen how people like Newton were not actually completely wrong although he was not as right as Euler, who in turn was not as right as Einstein. The principle here is what Isaac Azimov termed the 'Relativity of Wrong' in his, now sadly out of print, collection of essays on scientific progress of that name. However, the first essay from which the book takes its title in available online.[46]

Azimov used the example of a child who spells the word *sugar* as "pqzzf". This is clearly wrong, yet a child who spells the word "shuger" is also wrong, but less wrong than the first child. What then of a child who writes "sucrose" or "$C_{12}H_{22}O_{11}$" and disregards the spelling of *sugar* completely? This child might fail a formal spelling test but shows a degree of knowledge about the real thing under study far above that needed to simply spell the word.

Another example Azimov gives is that of the shape of earth:

> *...when people thought the earth was flat, they were wrong. When people thought the earth was spherical, they were wrong. But if you think that*

---

[46] (Azimov, 1989)

thinking the earth is spherical is just as wrong as thinking the earth is flat, then your view is wronger than both of them put together....

You will see this black and white thinking being used *ad nauseum* in creationist books and websites. There, the tactic is always and invariably to attack some aspect of science as though science having got something wrong no matter how slight, renders the entire body of science wrong. To these creationist propagandists, science is either completely right or completely wrong. So if it is wrong about, say, the exact evolution of the horse, or the precise details of how the first self-replicating molecules arose, it is also wrong about the Big Bang, human evolution, the age of the Universe, carbon dating, consciousness and love. If that were true it would also be wrong about electricity and how computers work, but somehow these media can still be used to tell the world via the Internet that science does not work.

But if 'right' and 'wrong' are not absolutes but different positions on a continuum, to what degree is 'flat' wrong as a description of the shape of Earth?

Isaac Azimov again:

In the early days of civilization, the general feeling was that the earth was flat. This was not because people were stupid, or because they were intent on believing silly things. They felt it was flat on the basis of sound evidence. It was not just a matter of "That's how it looks," because the earth does not look flat. It looks chaotically bumpy, with hills, valleys, ravines, cliffs, and so on.

Of course there are plains where, over limited areas, the earth's surface does look fairly flat. One of those plains is in the Tigris-Euphrates area, where the first historical civilization (one with writing) developed, that of the Sumerians.

Perhaps it was the appearance of the plain that persuaded the clever Sumerians to accept the generalization that the earth was flat; that if you somehow evened out all the elevations and depressions, you would be left with flatness. Contributing to the notion may have been the fact that stretches of water (ponds and lakes) looked pretty flat on quiet days.

Another way of looking at it is to ask what is the "curvature" of the earth's surface over a considerable length, how much does the surface deviate (on the average) from perfect flatness. The flat-earth theory would make it seem that the surface doesn't deviate from flatness at all, that its curvature is 0 to the mile.

Nowadays, of course, we are taught that the flat-earth theory is wrong; that it is all wrong, terribly wrong, absolutely. But it isn't. The curvature of the earth is nearly 0 per mile, so that although the flat-earth theory is wrong, it happens to be nearly right. That's why the theory lasted so long.

...

The curvature of such a sphere is about 0.000126 per mile, a quantity very close to 0 per mile, as you can see, and one not easily measured by the techniques at the disposal of the ancients. The tiny difference between 0 and 0.000126 accounts for the fact that it took so long to pass from the flat earth to the spherical earth.

Mind you, even a tiny difference, such as that between 0 and 0.000126, can be extremely important. That difference mounts up. The earth cannot be mapped over large areas with any accuracy at all if the difference isn't taken into account and if the earth isn't considered a sphere rather than a flat surface. Long ocean voyages can't be undertaken with any reasonable way of locating one's own position in the ocean unless the earth is considered spherical rather than flat.

Furthermore, the flat earth presupposes the possibility of an infinite earth, or of the existence of an "end" to the surface. The spherical earth, however, postulates an earth that is both endless and yet finite and it is the latter postulate that is consistent with all later findings.

So, although the flat-earth theory is only slightly wrong and is a credit to its inventors, all things considered, it is wrong enough to be discarded in favor of the spherical-earth theory.

Describing Earth as flat also gives rise to the problem of size. Flatness tells us nothing about how far it stretches so it is potentially infinite. If it is not infinite, it has an edge. As soon as we know the amount by which it deviates from flatness at a constant rate, we know both its size and the fact that it is finite and has no edge.

Azimov's example of the small differences adding up to make the big difference between a flat Earth with indeterminate limits if any, and a nearly spherical Earth which is finite but has no end, is a good analogy with evolution. Intuitively, when looked at on the small scale of a human lifetime, or even over several centuries, it seems there is no change and all species have always been like that.

Chaffinches and stoats; primroses and oak trees, all look the same to me now as they did when I was a child, and my mother, who was taught their names by her mother or father, told me their names too because they looked to me the same as they looked to grandmother. But if I could travel back in time to say, Ice Age Europe when all the ancestors of these species lived in Spain or Italy or maybe the Balkans, south of the ice sheets, they would probably not be recognisable to me. They would have adapted to a different environment. Yet there has never been a time when parents could be described as a different species to their offspring.

This was the mistake made by the same Bronze Age hill farmers who thought Earth was flat and the sky was a dome. We now know, because we have the evidence from long ago to give us a longer perspective, that accumulated small differences give rise to gradual change and diversification which can only be recognised with the right perspective. We now know that species have not remained static and unchanged but have been dynamically adjusting to environmental change to look like they were designed to fit.

Hypotheses, Experiments, Theories and Laws.
How then does all this doubt and uncertainty transform itself into useful scientific knowledge that we can put into practice?

Part of the problem here is that science uses a slightly different but more precise meanings of 'hypothesis' and 'theory' to that used in vernacular speech. In the vernacular, hypothesis and theory are pretty much interchangeable. Neither has a very definite meaning and sometimes they mean the same as a guess or a hunch, or just a vague feeling. Frequently in vernacular speech, 'theory' or 'hypothesis' means 'this is what I would like it to be' as people often try to fit their idea of reality into a consistent view of the world.

In science, a hypothesis is a suggested explanation for a phenomenon which is different to the current scientific theory, if there is one. A hypothesis also needs to be falsifiable in that there must be some theoretical way to disprove it. A hypothesis is never formally proven; it is only ever not falsified.

Given that science always proceeds by acknowledging that, as we saw above, its theories can be overturned and replaced with better ones, it is only necessary for a hypothesis to be repeatedly shown to be unfalsified for it to be provisionally accepted as the current best explanation. Normally, this would be by at least two independent researchers repeating the experiment exactly and getting close to the same results.

Experiments are designed to test the hypothesis exactly as stated, to check that predictions made by the hypothesis are correct. For this to be done, experiments must eliminate any personal bias from interpretation of the results and eliminate any false positives from the experimental method itself.

For example, in my early career as a medical research technician, one experiment included assaying samples of female guinea-pig serum for a particular hormone, progesterone. Repeated tests had shown we could measure to a high degree of accuracy the level of hormone in solutions of known strength of a solution of pure hormone of a given batch number supplied to us by the National Institute for Health, Bethesda, Maryland, USA.

The method we then used (in the early 1970s) was a state of the art technique but it was incredibly labour-intensive compared to today's assay methods. To measure the hormone in the serum we had to extract it by mixing the serum with a solvent, then carefully separating the solvent complete with extracted hormone from the serum. We then separated the hormone we needed from all the other hormones or other solvent-soluble substances which might be present and which could have interfered with the result, using thin-layer chromatography, so obtaining a pure sample to be measured. This was before we could even begin to measure the actual amount of hormone.

Every step of this extraction process included the risk of contamination or some unidentified substance being included in the extract, so we included two sets of blanks – one of pure, double-distilled water and one of just empty test tubes because we had found that empty tubes gave a small positive result and distilled water a slightly larger one.

We suspected though that this small positive result came from a minuscule amount of aldehyde in the ultra-pure solvent we were using. By including these controls, we were able to show that the hormone levels we were measuring were statistically significantly higher that the 'zero' results from water. Including empty test tubes confirmed that there had been no accidental contamination from other sources such as laboratory dust, etc.

What we were doing with each sample by this method was testing the 'null hypothesis'. The null hypothesis is a basic assumption in all experiments that the result of the experiment will not be significantly different to there being no effect. In the case of my samples of female guinea-pig serum, the null hypothesis is that there will be no difference between the results of the assay and the results of an assay where there is no hormone.

To make doubly sure, two samples of each serum were included in each assay and each serum was included in two different assays. Also included in each assay were duplicated samples of known dilutions of the standard pure sample from NIH. This gave us a calibration curve for known concentrations of progesterone, so our unknowns could be read off the graph plotted from these results. It also ensured our unknowns were within the range of maximum sensitivity of the assay.

Another version of the null hypothesis says that the result of the experiment is purely due to experimental error, bias, and/or personal prejudice, even subconsciously, or something in the method itself that produces the result. The empty tubes were there to show that the technique itself was not producing the results.

For an experiment to be regarded as a success the null hypothesis must be falsified, and that is what our water blanks were enabling us to show. For this reason, results are often presented in terms of a probability of being false! A result for a biological experiment where there is inherently more variability in the population than in, say, atoms of a given element, a probability of less than

0.05 is regarded as significant. This says that if we repeated this experiment exactly a thousand times, we would expect to get five false results and nine hundred and ninety-five true results on average.

Of course, you can never be certain with any single biological experiment that it is not one of the five in one thousand false ones. To ensure greater confidence, not only should you be able to repeat your results but another team somewhere else should be able to get the same results using your method. Only then does science have any real confidence in the results of research.

If you have been following the Higgs Boson story closely you may remember the CERN team expressed their confidence in the result as 'at the 5 sigma level'. This is another way of saying they were 99.99965% certain they had found the Higgs Boson; in other words there was a 3.5 in 1 million possibility of being wrong. Note: there was no declaration of certainty. It does not matter how often that test is performed, the possibility of it being another false positive result will never become zero. It will approach it so closely as to make it almost indistinguishable from zero, but it will never become zero (impossible to be wrong).

For everyday purposes though, and certainly with enough confidence to move on to the next steps in physics that this discovery has opened up, the Higgs Boson has been shown to exist (or proven, in the vernacular though non-scientific, sense).

A hypothesis then is an educated guess which seems to explain the observed phenomenon which can be used to make a prediction, and so can be experimentally falsified.

A theory is something else entirely in science. A theory, such as the Theory of Gravity, the Big Bang Theory, the Theory of Evolution, the Quantum Theory or Einstein's General Theory of Relativity, are not hypotheses. Theories are the widely accepted explanations for a phenomenon, including the entire body of supporting science in the form of observations, experimental results and variations within the interpretations of the evidence.

To quote from Wikipedia:

> *A scientific theory is a well-substantiated explanation of some aspect of the natural world that is acquired through the scientific method and repeatedly tested and confirmed through observation and experimentation* [47, 48, 49]. *As with most (if not all) forms of scientific knowledge, scientific theories are inductive in nature and aim for predictive power and explanatory capability.*
>
> *The strength of a scientific theory is related to the diversity of phenomena it can explain, and to its elegance and simplicity. See Occam's razor. As additional scientific evidence is gathered, a scientific theory may be rejected or modified if it does not fit the new empirical findings; in such circumstances, a more accurate theory is then desired. In certain cases, the less-accurate unmodified scientific theory can still be treated as a theory if it is useful (due to its sheer simplicity) as an approximation under specific conditions (e.g., Newton's laws of motion as an approximation to special relativity at velocities which are small relative to the speed of light).*
>
> *Scientific theories are usually testable and make falsifiable predictions.*[50] *They describe the causal elements responsible for a particular natural phenomenon, and are used to explain and predict aspects of the physical universe or specific areas of inquiry (e.g., electricity, chemistry, astronomy). Scientists use theories as a foundation to gain further scientific knowledge, as well as to accomplish goals such as inventing technology or curing disease. Scientific theories are the most reliable, rigorous, and comprehensive form of scientific knowledge.*[51] *This is significantly different from the common usage of the word "theory", which implies that something is a conjecture, hypothesis, or guess (i.e., unsubstantiated and speculative).*[52]

So when you see, as you regularly will, a creationist stating as a matter of fact, that 'Evolution is just a theory', often followed with '- just a guess with no

---

[47] (National Academies Press, 1999)
[48] (Winther, 2015)
[49] (American Association for the Advancement of Science, 1990)
[50] (Popper, 1963). Reprinted in (Schick, 2000)
[51] (Schafersman, 1997)
[52] (The National Academy of Sciences, 2008)

supporting evidence', you can be as certain as it is that the Higgs Boson has been found that they are either ignorant of the science or lying. In the case of professional creationists who write books and maintain disinformation websites for creationists, you can be certain they have had this error pointed out countless times. They cannot possibly be unaware that their statement is false and a deliberate misrepresentation of science intended to deceive their readers.

It seems to be a characteristic of professional creationists that having a claim shown to be false, is not considered a reason not to try to dupe someone else with it. This basic intellectual and moral dishonesty almost seems to define creationists as much as it does professional religious apologists who do not seem to see having an argument refuted any number of times as a reason not to continue to use it.

I will try to illustrate what a scientific theory is with a theory that is close to my love of science and in particular biology – the Theory of Evolution. The Theory of Evolution (TOE) is the body of science that seems to excite and distress religious fundamentalists the most.

Many fundamentalist creationists seem to assume that the entire TOE is contained in Charles Darwin's *'Origin of Species'* rather like a Christian assumes the whole of Christianity is contained in the Bible or a Muslim assumes the whole of Islam is contained in the Qur'an. In fact, about the only reason to read Darwin's *'Origin'* now is as a historical work and to enjoy the brilliance of the mind behind it. It has almost no value as a definitive textbook or reference work.

Like Newton, Darwin was nearly right but also wrong in many respects. Darwin did not know about genes or how information was passed to the next generation, nor did he know about plate tectonics. He believed, as did all his contemporaries, that Earth was very much younger than we now know it to be. He had the same cultural assumptions about racial superiority of Europeans that some people still hold to this day, although he did not translate that into racism in the sense of believing it was alright to treat the 'lesser races' as less than human. He was actually an enthusiastic supporter of the abolition of the slave trade and notoriously (if that's the right word) kind and considerate to his servants.

The modern TOE has its historical origins in Darwin's and Wallace's theory of evolution by natural selection, but now incorporates genetics and especially the structure of DNA, comparative anatomy and physiology, fossil records, cladistics, immunology, and even plate tectonics and cosmology. It is a tribute to the robustness of the theory that not a single major scientific advance has ever dented the basic principle of TOE but instead has strengthened it, as we see how well it meshes with other scientific disciplines.

I would go so far as the say that if a scientific theory appears to contradict evolution, it is vastly more likely that the scientific theory is wrong than that evolution is wrong. What creationists seem unable to grasp is that, so strongly supported is the TOE by diverse strands of science, when they tell us their religion disagrees with it, they might as well be telling us their religion is wrong. In fact, without realising it that is exactly what they are telling us.

The TOE has now been extended to non-biological systems. Wherever there is imperfect replication and selection, there will be evolutionary change. This change will inevitably be towards better fitness for whatever the selective environment is favouring. The direction of evolution will always be in the direction of greater fitness to produce more copies **in that environment**. The genetic algorithm is an accepted method for designing complex systems and developing new approaches to engineering problems as in, for example an aircraft wing where there must be an optimal balance between lift, drag, manoeuvrability and fuel consumption at different speeds and altitudes.[53, 54]

We can even make a plausible case for gods, religions, cultures, holy books and science itself being the product of an evolutionary process.

The TOE is no longer seriously questioned by mainstream biologists other than those with a book to sell or a particular extremist religious or political agenda to pursue. It sets the backdrop for all biological research, for a great deal of modern medicine, for embryology and for bioengineering (whatever you might think of it) and taxonomy. Comparative anatomy and physiology simply would not make sense without the TOE.

Of course there are disagreements, and rightly so, between for example those who think that selection operates more strongly at the group level, the

---

[53] (Mukesh, Pandiyarajan, Selvakumar, & Lingadurai, 2012)
[54] (Oyama, Obayashi, & Nakamura)

individual level or at the levels of individual genes. These are not necessarily mutually exclusive, incidentally. There were also arguments in the past about whether there was some other factor operating to give 'punctuated equilibrium' (PE) or whether natural selection accounted for all the fossil records, including apparently quite rapid changes over a short geological timespan. Some twenty years ago this debate raged between the American proponents of PE, the inspirational author, Stephen J Gould, and the proponent of Darwinian gradualism, the equally inspirational author Richard Dawkins.

Such is the stuff of science. So long as it stimulates debate, tests ideas and interests the audience, long may it continue as a side show. Never in doubt in this debate, however, was the fact that species have evolved from a common ancestor by an entirely natural process. The debate was only ever about the precise details.

The probable reason for the antipathy for evolutionary biology, especially amongst fundamentalist Christians and Muslims is because it goes to the heart of their beliefs about their relationship with their imaginary god. Both religions require the faithful to believe they are the special creation of an assumed creator of the Universe and were somehow created apart from all the other animals.

The fact that Christianity requires its followers to believe they were either, created from dirt (men) or from a rib cutting taken from a man (really?!) and in the case of Islam that they were both created out of mud, requires them to reject that they actually evolved in Africa from an ancestor in common with the other African apes.

They are also both required to believe that somehow they are unworthy creations and need to constantly praise their assumed creator and beg its forgiveness. They also have to believe they have a magic being or 'soul' living inside them which will be made to suffer hideously after they are dead unless they do so.

The reality is, however, that humans have been evolving by a natural process ever since they diverged from the other African apes and we are only beginning to discover the details of this fascinating story. We are in no sense an unworthy product of a fallen clod of earth; we are an ascended, evolved ape and the product of millions of generations of survivors. We have everything to be proud of and nothing to be ashamed of. It takes the callous psychopathy of the playground bully to tell a child otherwise.

What then is a scientific Law and why are theories not scientific Laws?

In science, the term Law is rather obsolete and tended to be used for early, fundamental discoveries that were universally true, or true within clearly defined conditions. They normally deal with specific, discrete cause and effect situations.

It would probably be possible to formulate it as a Law of Evolution that the frequency of beneficial alleles, in a population subject to imperfect replication of those alleles in a selective environment, will tend to increase. However that really only states the obvious and has little use outside a theoretical discussion of the mechanism of evolutionary change in a biological system.

More useful are those Laws which allow us to make accurate predictions, for example, The Law of Constant Composition (also called the Law of Definite Proportions) and the Law of Multiple Proportions which form the basis of analytical chemistry.

Some Laws, such as Hook's Law of Elasticity only holds over a certain range. A rubber band will obey Hook's Law up to a point, but, beyond that point Hook's Law will fail and there will be a point at which the rubber band will snap.

Perhaps the most famous example of a scientific Law is that derived from Einstein's Theory of Special Relativity, $e = mc^2$, where energy (e), mass (m) and the velocity of light in a vacuum (c) are in a constant relationship. A given mass of matter will always give the same amount of energy because the velocity of light in a vacuum is a universal constant.

To summarise then, in science:

- Laws express causal relationships which are either universally true or true within a known range of conditions.
- Theories are the accepted best explanations for observable phenomena together with the body of confirmatory experiments, evidence and fundamental Laws where appropriate.

- Hypotheses are the ideas which are tested and either falsified, or confirmed to a high degree of confidence through repeated testing and failure to falsify.

None of these are cast in tablets of stone because probably the only certainty in science is that there are no certainties. Laws are unlikely to be changed but can be if new information shows them to be inadequate. For example, the Law of Conservation of Mass had to be replaced with the Law of Conservation of Energy in view of Einstein's Relativity. Theories can be overthrown and will almost certainly be modified and will evolve in the light of new information; and hypotheses are made to be destroyed and will be abandoned or reformulated as necessary.

The last point to be made here is the distinction between a scientific Law and a judicial law which are often, probably deliberately, confused in the minds of non-scientific people. This confusion is often used to mislead creationists by telling them that laws need a lawmaker, as though the existence of scientific laws formulated by human beings are evidence of a magic lawmaker somewhere. The confusion here is that a scientific law is descriptive; it tells us what will happen in a given situation. Matter has no choice in the outcome so does not need to understand that it must obey the law or there will be consequences.

Drop a stone and it has no choice but to fall to the ground. This is a Law because it will always happen if you are standing on a planet with gravity. It is a fundamental law of mathematics that $1+1=2$. There is no law that makes one pebble and another pebble make two pebbles. $1+1=2$ simply describes the situation of one pebble next to another and expresses it as a useful model.

Judicial laws however are proscriptive or prescriptive. They are man-made rules that tell you what you can and cannot do or what you must or must not do and what the penalties are for non-compliance. We would not need judicial laws if people had no choices but we could then express their behaviour with scientific Laws.

7. Freedom from Delusion.

In the first five chapters we looked at reasons why faith is an unreliable tool at best when it comes to searching for the truth. At worst it will mislead you and leave you with no way to know whether you are right or wrong.

In Chapter 6 we have seen how, far from being the unreliable things doubt and uncertainty might intuitively seem to be, they are the only reliable means to discover truth. They liberate the mind and to give us the humility to accept there is still much that we do not know and there is still much to learn.

Doubt, uncertainty and the humility to accept our own ignorance have propelled humanity from the Stone Age to the Space Age. They have taken us from superstitious ignorance in a world which seemed full of incomprehensible magic, to the discovery of how the universe came to be the way it is. Even as I write this paragraph, the discovery of gravity waves was announced on the radio. Now the science books will need to be re-written because, as the announcer put it, 'this changes everything!'

With doubt and uncertainty you can fill an entire lifetime in a joyous quest for knowledge; with faith you can waste an entire lifetime pretending to know things you do not know and merely looking for comforting confirmation of bias. Some may believe the latter gives them certainty and purpose in life but it is the certainty of the ignorant and the purpose of the deluded.

Richard Dawkins, in *The God Delusion*, popularised the idea that religion and belief in gods is nothing more than a delusion; "a persistent false belief held in the face of strong contradictory evidence" In the words of Robert Pirsig, author of *Zen and the Art of Motorcycle Maintenance*, "when one person suffers from a delusion it is called insanity. When many people suffer from a delusion it is called religion."

But is the knowledge that belief through faith is merely a delusion, sufficient reason to stop believing?

Some people derive great comfort from the thought that someone is watching over them and has a plan for them. They seem to believe this even though what happens to them in life is indistinguishable from a life with no-one watching over them. I wonder though how much this belief affects their lives and the decisions they take.

I can understand people wanting to think that a lost parent or child or loved one is somehow still there, and can even see them and knows what they say and do. I can also understand the seductiveness of thinking death is not really the end. This becomes even more seductive when the life you are leading is miserable and hopeless compared to that of other people in the society around you and the 'afterlife' is going to be so much better... if only you abide by the rules.

In his book, *Godless*, Dan Barker tells how when he was an evangelical Christian, he was driving along a road when he suddenly felt he ought to take the next turning. Obviously, so he thought, God was telling him to turn off for some reason. God had a plan for him and was sending him on a mission. At each fork in the road something seems to be telling him to take one fork or the other. Was he being sent to minister to the spiritual needs of some community, maybe a person in need of spiritual guidance? His excitement mounted as he took turn after turn until he arrived at the end of the track.

There was no community in need of a pastor, no lost soul in need of saving, just a field. Still, maybe God had just been testing him to see if he would respond that way when really needed. So, pleased that God had tested him and that he had passed the test, he turned around, followed his way back to the road he had turned off, and continued his journey.

It had, of course all been a delusion. It would not have mattered what he had found at the end of the track. To him, **that** would have been why God sent him there. Confirmation bias would have ensured he reached the conclusion that confirmed his notion that he was God's valued servant and that God had a plan for him.

It is not just at the personal level that the delusion of faith affects people's lives but at the collective, community level too. It is noticeable that religiosity tends to increase and become more fundamental in highly stratified societies like the USA. In these societies there are large urban underclasses and a very large disparity between the income of the poor and the income of the very rich, with very little hope for people in the lowest strata of ever escaping from that situation. A 2012 Gallup poll conducted across 112 countries found, 'The more poverty a nation has, the higher the "religiosity" in that nation. In general, richer countries are less religious than poorer ones.'[55]

However, as the report also noted, the USA remains an outlier: it is comparatively rich yet sixty-five percent of people say religion is important in their lives compared to just thirty percent in France, twenty-seven percent in the United Kingdom, nineteen percent in Denmark and seventeen percent in Sweden. This difference had been explained in a 2009 study by Dr Tomas Rees, which found 'Income inequality, and hence personal insecurity, was an important determinant of religiosity'. [56]

It would seem then that rather than absolute income being the main determinant of religiosity, important though that it, relative poverty within a particular country is also a very important determinant. However, there is also a strong correlation between poverty and education. Many people remain poor because they lack education either from failures in the education system or because they live in a social background not conducive to educational achievement.

In the days before i-phones and e-readers, it used to be axiomatic that you could generally tell the social status of a person by looking at the number of adult books in their home. In many parts of the USA, many homes will have just one or two adult books often but not always including the Bible. In these homes there is no tradition of reading for the pleasure of reading or of using reference books to find things out.

The effect of education on religiosity was the subject of a 2008 study by Bruce Sacerdote and Edward L. Glaeser. They found:

> *In the United States, religious attendance rises sharply with education across individuals, but religious attendance declines sharply with education across denominations. This puzzle is explained if education both increases the returns to social connection and reduces the extent of religious belief. The positive effect of education on sociability explains the positive education-religion relationship. The negative effect of*

---
[55] (Crabtree S. , 2010)
[56] (Rees, 2009)

> *education on religious belief causes more educated individuals to sort into less fervent religions, which explains the negative relationship between education and religion across denominations. Cross-country differences in the impact of education on religious belief can explain the large cross-country variation in the education-religion connection. These cross-country differences in the education-belief relationship can be explained by political factors (such as communism) which lead some countries to use state-controlled education to discredit religion.* [57]

It seems then that there is a sort of unholy triple alliance between poverty, income inequality and (lack of) education which creates the conditions not only for people to be more religious, but to be more fundamentalist and fervent in their religion.

I suspect though, that religiosity plays a central role in this alliance and is not simply an incidental product of it. Religion teaches people to be satisfied with not knowing and to accept that somehow everything is the way it is because God or Allah wills it. You are poor because that was the role you have been allotted; you are at the bottom or the social strata because that is your allotted place. It is all part of God's plan and who are you to question God's plan?

This was actually taught to us as children at a village Church of England school in North Oxfordshire, England, where one of the popular hymns was the quite astonishingly blatant social and political propaganda hymn, *All Things Bright And Beautiful,* which contains the lines, 'The rich man in his castle, The poor man at his gate, God made them high and lowly, And ordered their estate.' This was a hymn aimed at children and wraps that obnoxious piece of snobbery inside verses singing about little birds and flowers.

It was written by Mrs Cecil Frances Alexander nee Humphreys, born in Dublin, the third child and second daughter of Major John Humphreys of Norfolk, land-agent to 4th Earl of Wicklow and later to the second Marquees of Abercorn. She was the wife of William Alexander, later Bishop of Armagh and Anglican primate of Ireland. It was written especially for children whom Mrs Alexander felt needed to be reminded not only what a lovely little planet God had provided for them but how he had thoughtfully provided them with a

---

[57] (Glaeser & Sacerdote, 2008)

neat social order, with the rich in their castles and the lowly at their gate so they knew their place in it.

This charming little piece of insidious social and anti-science propaganda was written in Ireland in 1848, the third and most devastating year of the Great Famine when between 500,000 and 1,000,000 'lowly' Irish men women and children were starving to death outside the gates, whilst their wealthy land owners in their castles were exporting food.[58]

Meanwhile the English gentleman parliament in London was refusing to distribute relief supplies for fear it would interfere with the law of supply and demand. God had also thoughtfully provided this law of supply and demand to help ensure the social order was maintained and the rich continued to get richer by living off the labours of the lower orders. What did a few hundred thousand dead Irish Catholic peasants matter, when there were plenty more where they came from?

Particularly insidious is the way it sets impressionable little children up with a twee little rhyme about flowers and little birds, before associating them with a rigid and God-given class system. These lucky little children would know their place and understand why they should stay in it.

The historical events in the UK and the rest of Europe were probably not insignificant factors in the mind of Mrs Cecil Frances Alexander in 1848. Events such as the French Revolution of February that year, the publication of the Communist Manifesto in the same month, workers uprisings throughout the Austro-Hungarian Empire and elsewhere. Probably the worst of all was a massive Chartist rally in London, audaciously demanding universal adult male suffrage and paid MPs, so you did not need to be rich to represent people in parliament. These were all within a few weeks of one another; events which had simultaneously concentrated the minds and slackened the bowels of the English ruling class.

How fortunate we were to have such a thoughtful ruling class to explain these things to us simple plebeians, and such a kind, caring Anglican Church to promulgate it down to the lower orders and ensure we got the lesson early in life when we were young and malleable.

---

[58] (Wikipedia, 2016)

And this all depends on a delusion and on people being persuaded to believe that somehow life is better because they may have jam tomorrow if they are very lucky, and just accept their suffering and non-aspirational lives humbly. A delusion moreover based on the absurd notion that faith is a sure and certain way to knowledge about something for which there is not a whiff of real evidence.

How many potential Leonardo da Vincis, Albert Einsteins, Pablo Picassos or Wolfgang Amadeus Mozarts have been lost to us because people knew their place and believed they were not entitled to more? How much more quickly could we have discovered modern medicines, radio, telephony and satellite navigation systems, if the full human potential had been released instead of humanity being required to don the mental straightjacket of religions in which people knew their place? It scarcely bears thinking about.

Even in highly educated academic circles for much of the Middle Ages, thinkers had to be extremely circumspect in any criticism of religion because, on a whim a pope, bishop or king could have them burned at the stake for heresy. There was little to be gained save self-respect, from looking too closely at religion and religious dogma rather than just accepting it and getting on with something less controversial.

A very good example of how religious dogma in the minds of even highly educated people of their time can be found in the writings of Francis Bacon (22 January 1561 – 9 April 1626). It shows how religion can influence their thinking and lead them to, in some cases, quite absurd and even inhumane policies. Francis Bacon was a leading thinker of his day and is regarded as the father of the scientific method.

His essay *Of Atheism* is frequently cited, usually uncritically, by theologians and Christian apologists. It is, as we shall see, the product of a straightjacketed mind combined with ignorance about real science (which had not been discovered then). Incidentally, notice how much of his argument is closely similar to that of creationists and religious apologists today, despite the enormous advances science has made to the sum total of human knowledge and understanding in the intervening years.

Let us examine some of it, especially to see how a leading thinker and advocate of scientific methodology, was none the less a child of his time, and was constrained by the limitations of knowledge and understanding, not to mention the political realities within which he operated.

> *I had rather believe all the fables in the Legend, and the Talmud, and the Alcoran* [Qur'an]*, than that this universal frame is without a mind. And therefore, God never wrought miracle, to convince atheism, because his ordinary works convince it.*

Bacon might well have rather believed the 'universal frame' has a mind but then he knew little or nothing of modern science especially cosmology, Relativity or Quantum Theory. He knew nothing of the chaos which characterises the underlying structure of the cosmos, nor of Chaos Theory, which explains how structure and order is an emergent property of chaos, especially when given direction by gravity.

Instead, baffled by the apparent order and appearance of design, Bacon opted for the only theory which seemed to explain it – a god did it. As we shall see in a moment, Bacon's understanding of how the world was constructed was primitive, to say the least.

In reality, Bacon was opting for the God of the Gaps and the argument from ignorance. Because he could not understand it, he assumed it was not understandable and therefore needed something to fill that gap. Of course there was only one god allowed. The penalty for suggesting another one was death at worst or ruin and disgrace at best.

> *It is true, that a little philosophy inclineth man's mind to atheism; but depth in philosophy bringeth men's minds about to religion. For while the mind of man looketh upon second causes scattered, it may sometimes rest in them, and go no further; but when it beholdeth the chain of them, confederate and linked together, it must needs fly to Providence and Deity.*

So, the more you think about it the more ignorant you realise you are and so the bigger the gap you discover to fit your preferred god in. It is hard to believe it would not have occurred to Bacon that this same argument can be used for **any** god of your choice, but he would have been acutely aware of the dangers of saying so.

> *Nay, even that school which is most accused of atheism doth most demonstrate religion; that is, the school of Leucippus and Democritus and Epicurus. For it is a thousand times more credible, that four mutable elements, and one immutable fifth essence, duly and eternally placed, need no God, than that an army of infinite small portions, or seeds unplaced, should have produced this order and beauty, without a divine marshal.*

Four mutable elements and one immutable fifth essence? Bacon's false conclusions are probably best explained by this revelation of the limitations of scientific knowledge of the times. How on earth could he have understood the universe when viewing it through this inadequate little telescope?

> *...Therefore, as atheism is in all respects hateful, so in this, that it depriveth human nature of the means to exalt itself, above human frailty. As it is in particular persons, so it is in nations. Never was there such a state for magnanimity as Rome. Of this state hear what Cicero saith: Quam volumus licet, patres conscripti, nos amemus, tamen nec numero Hispanos, nec robore Gallos, nec calliditate Poenos, nec artibus Graecos, nec denique hoc ipso hujus gentis et terrae domestico nativoque sensu Italos ipsos et Latinos; sed pietate, ad religione, atque hac una sapientia, quod deorum immortalium numine omnia regi gubernarique perspeximus, omnes gentes nationesque superavimus.*[Which roughly translates as: We know better that all those foreigners and even the locals. Our religion is right and bestest so there!]

This is not the work of a brilliant philosopher using the scientific method to prove there must be a god and that the only possible god is the Christian one. This is the work of someone busking it as a political propagandist in early seventeenth century England. Bacon knew which side his bread was buttered. He was trying to curry favour with the establishment of the day and to avoid the pitfall of saying anything which could be considered blasphemous, so ending up tied to a stake and surrounded by burning faggots, in the time-honoured way of resolving theological difference.

Bacon was constrained as much by his primitive view of the Universe, given the limited knowledge of the time, as by the straightjacket imposed on him by the political and religious culture in what amounted to a fundamentalist Christian theocracy. Like any seventeenth century upper class Englishman he carried the predominant cultural baggage and subscribed to the same cultural norms and unquestioning assumptions of the time. These assumptions included the 'knowledge' that there was a god, that the 'natural order' could only be explained by a god, and that the English naturally had the one true god and the one true religion.

How could God have arranged it otherwise?

Bacon's delusion lies in the fact that he believes he has evidence for a god (although he never does more than take it as a given that this god is the one described in the Bible). His 'evidence' is primarily the Bible itself and also the appearance of design in the Universe which looked like it was made for humans. In reality, this amounts to no more than confirmation bias and our old friend, the 'I do not know, therefore God!' argument. Bacon's god, like the god almost all theists, was exactly designed to fit the gap in his knowledge and understanding like a puddle fits the hole it is in. Because it fitted so perfectly that confirmed it, or so he felt.

The degree to which people's understanding of the world around them is conditioned by religious delusion can be seen from the results of a 2014 Pew Research Center US Religious Landscape study[59]. This study found that there was a wide difference in opinion on the matter of human evolution between members of different religions and even between different Christian churches.

In the USA, fifty-seven percent of Evangelical Protestants, seventy-four percent of Jehovah's Witnesses, forty-five percent of 'Historically Black' Protestants and fifty-two percent of Mormons do not believe humans have evolved at all but were created as they are today. Twenty-nine percent of Catholics agreed with that view despite the official teaching of the Catholic Church which accepts the Theory of Evolution as an established fact. The figure for those not believing in evolution falls to around thirty percent for Mainline Protestants and Orthodox Christians.

US Muslims are almost evenly divided on the issue, with forty-one percent not accepting evolution. Meanwhile, the equivalent figure for Buddhists, Hindus, Jews and the religiously unaffiliated or 'nones' is only thirteen, seventeen, sixteen and fifteen percent respectively.

---

[59] (Pew Research Center, 2014)

So we can see a wide difference between different faiths and denominations, yet on average across these groups there will be the same access to the same scientific data. Clearly, views on a fundamental aspect of human biology are determined more by religious beliefs than by hard evidence, and yet as we have seen above there is no factual basis for those religious beliefs in the first place.

The point is brought home even more sharply by the fact, as shown in another Pew Research Center survey[60], that ninety-eight of scientists associated with the American Association for the Advancement of Science (AAAS) believe that humans have evolved by a natural process. This figure rises even further to ninety-nine when just those working in biomedical science are surveyed. A different section of the same survey[61] also showed that only sixty-six percent of Americans think that scientists believe in evolution, showing, perhaps, that despite evidence to the contrary, people with religiously-conditioned views about science subjects actually believe that their opinions have some scientific basis.

Sam Harris has said:

> *While believing strongly, without evidence, is considered a mark of madness or stupidity in any other area of our lives, faith in God still holds immense prestige in our society. Religion is the one area of our discourse where it is considered noble to pretend to be certain about things no human being could possibly be certain about. It is telling that this aura of nobility extends only to those faiths that still have many subscribers. Anyone caught worshipping Poseidon, even at sea, will be thought insane.*[62]

Without evidence for gods, why do people become so deluded in their belief that they exist that they allow it to control their entire lives and even feel it gives them some sort of meaning and purpose?

The origins of the god delusion are probably in the propensity of children to believe the authority figures around them, especially their parents. There are in fact very good evolutionary reasons why children believe their parents. It is much better in terms of long-term survival to not go too close to the fire, not go

---

[60] (Pew Research Center, 2015)
[61] (Pew Research Center, 2015)
[62] (Peters, 2012)

down to the water hole to watch the crocodiles or not touch a snake when your parents have told you not to. They are older and wiser, so it stands to reason they know best.

So the children who were open to believing what authority figures told them, would have left more descendants than those who got eaten by the crocodiles, fell in the fire or got bitten by a snake. But if it stands to reason that parents know best, it stands to reason that their gods exist and should be worshipped in a particular way on a particular day in a particular church, mosque, synagogue or temple, does it not?

It stands to reason also that you will be thrown in a fiery pit or you will be reincarnated as a lower caste person, if you do not obey God and do exactly as he says, or if you even doubt the religion or question the truth of the holy book.

And it stands to reason that your particular god created you and everything else and so you and everything else are evidence for your particular god. If your particular god wrote your particular holy book. and said in it that it was his inerrant word, it stands to reason that this is so because your parents said so when you were a child.

My father died suddenly when he was fifty-three years old. I am now considerably older than he was as I last remember him. In fact my eldest son is closer to his age than I am. Yet I find it extremely difficult to think of my father as someone who I am older and wiser than. In my mind, he is still an authority figure (not in the authoritarian sense but in terms of his knowledge and wisdom) and someone whose approval was important to me.

I just about remember my maternal grandfather. He was extremely wise and even knew more than my mother and father who deferred to his greater wisdom! And just imagine how wise **his** grandfather was! My grandfather even used to quote his old sayings!

My suspicion is that this natural deference to our parents and the innate respect we have for them, and even more so for our grandparents, is the origin of cults of ancestor worship. It is one of the reasons people tend to think that those born before us must be wiser than us. Project that back hundreds or thousands of years and you are inclined to think that the 'wisdom of the ancients' is sacred truth. So, the people who wrote the ancient 'holy' books were extremely wise and knowledgeable, were they not?

This deference to the authority of our parents and grandparents, natural though it is for very good evolutionary reasons, runs completely contrary to the fact that the sum total of human knowledge **increases** over time; it does not diminish. We are vastly more knowledgeable today than we were even a generation ago, let alone several thousand years ago. The 'science' in the holy books is not deep wisdom; it is shallow ignorance. It was written by people who knew no better. We know much better than that now.

I was brought up as an Anglican Christian. I have no recollection at all of when I first heard of God or Jesus, or was told that the Bible was a sacred book. But I remember touching the family Bible with great reverence in the 'knowledge' that I was being watched particularly closely. I thought I knew someone was watching my every move and knew my most secret thoughts and paid special attention when I was in church. Yet I have not the least idea **why** I believed those things.

They simply seemed like facts of life, like the fact that day followed night. If you had asked me why I believed in God I would probably have said, 'Because it is true!' and I would have thought that reason enough. I would not have been able to tell you what convinced me because I was never reasoned into belief in the first place. I had belief without reason. I had 'faith'. I had no choice!

I remember very clearly though when I realised I did not believe in gods and what convinced me there were none. I know the thought processes that led me to that conclusion. I absolutely did not go through the same reasoning process in order to believe in the first place. So far as I was aware, I had always believed in exactly the same god as my parents and knew I had to go to the same church as they did and that we had the one true religion.

Children simply wear with pride whatever labels their parents put on them. It is part of what gives them their personal, family and group identity. The evidence for this is in the geographical distribution of religions. It is an evolved psychological and cultural process giving group affiliation and cohesion.

Faith is put into the minds of children without their permission.

But if religious delusion is a bad thing, should adaptive evolution not have eliminated it early on in human evolution?

The answer of course is no. Simply because an adaptive feature evolves in a given environment does not mean it will necessarily give advantage in a different environment. Giraffes have a superbly adapted neck for living where their preferred food is at the top of tall trees (which are tall incidentally because it is an adaptive advantage to them to not be eaten by giraffes). If, however, something eradicated these tall trees, giraffes would be hopelessly maladapted and their long necks could well cause their extinction.

So the answer is that it may not always have been harmful and divisive for small groups to be religious, the way it is today in multicultural, multi-ethnic societies and globalisation.

When humans consisted of small extended family groups as anthropologists believe, it would probably have been more beneficial to have everyone agreeing on the need for religious rituals and ceremonies if only because group activity produced social cohesion. Additionally, the thought that a judgmental deity is watching would have made it easier to enforce group rules and deter free-loaders. In other words, religions would have played a useful role in human cultural development and the development of ethics.

The fact that ethics evolved for fitting us to live in small social groups can be seen in the mind experiment, Singer's Dilemma[63], devised by Peter Singer, author of *The Life You Can Save*:

Imagine you are walking near a village pond wearing a thousand dollar suit or dress and you notice a child in the pod obviously in trouble and out of his or her depth. You are the only one who can help and you have no time to undress, but if you jump in the pond you will ruin the thousand dollar suit or dress.

What would you do?

Most people would recoil at the suggestion that you should save the suit and let the child die. I suspect most decent people would save the child. Is a child's life not worth infinitely more than a thousand dollars? We even have a term

---

[63] (Singer, 2009) page.3.

for people who hold the lives of others in little value – we call them sociopaths and recognise it as a psychological disorder.

But you can save many starving children far away by donating a thousand dollars. Why then do so few people save the starving children? How are these two situations different?

The simple answer is that we feel we have a moral obligation to those we can immediately help because they are in our social group even if just because we are physically near to them. We do not innately feel such a strong moral obligation to people a long way away and who are not 'one of us'.

The simple, but maybe disturbing, truth is that we do not have a universally objective 'moral' that every child's life is worth more than a thousand dollars. Our morals are subjective and weighted in favour of those who are part of our immediate group, tribe, clan, etc.

But we do not now live in small groups but is very large conurbations and diverse, multi-ethnic, multi-cultural societies consisting of tens or hundreds of millions of people; even billions of people. Many of these societies are already ghettoised because of language, religion and cultural origins, yet we still have cultural memes fitted for forming and maintaining exclusive groups with in-group versus out-group morality, and see the out-group as a threat. As Sam Harris says:

> *Incompatible religious doctrines have balkanized our world into separate moral communities, and these divisions have become a continuous source of bloodshed. Indeed, religion is as much a living spring of violence today as it has been at any time in the past.* [64]

How much of this innately differential morality lies behind nationalism, xenophobia, social exclusion, inter-communal conflict and mutual distrust and hostility? Religions are not now sources of either peace or social cohesion for the simple reason that our technological development has outstripped our memetic evolution, leaving us saddled with religions that are no longer fit for purpose.

---

[64] (Peters, 2012)

So we can be reasonably sure that the propensity to be religious evolved, but for something to evolve does not necessarily mean there was an adaptive advantage to it. It could be that religions are the result of the evolution of other psychological processes that also happened to create the propensity to be religious.

One such mechanism was suggested in a 2009 research paper by Kevin R Foster and Hanna Kokko. They applied the recognised psychological phenomenon of superstitious behaviour arising from mistaken association between cause and effect to human evolutionary biology. They showed that where the risk from mistaken association between events like a rustle in the grass and potential danger is low compared to the risk of ignoring it, counterintuitively, there will be evolutionary advantage in frequently making mistakes. In the authors' words:

> ... our work suggests that the acquisition of new information through learning, copying and hearsay is all underlain by the innate and adaptive propensities to act on uncertainties. In particular, the inability of individuals—human or otherwise—to assign causal probabilities to all sets of events that occur around them will often force them to lump causal associations with non-causal ones. From here, the evolutionary rationale for superstition is clear: natural selection will favour strategies that make many incorrect causal associations in order to establish those that are essential for survival and reproduction. [65]

Basically, because it was an evolutionary advantage for us to make superstitious-like responses to perceived threats, so we evolved the ability to make these sorts of mistakes. Hence, our brains were ready to make a false association between say crop failures and an angry invisible spirit, or between rituals to appease these spirits and success at bringing about a desired outcome that would have happened anyway.

In other words, it is entirely possible that the propensity to develop religions, and so to develop all manner of religions according to local conditions, was an incidental consequence of us evolving the propensity to over-react when the risk is low but the rewards for occasional success are high.

---

[65] (Foster & Kokko, 2009)

In human evolutionary terms, religions might well be an understandable mistake.

But this explanation presupposes an existing belief in deities of some sort in order to mistakenly ascribe effects to them in the first place. So where did this idea of gods come from? I have a hypothesis which I will present here, not as a fully worked out scientific theory with supporting evidence but as an example of how it **could** have happened.

First we need to go back again to the plains of Africa again, to a time when our ancestors were living pretty much as their other ape cousins still do. Just as with the other African ape species, we would probably have lived in small groups of related individuals, each group dominated by an alpha male.

This alpha male would have won his 'right' to be leader and the size of the group would have been related to how many individuals this alpha male (and maybe his alpha female mate) could exert control over. The alpha male would have had first pick of the females and would have enforced this right, maybe through a group of loyal supporters, by the sanction of physical punishment against those who infringed his right or who threatened his dominance.

The idea that the alpha male had this right would have been passed on from one generation to the next as a group norm or ethic. In evolutionary terms, there would be an advantage in the alpha male passing on the genes which enabled him to dominate and the group would have benefited by being more likely to be led by a strong male able to dominate and lead. However, there would have been an evolutionary arms race between these 'alpha male' genes and genes which predisposed to illicit sexual activity, since these genes would have enjoyed the protection of the alpha male – classic free-loaders which are predictable consequences of game theory applied to evolutionary arms races.

Whether these 'genes' were actual DNA genes or memes, inherited as part of group culture, is immaterial. The fact is that human groups would have been evolving by gene-meme co-evolution. Replicators have no concern for the nature of the other replicators with which they form alliances because alliances form naturally out of mutual self-interest.

The plains of Africa have very many rocky out-crops which offer shelter and which are good vantage points from which to survey the surrounding plain.

These outcrops also give the alpha male good vantage points from which to survey the group and keep an eye on what is going on: who is doing what and with whom, with particular regard to illicit sexual activity. Alternatively, other males and females will be trying to evade his watchful eye, and those of his 'enforcers'.

It is easy to see how this idea of a dominant alpha male, the strong leader on whom the group depends, and the vengeful deliverer of pain and suffering for any transgression of the group norms came to evolve in human culture. It is easy to see too why this alpha male takes a special interest in the sexual activities of his 'subjects', and is especially concerned that females remain inactive until he has had his turn, or at least sanctioned their mating.

Dominating his group through controlling their sexual activity ensures the alpha male's genes get priority and he can also use this control as a reward system to ensure obedience. Meanwhile other selection forces are ensuring continued 'illicit' sexual activity, even making this thrilling and exciting.

Now, move on two or three million years and remove humans from the East African plains. Place them now in larger nomadic tribes or into settled farming communities and towns across Africa, Europe and Asia and into the Americas. Now there is no place for a single alpha male to sit and watch the whole group and the group is too large or diverse for him to dominate it, yet he still exists in the culture.

The memes which arose on the plains of Africa are still being replicated down through the generations. So many of our cultural ideas have been conditioned by the alpha male's presence and have evolved in an environment in which he exists, but the physical reality of the alpha male has now been replaced by the cultural idea of one.

The alpha male now sits on some imaginary vantage point overlooking the tribe, still the benevolent protector and leader, the guardian of the law, and the vengeful enforcer of his right to grant permission for sexual activity and for whose permission all, but especially the females, must wait until he grants it through the symbolic ceremony of marriage.

The alpha male's loyal enforcers still exist though. They have become a self-selecting band which acts as though the alpha male still exists and whose claim to power and authority is that they represent him and are doing his bidding. They have become his priesthood.

Here we have the almost universal character of the slightly different forms of the Abrahamic god – the aloof, protective father-figure who makes and enforces the laws and metes out punishment; who loves his people but can be capriciously vengeful and who especially takes a very close, obsessive interest in our sex lives and tells us who can mate with who, when and how. He closely resembles the Late Bronze Age tribal chief who would have been the direct homologues of the pre-human alpha male.

One consequence of this is the tension, especially in females as they mature, between the cultural demand that they stay virgins until they have permission to have sex and the powerful biological drive to have sex. This tension still almost completely dominates some highly religious cultures and even determines their mode of dress. Ayaan Hirsi Ali, the atheist former Muslim and feminist writer, cites this tension as one of the things that made her begin to question Islam:

> *Ultimately, I think, it was books, and boys, that saved me. No matter how hard I tried to submit to Allah's will, I still felt desire — sexual desire, urgent and real, which even the vision of Hellfire could not suppress.* [66]

I think we can now see clearly how the idea of gods arose in the human meme pools we call culture, how the assumption that these gods exist led to religion and so why what Richard Dawkins' called the God delusion came to be such a dominant theme in almost all human cultures. At no time was there a moment when, either individually or collectively, mankind saw clear definitive evidence for any gods, although myths abound in which people allegedly saw the gods they already believed in, as Greek, Roman, Egyptian and Hebrew mythology shows.

Yet, as a direct and probably accidental, consequence of our genetic and memetic evolution, we have ended up with well over half of mankind suffering from one form or another of this god delusion, not because it is beneficial now but because it was possibly once beneficial. We are like giraffes struggling to cope with a maladapted long neck when the tall trees have gone.

---

[66] Ayaan Hirsi Ali; *How (and Why) I Became an Infidel*. From (Hitchens, The Portable Atheist: Essential Reading for the Nonbeliever, 2007) (pp. 477-480).

Freedom from Delusion

People still kill one another and have been killing one another for thousands of years, over which delusion exactly is the right delusion. Otherwise sane adults of apparently normal intelligence allow themselves to be turned into the delivery system for weapons of mass destruction. They do this in order to strike a mighty blow for their particular delusion by randomly killing people in the hope that those killed will include some people who have a different delusion – and of course because they have been promised a wonderful reward.

Combine the grotesque obscenity (I do not think that is too strong a description) of the belief that life is merely a cage from which we should seek to escape to a better life in a better place, with possession of nuclear, biological and chemical weapons, and this malevolent delusion has the power to destroy life on the planet as we know it. All in the name of an imaginary friend for whom there is not now and never has been the smallest shred of evidence.

Writing in the Guardian in November 2013, Susan Blackmore, atheist, psychologist and author of *The Meme Machine,* explained the harm done by religion with:

> *When you see religions as mind viruses that evolved over thousands of years in competition with other, similar, mind viruses, it's easy to see why they have acquired the powerful adaptations they have. Just as animals acquired teeth and claws, beaks and jaws, mimicry and trickery, so religions have acquired their own weapons and tricks. They protect themselves with threats and promises – and not just any old threats and promises. Some are promises of everlasting pain or eternal bliss – only you can't check whether they're true because you'll only find out after you're dead. Others are immediate threats that can be checked – that if you reject a belief you never chose in the first place but were landed with as a baby, you'll be killed. And this is happening even here in Britain. The founder of the Council of Ex-Muslims of Britain has had numerous death threats for trying to help Muslims let go of their imposed beliefs.*
>
> ...
>
> *A really clever trick – and I'm not sure how the great religions have managed to pull this one off – is to make the rest of us feel that we ought to respect people for believing impossible things on faith, and that we should not laugh at them for fear of offending them. In a society that*

> *strives for honesty and openness, that values scientific and historical truth, and that encourages the search for knowledge, this is outrageous – and it's scary that we still fall for it.*
>
> *Then there's the cost of believing. Many are tempted by Pascal's Wager: if I deny that God exists and I'm wrong, oops I might really go to hell, but if I believe in him and I'm wrong there is no problem. But there is a problem – the enormous cost of belief. There is not only the mental and intellectual burden of having to take on false, disturbing and incompatible beliefs, but the cost in time and money. Religious memes capture people's time to get themselves spread. Just as the common cold virus makes people sneeze to get itself spread, so religions make people sings hymns and say prayers, and chant and so spread the word of God. They also induce them to part with large sums of money to build glorious mosques, churches and synagogues and to pay the wages of priests who in turn spread the word of God.*
>
> *And how did they get this way? They got this way because less effective versions of the religions, with less dangerous tricks and weapons, failed to infect enough people. .* [67]

Despite all that, and even knowing that religion is delusional and probably a parasitic memeplex, is there not still a case for maintaining this delusion, if it leads to a moral, peaceful and loving society?

Astonishingly, despite the troubles in the world today as major religions are squaring up to one another in the Middle East; despite atrocities being committed daily throughout the world in the name of one or other religion; despite the fact that refugees are pouring into Europe and elsewhere to find peace and stability, this argument is still advanced for allowing religions to continue unchallenged.

The argument that religion is required for a moral society quite simply runs counter to the available evidence. It amounts to little more than the argument that my religion makes me your moral superior; 'I'm holier than thou!' in disguise.

---

[67] (Blackmore, 2007)

The difficulty is in defining moral behaviour in the first place. Most dictionaries I have checked seem to be quite vague and subjective, using definitions such as, 'Principles concerning the distinction between right and wrong or good and bad behaviour', without much consideration about what 'right' or 'wrong' behaviour is. The *Stanford Encyclopedia of Philosophy* puts the problem this way:

> *There does not seem to be much reason to think that a single definition of morality will be applicable to all moral discussions. One reason for this is that "morality" seems to be used in two distinct broad senses: a descriptive sense and a normative sense. More particularly, the term "morality" can be used either*
>
> 1. *descriptively to refer to certain codes of conduct put forward by a society or a group (such as a religion), or accepted by an individual for her own behavior, or*
> 2. *normatively to refer to a code of conduct that, given specified conditions, would be put forward by all rational persons.*
>
> *Which of these two senses of "morality" a theorist is using plays a crucial, although sometimes unacknowledged, role in the development of an ethical theory. If one uses "morality" in its descriptive sense, and therefore uses it to refer to codes of conduct actually put forward by distinct groups or societies, one will almost certainly deny that there is a universal morality that applies to all human beings. The descriptive use of "morality" is the one used by anthropologists when they report on the morality of the societies that they study. Recently, some comparative and evolutionary psychologists (Haidt 2006; Hauser 2006; De Waal 1996) have taken morality, or a close anticipation of it, to be present among groups of non-human animals: primarily, but not exclusively, other primates.*

Religious apologists on the other hand will not only claim that there are objective morals but that their particular god is the source of them and they can only be found in their particular holy book.

But when we examine the behaviour of the clerics and priests of these diverse religions, we find examples of behaviour that are difficult to reconcile with any reasonable notion of moral good. We find child-raping priests; advocates of mass murder; advocates of repression, persecution, holy wars and jihads. We find a church organisation more interested in protecting and defending miscreant priests and imams and obstructing the national law enforcement agencies by withholding information and by transferring miscreant priests out of their jurisdiction altogether.

We find a Vatican rife with financial corruption and self-serving in-fighting, and indulging in sexual practices they loudly condemn in others. More importantly, we find a church which not only fails to advocate for individual liberty, for gender equality, for freedom of conscience and for extension of human rights, but which actively and openly campaigns against them and demands the right to discriminate.

What we find is a growing tension between the old, inadequate morality of the times in which the sacred holy books were written and the needs and desires of a modern, urbanised and technologically advanced society. People are no longer willing to tolerate an imposed and obviously immoral code of behaviour.

The problem is that religions are stuck with their circular definitions of right and wrong based on what their holy books say, and they regard their holy books as 'right' because they contain objective morals. Meanwhile, human culture has moved on and increasingly views that which once passed for morality as decidedly immoral.

It is an instructive enterprise to ask a devout Christian or Muslim to provide empirical proof that their holy book was not written by Satan. Invariably, they will quote from the book, ignoring the fact that had Satan been real and had he written the book, whatever they quote could have been written in it specifically to mislead them.

Logically, of course, simply by using the books themselves, it is impossible to disprove that proposition, just as it is impossible to prove that a benevolent god wrote it, so any appeals to these books as sources of objective morals is immediately flawed

But the morality of the holy books is a very strange thing anyway. In the Bible for example, apart from a few nods towards the basic rules common to all human societies, there is actually nothing much about how we should treat one another. Rather, it is not more about defending the power and influence of the priesthood and obeying the arbitrary dress code and food taboos.

What specific rules there are, such as killing homosexuals, witches, unruly children and daughters who are not virgins, seem barbaric in the extreme now. Racism is rife, as is support for slavery and repression and even ownership, of women. Rape victims are to be blamed for being raped while the rapist can buy his victim from her father for a small sum. Rape is a legitimate way to obtain wives!

Anyone with a disability or disfigurement, however slight, is condemned as an abomination and the entire human race is condemned as unworthy, shameful and in need of forgiveness for simply being born while natural sexual desire is riddled with guilt. Children are to be condemned for things their grandparents did and trial, condemnation and execution are peremptory and mandatory with no room for mercy or arguments in mitigation.

Perhaps the most noticeable thing about these biblical morals is how so many of them would rightly result in a prison sentence if obeyed in any civilised modern society. Some of them are considered so heinous that the law calls for the death penalty even. It is probable that if the Bible were published for the first time today, its author and publisher would face prosecution for a number of crimes, including incitement to commit murder, incitement to racism and other hate crimes.

There is not a word against child abuse, against misogyny, racism, slavery or disability discrimination. There is no mention of universal human rights, of the right to life, liberty and the pursuit of happiness, of the right to elect and remove our leaders, nor of the right to free trial. All of these things have been won by a people who saw the old morality as wrong, and usually in the teeth of clerical opposition, or at least official opposition from the established churches.

To be fair though, others who claimed to be finding inspiration from the same holy books discerned an opposite set of 'objective' morals in it, and enthusiastically supported the abolition of things the Bible calls for such as slavery. One might have expected an omnipotent god to have put his message in a less ambiguous form.

For a supposed book of absolute objective morals, the Bible, like the Qur'an is crude and simplistic and lacks the subtlety needed for any half-decent moral code. Take for example the unambiguous 'Thou shalt not kill' commandment. Notwithstanding that this is followed almost immediately with instructions to go on a genocide and land-grabbing spree, it is simply too crude.

To illustrate this, try the following mind experiment:

You are standing next to a lever than can change a set of points on a rail track. You see a runaway truck coming down the line heading straight for a group of six workmen on the track who will be killed if the truck hits them. There is a single workman on the other line. You can throw the lever to divert the truck away from the six but this will surely kill the one workman.

What would you do? Your action will kill one person but your inaction will kill six. Clearly, there is not a morally perfect answer to this dilemma because failing to save six when you had absolute power to, is surely morally reprehensible, is it not? Is failing to save six lives more morally reprehensible than deliberately sacrificing one?

Try as you might, you will not find a morally perfect answer to this dilemma in any holy 'book of objective morals', which is exactly why theologians can be rolled out to support either side in, for example, the capital punishment debate or the morality of taking military action in national self-defence, or even wars of aggression. There is no explicit concept of the greater good in the Bible.

One only need read the convoluted logic of apologists like Dr William Lane Craig when he tries to make genocide and infanticide look like moral acts, to know that there is something deeply flawed in the notion that the Bible is a book of objective morals. The dangers of abdicating responsibility for your own morality in favour of a book which you have arbitrarily designated as 'moral', regardless of its actual content, should be readily understandable. This is the same faith-based morality that led to the Srebrenica massacre and led the Abbott commander in charge of the siege of Bezier to order the slaughter of the entire population of the town so that 'God will recognise his own'

Try this mental exercise. First read this passage from:

And, behold, a certain lawyer stood up, and tempted him, saying, Master, what shall I do to inherit eternal life?

He said unto him, What is written in the law? how readest thou?

And he answering said, Thou shalt love the Lord thy God with all thy heart, and with all thy soul, and with all thy strength, and with all thy mind; and thy neighbour as thyself.

And he said unto him, Thou hast answered right: this do, and thou shalt live.

But he, willing to justify himself, said unto Jesus, And who is my neighbour?

And Jesus answering said, A certain man went down from Jerusalem to Jericho, and fell among thieves, which stripped him of his raiment, and wounded him, and departed, leaving him half dead.

And by chance there came down a certain priest that way: and when he saw him, he passed by on the other side. And likewise a Levite, when he was at the place, came and looked on him, and passed by on the other side.

But a certain Samaritan, as he journeyed, came where he was: and when he saw him, he had compassion on him, And went to him, and bound up his wounds, pouring in oil and wine, and set him on his own beast, and brought him to an inn, and took care of him.

And on the morrow when he departed, he took out two pence, and gave them to the host, and said unto him, Take care of him; and whatsoever thou spendest more, when I come again, I will repay thee.

Which now of these three, thinkest thou, was neighbour unto him that fell among the thieves? And he said, He that shewed mercy on him. Then said Jesus unto him, Go, and do thou likewise.

Was the 'Good Samaritan' good because he did a good thing, or was he good simply because Jesus arbitrarily designated his act as good without reference to some external standard of goodness, as a god who defines objective morals must?

If the former, Jesus is acknowledging good morals exist and using an example of morality to illustrate a point with a parable, knowing that the lawyer would recognise it. If the latter, then what if Jesus had equally arbitrarily advocated passing by on the other side, or even joining in with the thieves?

If God arbitrarily defines morals then why would he not define things we instinctively find morally repugnant as moral?

Traditionally, Christians take not only the dubious rules as laid down in the Pentateuch but also the so-called Beatitudes from the Sermon on the Mount as the basis of Christian morality. However, any critical reading of these will show, as Dan Barker points out in *Godless: How an Evangelical Preacher Became One of America's Leading Atheists*[68], none of the beatitudes are truly moral because they are all conditional on a future reward.

It is manifestly obvious to an outsider that very few if any Christians, Jews or Muslims follow the instructions in their holy books to the full, but cherry-pick the convenient parts that fit in with the morality of the culture in which they live.

It would now be highly unusual, for example, to find a girl living in an economically developed country who self-identifies as Christian, who is a virgin on her wedding night. If we enforced the Levitical laws, public stoning of teenage girls would be a daily spectacle in every town and village.

Sexual activity between couples even recreationally is now the norm in Western cultures yet the Bible explicitly instructs that women who are not virgins on their wedding night are to be stoned to death. Virginity is no longer regarded as something to be prized and casual sexual activity is widely regarded as normal and healthy between consenting couples.

Some years ago we were in Istanbul, on a very enjoyable coach trip with a guide who had identified herself to us as an Armenian Christian. Chatting to her over lunch, she was astonished to learn that in the UK now, most couples will have cohabited for some time before marriage, might have a child or two

---

[68] (Barker, Godles: How an Evangelical Preacher Became on of America's Leading Atheists, 2009)

before they marry, if they ever do marry, and that both will normally have had several sexual partners before they became a couple.

She was surprised to learn that our teenage children might well bring sexual partners home to sleep with and that we now take it for granted that they will be sexually active before marriage, just as we were in fact, though we were less open about it to our parents.

The significant thing was that she was envious of our freedom and lack of hypocrisy and saw this as something desirable, not something wrong. To her, in secular but deeply conservative Turkey, Western sexual freedom was not a sign of moral decadence but progressive and liberating.

Sexual morality has been a changing thing in the West for the last fifty years or more, not so much in the privacy of our bedrooms as in the public acceptance of it. In my grandparents' and parents' generation, pre-marital sex was normal but surreptitious and riddled with guilt. That it was normal can be seen from any casual perusal of parish baptismal records where single-mother baptisms were commonplace before contraception became available. First pregnancies were often 'short' with a baby being born within a few months of marriage. But the girl who was abandoned by her lover bore the shame and stigma of an 'illegitimate' child which often tarnished her (and her child) for life, condemned as immoral by the sanctimonious hypocrites who had almost certainly managed to get away with it themselves.

Where was the objective morality in a creed that condemns a girl for making love and her child for being born? Or worse still condemns an abused girl for having to suffer the consequence of abuse? This is a hypocritical 'morality' from which we have liberated ourselves. Recreational sex and the act of making love are now enjoyable, shared experiences, free from the guilt and shame that they always should have been, had not sanctimonious religious hypocrites tried to take control of them and impose their unhealthy sexually dysfunctional views on the rest of us.

The Abrahamic faiths, especially Catholic Christianity, often resemble unhealthy sex cults where sex and sexuality are all-consuming obsessions. Instead of sex being the loving, bonding and recreational activity it has clearly evolved to be in humans, it is loaded with shame, guilt and embarrassment.

This obsession leads many devout Christians to avoid sex with the same unhealthy obsession that an anorexic avoids food.

Simply recognising that women are potentially sexually receptive at most times in their monthly cycle and that post-menopausal women not only retain a sexual appetite but often find it enhanced, should tell anyone that sex is not just for reproduction. In humans, as with some other sentient species, sex is not even mostly for procreation but serves other important social functions.

How does a belief in a creator god lead people to conclude that something it supposedly created and gave humans the equipment and psychological drives for, is a sinful thing which should be avoided? The answer to this may well lie in the way the idea of gods evolved from the alpha male of pre-human ancestors who had the right to mate with the females and so took a close interest in the sexual activity of others.

In matters of sex and sexuality, the delusion of faith has often been a source of a great deal of anxiety and mental turmoil. People have struggled to reconcile their own natural urges with the demands of the faith they subscribe to and the unnatural sexual rules it tries to impose. Even worse is the struggle to live with the burden of guilt and the fear of Hellfire that giving in to those natural desires and actually physically loving another human being to the full has imposed on them.

Imagine the terror of a devout elderly man or woman facing the prospect of death, knowing that as a sixteen year-old he or she enjoyed the 'sin' of masturbating, or once allowed someone of the opposite sex, or even the same sex, to touch his or her genitalia, or even 'worse' had sexual intercourse with them. Horror of horrors, they might even have enjoyed it, thought about it a great deal and wanted to do it again! What obscene creed condemns people to a lifetime of fear, anguish and guilt over something so pleasurable, primary and loving as consensual sex?

As Bertrand Russell pointed out in *Why I Am Not A Christian*:

> *You may think that I am going too far when I say that that is still so. I do not think that I am. Take one fact. You will bear with me if I mention it. It is not a pleasant fact, but the churches compel one to mention facts that are not pleasant. Supposing that in this world that we live in today an*

inexperienced girl is married to a syphilitic man; in that case the Catholic Church says, "This is an indissoluble sacrament. You must endure celibacy or stay together. And if you stay together, you must not use birth control to prevent the birth of syphilitic children." Nobody whose natural sympathies have not been warped by dogma, or whose moral nature was not absolutely dead to all sense of suffering, could maintain that it is right and proper that that state of things should continue.

That is only an example. There are a great many ways in which, at the present moment, the church, by its insistence upon what it chooses to call morality, inflicts upon all sorts of people undeserved and unnecessary suffering. And of course, as we know, it is in its major part an opponent still of progress and improvement in all the ways that diminish suffering in the world, because it has chosen to label as morality a certain narrow set of rules of conduct which have nothing to do with human happiness; and when you say that this or that ought to be done because it would make for human happiness, they think that has nothing to do with the matter at all. "What has human happiness to do with morals? The object of morals is not to make people happy."

The churches' insistence on a perverse sexual morality, based not on nature or ideas which associate morals with human happiness, is the cause of much misery.

Russell was talking and writing in 1927, when the church had much more power than it does now in the twenty-first century. We are no more sexual in our desires now; what we are is less deluded in our religion so the irrational delusion no longer imposes guilt and a harmful mental tension. As the psychological grip of the god delusion slackens, so we are becoming freer to enjoy sex and our sexuality. Associating love and sexuality with guilt and shame is probably one of the great crimes against humanity that religions have committed.

A measure of this change can be seen in the May 2015 referendum on the question of the legalisation of same-sex marriage held in the Irish Republic.[69] Ireland had traditionally been a highly conservative, Catholic country where

---

[69] (Irish Times, 2015)

the Catholic Church was held in high esteem and could effectively veto legislation with a condemnatory letter. Following major child-abuse scandals involving Catholic priests and nuns, and systematic cover-ups going to the highest levels in the Irish Catholic Church, and the publication of the Cloyne Report[70] into clerical abuse, church attendance has fallen drastically and self-identified non-belief or non-affiliation has increased dramatically.

Despite hysterical opposition by the Catholic Church to the idea of same-sex marriage, Ireland voted almost 2:1 to legalise it. Even holding such a referendum in Ireland would have been unthinkable just twenty years ago.

We are seeing similar changes throughout most of Europe where the old dogmas of religion are being dumped in favour of a more inclusive, humanitarian ethic based on Humanist principles, whether consciously or unconsciously. This is a direct consequence of the increase in outright atheism and disaffiliation from established religions. As the evidence from repeated polls of the same cohort of people shows, disaffiliation is often a stage on the way to outright rejection of religion.

Freed from the god delusion, people become free to exercise their own judgement based on their innate empathy. In effect, people are once again reclaiming the right to determine their own morals from the religions which hijacked it in the Early Middle Ages – a time which is so aptly referred to as the Dark Ages.

How the churches (and I include the mosques and synagogues in that term) managed to get away with the absurd claim that gods hand down morals and so we should look to the clergy for moral guidance because only they understand the minds of gods, is something of a mystery. It should have been manifestly obvious to anyone but the most parochial and ignorant of people that the facts simply do not support that view.

If morals come from gods, and especially if you believe there is only one god, you should see one of two things:

1. Universal moral codes. In other words, all societies and cultures should have the same God-given set of morals and ethics, or

---

[70] (Department of Justice and Equality, 2011)

2. Moral behaviour only in the area with the 'one true god' with anarchy and rampant immorality elsewhere.

The fact that we see neither should have been a clue. What we see is some broad similarities amounting to universal basic ethics like killing being wrong (usually), treating other people with respect (usually), not stealing, caring for and not exploiting children, etc., etc.

We also see major differences in detail and some major inconsistencies between even the Abrahamic religions. Judaism prohibits mixing meat and dairy products; Islam prohibits figurative art and some Christians indulge in ritual cannibalism, eating wafers and drinking wine that they believe literally turns into the flesh and blood of their religion's legendary founder, Jesus. Hindus have a caste system with its 'untouchables' and even some Buddhists spurn those born with disabilities as having done wrong in a previous life.

What we see, in fact, is exactly what we would expect to see if morals had evolved over time from a stem moral code, in an exact analogy with an evolving biological population as it diversified and speciated and adapted to local environmental factors, with the survival of those moral codes which produced the most descendants.

I will illustrate how social ethics evolve differently in different places with something I noticed a few years ago during a visit to Naples, Italy.

If you have never driven there, it is something of an experience to put it mildly. Basically, the traffic is chaotic. The road-markings are absent or indistinct and are mostly ignored anyway as are speed limits, pedestrian crossings and red traffic lights by the first half dozen cars. People live in tenement blocks with no off-street parking, so roads are lined with parked cars – in fact, for the average visitor, parking is almost non-existent. This makes all but the widest roads barely wide enough for two cars to pass and yet slowing down seems to be regarded as something for softies. Driving is competitive, so you will be overtaken on either side if there is room, raced away from traffic lights, cut up on junctions, and nine out of ten cars will be battle-scarred.

Horns are used frequently and yet headlights are rarely flashed. On the one occasion I flashed a car with a short flash, which in the UK unofficially means, 'Go ahead, I'm giving way to you', I got a stare that would have turned a cockatrice to stone. Yet road-rage is rare, if my experience is anything to go by. The Neapolitans are generally actually considerate and helpful people, or so I found. It took me a couple of days to work out what was going on; then it became much easier to drive. When in Naples, do as the Neapolitans do!

In Naples, you expect a car to pull out of a turning or to turn across your path because they assume you will give way to them. It is a social norm which is taken so much for granted that no one thinks anything of it. It is a bit like the old rule of the road you still see quite a lot in France where you give way to someone pulling out from the right. You are expected to push into a small gap or overtake either side if there is room. It is not meant to be aggressive and it is not taken as such. In the UK what could easily end up as a road-rage incident is the norm in Naples.

On the other hand, flashing your headlights in Naples is a big no-no. That is the equivalent of a rude stare and is assumed to be aggressive. In the UK, it is a sign of courtesy unless you give a long flash, or flash from behind, then it is aggressive. We all know this and take it for granted – short flash to give way; long flash to get out of my way.

In the UK we hardly ever sound a horn unless it is in anger. In Naples, a short toot simply means take care; normally given when you want to warn of your presence – as a courtesy more than anything (in fact what it should mean in the UK according to the Highway Code, except that no-one uses it that way) and with much less of the aggressive connotations it has in the UK.

So, in two European countries, both predominantly culturally Christian and both of which have had the motor car for about the same length of time, two very different cultures have developed so far as driving, sounding horns and flashing headlights are concerned. These two different sets of ethics have evolved in less than a hundred years and mostly in the last fifty. One uses the horn extensively, assumes the right to cross another car's path and hardly ever flashes headlights because that shows aggression; the other flashes headlights as a courtesy, only normally sounds the horn in aggression and crossing another car's path, unless given permission to, is a big insult which may well get an aggressive retaliation.

It is fair to assume that these have evolved as extensions of the human voice for a horn and a stare for headlights. Clearly, they must have had different nuances pre-motorcar to have acquired different meanings in the context of driving today. Then there is the assumed courtesy of giving way in Naples which is mostly absent in Britain although it is okay when permission has been given – and permission is often given.

Nowhere in this evolution of driving ethics is there anything in the Bible that was not basic to all human cultures already and nowhere has religion contributed to their development. Never to my knowledge has the Pope or the Archbishop of Canterbury ever expressed an opinion on the use of horns or headlights and there is no theological doctrine concerning giving way at a road junction. Yet we have evolved ethics, and two very different sets of ethics, in such a short space of time. We even take driving on the right or the left respectively as absolutely basic, right and proper with the assumption that it is based on some sound reasoning or other.

With very simple, everyday examples such as this we can see clear evidence of the evolution of morality in cultures and no evidence whatsoever of them having been handed down by a deity at some point in the past. Presumably, if you subscribe to that notion, you believe that humans suddenly realised killing, stealing and coveting a neighbour's wife or his oxen were wrong, having been happily doing so for generations. You would also expect historical evidence of this sudden change, yet no such evidence exists.

In fact a mere glance at the statistics shows us that, far from religious societies being paragons of morality and atheistic societies being lawless and violent, almost exactly the opposite is found. Counties like Sweden, Denmark, The United Kingdom and The Czech Republic where atheism is the largest demographic, have lower rates of crime than in the more religious parts of the world. A notable example is the USA where some eighty plus percent of the population profess to be religious yet the crime rate and prison population is the highest in the developed world.

In August 2015, Herman Mehta released figures provide by the US Federal Bureau of Prisons in response to a Freedom of Information request.[71] These showed that self-identified atheists formed just one tenth of one percent of the prison population in the USA as a whole, with fifty-five out of one hundred and thirty-five prisons reporting no atheists at all. This compares with a Pew

---

[71] (Mehta, 2015)

Research survey which reported that atheists now make up just over three percent of the population. On these figures, a believer is over thirty times more likely than an atheist to be convicted of an imprisonable offence in the USA.

Although this probably does not account for all the reason religiosity and criminality seem to be correlated, and studies have not always shown a consistent correlation, there is probably a psychological process known as 'moral self-licensing' which may account for some of it[72]. Moral self-licensing is where the individual feels entitled, because of their piety, to a little relaxation or suspension of the rules now and then, rather like a well-earned holiday from work. The concept of moral self-licensing was expressed in a 2013 paper by Brañas-Garza, et al., with:

> *Research on moral cleansing and moral self-licensing has introduced dynamic considerations in the theory of moral behavior. Past bad actions trigger negative feelings that make people more likely to engage in future moral behavior to offset them. Symmetrically, past good deeds favor a positive self-perception that creates licensing effects, leading people to engage in behavior that is less likely to be moral. In short, a deviation from a "normal state of being" is balanced with a subsequent action that compensates the prior behavior.* [73]

Here we can see believing that morals come from a deity leads some people to assume that this deity will grant special dispensation to favoured followers (just like an alpha male boss of a pre-human tribe of apes might have done) and that doing good serves to build up credit that can be drawn upon later. The alternative explanation is that piety is merely being used as a cover to lure people into false trust in the hope that they would not consider the individual capable of that sort of behaviour. How much of this lies behind the excessive piety of the typical televangelist multi-millionaire or Jesus-loving pastor of a mega-church?

Freedom from the god delusion frees us to make our own morals, free from the tensions and worries of transgressing the arbitrary rules of a judgmental and potentially dangerous, imaginary observing deity. It also forces us to take personal responsibility for our own actions. We have to take personal

---

[72] (Blanken, Van de Ven, & Zeelenberg, 2015)
[73] (Brañas-Garza, Bucheli, Espinosa, & García-Muñoz, 2013)

responsibility for our relationships with others, for our place in a civilised society and our role in keeping it that way. It means we do not have the pusillanimous option having our transgression-counter zeroed by having a few words with an imaginary friend or by attending Church or Mosque and saying the right magic spells. We need to make amends to the actual victims of our transgressions.

When people do not have a god or a holy book to blame, they only have themselves. The realisation of this does not make people less moral; as the evidence shows it makes them more moral. This view was vindicated recently in the results of a November 2014 Survation opinion poll conducted for Huffington Post[74] which showed that in the UK, where atheism has been growing steadily and is now the largest single demographic by far (sixty-one percent in this survey), only six percent of people think atheists are less moral than religious people. Only twenty percent of 'very religious' Christians thought Christians were more moral than atheists.

The same poll also found that over half (fifty-two percent) of those interviewed saw religion as harmful in society while only twenty-four percent saw it as a force for good. Where atheism is becoming the norm, experience is showing people that you do not need God to be good. In very many cases, not having a deity or a holy book to blame makes people better human beings.

Just as religion should never have had ownership of the institution of the interpersonal relationships that we call marriage, so it should never have been allowed to take ownership of morals and ethics. It should not have been able to offer the easy option of confession to a priest or deity in place of recompense to those we have wronged. The growing evidence is that freedom from the god delusion produces kinder, more caring and considerate people and produces a more peaceful, more inclusive and more human society.

---

[74] (Owen, Katy)

8. Freedom of Intellectual Honesty.

Freedom from the delusion of faith creates the opportunity to be as rigorously intellectually honest as you can to be, but what exactly is intellectual honesty?

Wikipedia defines intellectual honesty as:

Intellectual honesty is an applied method of problem solving, characterized by an unbiased, honest attitude, which can be demonstrated in a number of different ways:

- *One's personal beliefs do not interfere with the pursuit of truth;*
- *Relevant facts and information are not purposefully omitted even when such things may contradict one's hypothesis;*
- *Facts are presented in an unbiased manner, and not twisted to give misleading impressions or to support one view over another;*
- *References, or earlier work, are acknowledged where possible, and plagiarism is avoided.*

Harvard ethicist Louis M. Guenin describes the "kernel" of intellectual honesty to be "a virtuous disposition to eschew deception when given an incentive for deception."[75]

Intentionally committed fallacies in debates and reasoning are called ***intellectual dishonesty.***

Immediately, we can see that personal beliefs can prevent a person being Intellectually honest, unless those personal beliefs are consciously put to one side.

In June 2015 a question was posted in Research Gate, an online networking site for research scientists, asking what intellectual honesty is, exactly. The replies included:

---

[75] (Front Matter, 2005).

What most attracts me to Science and scientific studies is exactly the quest for Truth and Honesty. And the love for simple, accurate facts, acknowledged through honest research.

It is my belief that Science and Honesty work together and complement as an integrating part of each other.

There is no Science without honesty.

From my own perspective, intellectual honesty means frank admission of the strengths and weaknesses of a theory.

For me intellectual honesty is to disseminate and debate what we know as scientists or intellectuals, criticize what is not working in the right way, and point to what is wrong, weak or not objective, and acknowledging the good or best ideas and works. And among all be able to say "I don't know; it is not in my competency", or "sorry, I was wrong and I should correct it". [76]

The overwhelming impression from these replies is that scientists consider rigorous intellectual honesty to be fundamental not only in its application of the scientific method but in the way scientific findings are presented and debated. Intellectual honesty is not an optional extra but the very stuff of science.

The last reply quoted above includes the willingness to admit to ignorance and the willingness to admit to being wrong. Both of these are prerequisites to acquiring, objectively evaluating and accepting new knowledge, and both depend on the humility to accept one's limitations and inadequacies.

I have no doubt at all that many religious people can be as intellectually honest as an atheist when it comes to science and will never try to insert their own personal beliefs into their findings, however subtly. Indeed, the scientific

---

[76] (Research Gate, 2015)

method, including the peer-review process, should if followed correctly, eliminate superstition and personal beliefs.

My concern is not with scientific research, but in the way that many religious people conduct themselves in everyday life; where they follow less intellectually rigorous but influential professions such as journalism, politics, healthcare and teaching. Here the delusion of faith can not only prevent intellectual honesty but can positively encourage intellectual dishonesty.

Should we include professional and lay preachers, theologians and religious apologists in the above list? Perhaps the question is why we would expect these groups **not** to be intellectually honest. Why do we take it for granted that a priest is not going to admit that he does not actually know if his religious claims are true because he simply does not have the evidential basis for even provisional belief pending more information? Would you expect to find doubt and uncertainty expressed from a pulpit like you would from a scientific presentation from a podium?

How can we expect intellectual honesty in professions which adhere to a delusion that they know the truth with complete certainty and that this truth is eternal and unchanging? How can that approach allow for new information, for revision and re-evaluation of existing opinions and abandoning old beliefs if the new evidence demands it?

The example of the Young Earth Creationist Kurt Wise is often cited approvingly in religious circles and even Richard Dawkins in *The God Delusion* pays tribute to him as an 'honest creationist' but nevertheless criticised his intellectual dishonesty.

According to Kurt Wise's Wikipedia entry:

> *Wise has said he believes, according to a literal reading of the Bible, 'that the earth is young, and the universe is young, I would suggest that it's less than ten thousand years in age.' He believes that science can be used to support and demonstrate these claims. Despite believing that science supports his position, Wise has written that:*
>
>> *Although there are scientific reasons for accepting a young earth, I am a young age creationist because that is my understanding of the*

> *Scripture. As I shared with my professors years ago when I was in college, if all the evidence in the universe turns against creationism, I would be the first to admit it, but I would still be a creationist because that is what the Word of God seems to indicate.*[77]

Later, as a sophomore in high school, he took a newly purchased Bible and a pair of scissors and cut out every verse which could not be interpreted literally if scientific determinations on the age of the earth and evolution were true. He pursued this task with a flashlight under the covers of his bed for several months; at the end, he had removed so much material that "with the cover of the Bible taken off, I attempted to physically lift the Bible from the bed between two fingers. Yet, try as I might, and even with the benefit of intact margins throughout the pages of Scripture, I found it impossible to pick up the Bible without it being rent in two."[78] *Wise decided to reject evolution instead of Biblical literalism, deciding:*

> *...that the rejection of evolution does not necessarily involve the rejection of all of science. In fact, I have come to learn that science owes its very existence and rationale to the claims of Scripture. On the other hand, I have also learned that evolution is not the only claim of modern science which must be rejected if Scripture is assumed to be true.*[79]

Richard Dawkins' response to this included:

> *Kurt Wise doesn't need the challenge; he volunteers that, even if all the evidence in the universe flatly contradicted Scripture, and even if he had reached the point of admitting this to himself, he would still take his stand on Scripture and deny the evidence. This leaves me, as a scientist, speechless... We have it on the authority of a man who may well be creationism's most highly qualified and most intelligent scientist that no evidence, no matter how overwhelming, no matter how all-embracing, no matter how devastatingly convincing, can ever make any difference.*[80]

---

[77] (Wise)
[78] Ibid.
[79] (Wikipedia, 2016)
[80] (Dawkins, Sadly, an Honest Creationist, 2001)

Freedom of Intellectual Honesty

Very clearly if Kurt Wise is typical, a prerequisite of fundamentalist Bible literalist creationism is the abandonment of intellectual honesty. Sadly, creationists such as Kurt Wise never seem to ask themselves why this deliberate dishonesty would be required by a god of truth and personal integrity. Nor do they ask themselves why the Bible should need to be deemed to be superior to the evidence in the entire rest of 'creation'; a creation that they believe their god to be as responsible for as they believe it to be for the Bible.

On what basis do they make that decision and from what evidence does that conclusion flow? Why did they conclude that all the physical evidence is unreliable and could be misleading, yet the Bible cannot be questioned? It must be obvious to anyone that it is far easier for a book to be man-made and so more likely to unreliable than it is for the physical evidence in nature.

The only answer is because they feel themselves able and qualified to declare by fiat what is true and what is not. This is nothing short of arrogant narcissism; the 'sins' of pride and vanity writ large. It is the epitome of intellectual dishonesty; a triumph for personal bias and the antithesis of all that science stands for. Yet they lay claim to the title 'creation scientists' and demand to be taken seriously by the scientific establishment, by educators, by legislators and by ordinary people.

The intellectual dishonesty of faith causes people to try to shoehorn reality into their delusional view of what reality ought to be. It is a small but logically fallacious jump to concluding that, because this is the way things ought to be, this is the way things are. This psychological process is an attempt to overcome the cognitive dissonance between what you would like to think is true and what reality is telling you is actually true. Close your mind to reality and just pretend things are different.

Cognitive Dissonance Theory was developed in 1957 by Leon Festinger[81], who reasoned that we try to maintain consistency in our attitudes and beliefs where any two cognitions conflict. These conflicting cognitions produce a dissonance. The more difficult it becomes to reconcile them, the more uncomfortable this dissonance becomes, so creating a significant motivational force to eliminate it. The fear that this might be leading you to Hellfire is a

---

[81] (Festinger, 1957)

powerful motivator to accept any reconciliation, no matter how tenuous or illogical.

Festinger's theory arose from a study of a religious cult which believed Earth was about to be destroyed by a flood on a given date. Needless to say, this never happened. Cult members then had the conflicting cognitions that the Earth should have been destroyed and the fact that it never happened. Festinger noticed that the fringe members of the cult were much more inclined to accept that they were wrong; however, the core cult members refused to accept it. They concluded that they were right but that God had cancelled the flood due to their devotion and piety.

This is almost an exact parallel with 'The Great Disappointment 'of 1844[82] when William Miller, a fundamentalist Baptist preacher, managed to persuade thousands of people that Jesus would be returning that year. After several revisions, especially when predicted dates in March and April of that year passed, Miller settled on October 22, 1844.

Many Millerites sold all their possessions and, on the predicted day, thousands of them gathered on a hill to wait for the glorious moment. It stood to reason to them that when Jesus returns to Earth he will land on a hill in America, obviously.

You might think that when the inevitable happened – i.e. nothing at all – the Millerites would have accepted that they were wrong. Some did, of course, but many of them concluded, like the flood cult studied by Festinger, that they had really been right all along but God had been so impressed by their piety that he had postponed Jesus' return to give them time to win over more converts. So the modern fundamentalist Christian cult of the Seventh Day Adventists was born. The great day is still eagerly awaited. Meanwhile cult members are busying themselves trying to win more converts in the belief that this will buy them more time to… er… win more converts.

According to Saul McLeod, wring in Simply Psychology:

Dissonance can be reduced in one of three ways:

---

[82] (Wikipedia, 2016)

First, individuals can change one or more of the attitudes, behavior, beliefs etc. so as to make the relationship between the two elements a consonant one. When one of the dissonant elements is a behavior, the individual can change or eliminate the behavior. However, this mode of dissonance reduction frequently presents problems for people, as it is often difficult for people to change well-learned behavioral responses (e.g. giving up smoking).

A second (cognitive) method of reducing dissonance is to acquire new information that outweighs the dissonant beliefs. For example, thinking smoking causes lung cancer will cause dissonance if a person smokes. However, new information such as "research has not proved definitely that smoking causes lung cancer" may reduce the dissonance.

A third way to reduce dissonance is to reduce the importance of the cognitions (i.e. beliefs, attitudes). A person could convince themself that it is better to "live for today" than to "save for tomorrow." In other words, he could tell himself that a short life filled with smoking and sensual pleasures is better than a long life devoid of such joys. In this way, he would be decreasing the importance of the dissonant cognition (smoking is bad for ones health).

Notice that dissonance theory does not state that these modes of dissonance reduction will actually work, only that individuals who are in a state of cognitive dissonance will take steps to reduce the extent of their dissonance. One of the points that dissonance theorists are fond of making is that people will go to all sorts of lengths to reduce dissonance. [83]

Applying this to the situation where, for example, a religious person has two conflicting cognitions:

1. A consistent view that everything was created exactly as we see it today, by a deity a few thousand years ago.
2. Scientific evidence that a fossil of a long-extinct animal such as a plesiosaur is 100 million years old.

---

[83] (McLeod, Cognitive Dissonance, 2014)

Clearly, there will be a dissonance between the scientific evidence and the view this person already holds. Something has to give here:

They could change their attitude by accepting that the evidence of the plesiosaur means their existing view was wrong and needs changing. However, what if this person's membership of a social group requires her to hold to a creationist view? What if this person is seriously afraid of what her particular version of God might think? What if this person is a well-known creationist or has strongly identified with creationism in online debate forums? Clearly, abandoning an old, cherished set of beliefs on the evidence of one fossil is going to be very difficult.

They could try to find new information. For example an article on a creationist website claiming that the dating methods scientists use are all wrong or claiming that many 'fossils' are forgeries and that evolutionary biologists try to mislead people. They might even find an article claiming that plesiosaurs were alive very recently. Would he or she be likely to check the scientific evidence if any behind those claims?

Lastly, they could reduce the importance of the fossil by simply dismissing it as an obvious mistake or even, as is being encouraged by the creation industry today, to simply declare that no evidence could ever outweigh the account of creation given in this or that holy book, therefore the existing view trumps the fossil evidence.

Unless this person is prepared to abandon creationism altogether – and that might mean risking the wrath of God – are they likely to look more deeply at the science when this would increase, not decrease the dissonance? It at least renders that possibility less likely.

Note Saul McLeod's comment above that people will go to all sorts of lengths to reduce dissonance. What they very often will not do, and especially noticeably in the lunatic fringe cults like creationism, is change their view. Yet there is still that very clear scientific evidence that their view **must** be wrong. There is actually no rational, intellectually honest way to hold to Young Earth Creationism and to accept the scientific facts. Never the less, the cognitive dissonance has been dissipated and that is the important thing. The creationist might even feel vindicated and strengthened in their belief because they 'won' the debate.

Freedom of Intellectual Honesty

How can a deluded fundamentalist hope to have a real, as opposed to an imaginary, understanding of the world about them? How can they hope to understand the details of why living things are the way they are, why they are different to one another and how they interact with the other livings things to form a changing, evolving ecosystem of almost infinite variety and interest?

A proper understanding and appreciation of something they believe their god created is denied to them because it has to be made, at almost all costs, to fit in with their evidence-free view of the world. The whole of nature and the whole of science have to be dismissed, distorted or misrepresented to make it fit their requirements so that their received opinion can remain pristine and unadulterated.

If the sound scientific evidence of a 100 million year old fossil can simply be waved aside, if they can be persuaded to look at it at all, what evidence would convince them that Earth is more than a few thousand years old?

The answer of course, is none whatsoever. Their opinion trumps even evidence itself. This takes an astounding level of arrogance and intellectual dishonesty.

Religious delusion then, makes people biased. It makes people lose objectivity both in how they see and interpret the world around them, and in how they present it to others. This causes them to be dishonest both to themselves and to others while somehow believing they are presenting the truth and being true to themselves.

Of course we cannot and should not rule out deliberate dishonesty and intentional deception, but I am not talking here so much about the frauds that deliberately set out to deceive for money or for political power and influence. These charlatans, on which so much of the creation industry depends, deliberately misrepresent science. They will carefully and methodically trawl through scientific sources, looking for partial quotes that seem, lifted out of the context in which they were written, to say something other than what the authors actually said. They are not suffering from delusion so much as greed and psychopathy. They have no more interest in the truth than a dishonest used-car salesman, snake-oil peddler or confidence trickster.

Those I am talking about here are the people who allow the delusion of faith to influence their relationship with other people or to cloud their vision of the world about them; to filter it through a distorting lens of religious bias. This distorted view, and the constant demands for confirmation because so little is ever forthcoming in the reality around them, makes people vulnerable. They become prey to the charlatans and cheats and vulnerable to being manipulated and controlled psychologically and emotionally by people who have learned to exploit them.

The creation industry, especially in the USA, like many of the fundamentalist churches and television 'ministries', is a vast, multi-billion dollar industry in which the leading lights are rich beyond the wildest dreams of those they persuade to send them money. Entire websites are devoted to spreading disinformation and confusion about science and the scientific method, sometimes with the transparently obvious objective of undermining public confidence in science itself. Organisations such as the Jehovah's Witnesses depend for much of their income on the money collected by going from door to door handing out pamphlets and brochures containing blatantly false claims and carefully worded distortions of science designed to mislead, in the apparent belief that this is what God wants.

In the January 2015 edition of *Awake!* the Jehovah's Witness online magazine, in an article entitled, *How Did Life Begin?* the article opened with:

> *How would you complete the following sentence?*
>
> *LIFE IS THE RESULT OF* _____.
>
> *SOME might assume that a scientifically-minded person would pick "evolution" and that a religious person would pick "creation."*
>
> *But not always.*
>
> *Rama Singh, professor of biology at Canada's McMaster University, says: "The opposition to evolution goes beyond religious fundamentalism and includes a great many people from educated sections of the population."*

> *Why is it that even some scientifically-minded people have trouble accepting evolution as the origin of life? To answer that, consider two questions that baffle many researchers:*
>
> *(1) How did life get its start? and*
> *(2) How did living things develop?* [84],

Apart from the obvious confusion of abiogenesis with evolution, something which is persistently done by creationists despite countless corrections, this quite clearly and deliberately gives the impression that the noted biologist, Professor Rama Singh, does not support evolution but instead supports the version of creationism promoted by the Jehovah's Witnesses. It also implies that Professor Singh thinks there are a large number of other scientists who agree with that view.

In fact, the truth is diametrically opposite, as Professor Singh stated in an open letter to the editor of *Awake!* magazine, now taken down but originally published at: http://evol.mcmaster.ca/~brian/evoldir/Other/Awake.letter:

> *I am writing to protest your Awake Magazine article, "The origin of life – five questions worth asking", dated January, 2015", in which you have misquoted me by taking half a sentence out of context from my article on evolution. Contrary to what you imply, I do not support a creationist view, nor do I suggest that even a minority of scientists support such a view. Anyone who reads my article can see that I fully support the theory of evolution (Singh 2011).*
>
> *In my article, I follow the paragraph from which you have misquoted me with material showing why the facts of evolution are hard to comprehend for many people. My article is meant for people who want to understand evolution but who do not have the expertise to do so, not for creationists like you who oppose evolution on religious grounds.*
>
> *Your misquotation amounts to intellectual dishonesty and reflects on your character and dignity as editor as well as a man of God...*

The article has now been amended to remove the misleading quote by Professor Singh and to replace it by a similar one by an 'entomologist' only

---

[84] (Jehovah's Witnesses)

identified as 'Gerard'. No apology to Professor Singh seems to have been published, but his letter is no longer online.

It is hard to believe that this was simply the result of an accidental misreading of Professor Singh's article and that a genuine mistake had been made. That however only leaves one alternative; that this was a deliberate attempt to mislead readers, not only about Professor Singh's opinion but about the scale of the opposition to the theory of evolution in the scientific community. A persistent theme of creationism is that the Theory of Evolution is a theory in crisis which is rapidly losing support in the scientific community in favour of one or other creationist explanation.

It might be easier to dismiss this example as a simple, honest mistake, but the Jehovah's Witnesses have a long and documented history of using deliberate misquotes. The online, pro-science resource, Rational Wiki[85], lists hundreds of such examples, many of them taken from the Jehovah's Witness 1985 publication, *Life — How Did It Get Here? By Evolution or by Creation?*[86] For example, on page 73, trying to show that there are no intermediates between fish and amphibians, they quote the respected British television presenter, David Attenborough, with:

> *David Attenborough disqualifies both the lungfish and the coelacanth "because the bones of their skulls are so different from those of the first fossil amphibians that the one cannot be derived from the other."*

What David Attenborough actually said was:

> *But neither fish can be regarded as the one whose descendants eventually colonised the land permanently. Both are disqualified because the bones of their skulls are so different from those of the first fossil amphibians that the one cannot be derived from the other.*
>
> *However, there is a third fish found in the deposits of that early and critical period. It belongs to the same broad group as the coelacanths and the lungfish. It has leg-like fins with fleshy bases like the coelacanth; it seems very likely that it had air-breathing pouches from its gut like a lungfish. Its skull, however, has the crucial feature which neither the*

---

[85] (RationalWiki, 2015)
[86] (RationalWiki, 2016)

coelacanth nor the lungfish possess--a passage linking its nostrils with the roof of its mouth. All land vertebrates have this feature and it is this which confirms that this fish is indeed very close to the ancestral line.

This creature is called Eusthenopteron. Its fossils have been investigated by cutting them into thin slices, a technique that has revealed a great deal about its anatomy, even down to the details of the structure of its blood vessels. When the fins of fossil specimens are carefully dissected, the lobes at the base are found to be supported by one stout bone close to the body, two bones joined to it and finally a group of small bones and digits--the pattern that is found in the limbs of all land vertebrates.[87]

Far from saying there are no intermediates between amphibians and fish, David Attenborough gave an example of one; exactly the opposite of what the authors of the Jehovah's Witnesses propaganda tract were trying to persuade their readers to believe. If this does not contravene the biblical commandment to not bear false witness then it is difficult to believe anything could in their eyes.

With instance after instance of this sort of quote mining in a single publication, it becomes impossible to excuse them as unintentional mistakes or even just sloppy journalism. This is a deliberate and systematic attempt to mislead those who are ignorant of the real science and too lazy to check, and to exploit the gullibility of those who have been conditioned to believe that Christians are too honest and concerned about what God thinks to deliberately lie.

Why would someone set out to deliberately mislead? Surely, if someone genuinely believed that science was wrong they would tell the truth about it. The only reason to try to mislead others about science is because you know that science is right, but you want other people to think otherwise. This betrays a sinister, hidden agenda which depends on other people believing something you know to be untrue. I would venture to suggest a motive might be found in the dependence of the Jehovah's Witnesses on the income from the donations of those who have so been misled.

This form of deception is facilitated by the delusion of faith. It sets up the deluded both to want to believe their delusion is not a delusion at all but has

---

[87] (Attenborough, 1979)

good scientific support, and also to be disinclined to believe that people who purport to be devout Christians would deliberately lie.

Consequently, creationist dupes shell out billions of dollars to be fed this spurious confirmation for their bias. In return they get to feel that their scientific ignorance is no barrier at all to believing that they know the real truth. They feel they know so much better than all those wacky scientists who go to all that trouble with learning and study but still get things wrong. This must be a seductive lure to people who struggled with learning proper science at school or were too lazy to bother.

And creationist pseudo-scientists laugh all the way to the bank.

The question then is why do religious people lie especially to defend their faith and about their own religiosity? The answer probably lies in what they are getting out of their membership of a particular religion or church affiliation rather than what they really believe. To many people, it seems that their 'faith' is more a cultural identifier or badge rather than a statement of what they really believe, even if they do not admit this to themselves.

There is also the aspiration in countries like the USA where being religious is still associated in people's minds with being a good person, to want to be thought of as good. It could well be then that there is a big difference in what a person actually believes and what they say they believe, biased in favour of claiming to be religious, when in fact the apparent faith delusion is not that strong.

For example, studies have shown that there is a big difference between those Americans who report attending a place of worship at least once a week (always around forty percent) and those actually attending once a week (closer to twenty percent). As Kirk Hadaway, a sociologist at the United Church of Christ, reported in the magazine, *Christian Century*:

> *Americans misreport how often they vote, how much they give to charity, and how frequently they use illegal drugs. People are not entirely accurate in their self-reports about other areas as well. Males exaggerate their number of sexual partners, university workers are not very honest about reporting how many photocopies they make. Actual attendance at*

> *museums, symphonies and operas does not match survey results. We should not expect religious behavior to be immune to such misreporting.*"[88]

This statement was supported by solid evidence collected by Hadaway and others:

> *The underlying issue is that for the past half-century Gallup and other polling enterprises have relied on self-reporting to determine attendance at worship. Unfortunately, "there's a well-known tendency for individuals in self-report surveys to exaggerate what they perceive to be socially desirable behavior," Mark Chaves, now at the University of Arizona, told Richard Chapman of the Chicago Sun-Times in December of 1994. No behavior is more "socially desirable" than church attendance, but pollsters have rarely addressed this shortcoming in their press releases.*

> *In 1993, Chaves, Kirk Hadaway of the United Church of Christ, and Penny Marler of Samford University ignited the debate about "overrepresentation" by reporting the results of a study of church attendance by Protestants in Ashtabula County, Ohio, and in 18 Roman Catholic dioceses around the country. Instead of using telephone polling, the researchers counted heads at services and in parking lots, and checked with pastors. They then estimated that 20 percent rather than 40 percent of Protestants, and 28 percent rather than 50 percent of Catholics, attend church weekly. The study, "What the Polls Don't Show: A Closer Look at U.S. Church Attendance," appeared in the American Sociological Review.*[89]

Taking this vast over-reporting by Christians, far from church attendances remaining more or less steady as a proportion of the population since the 1960s and against a reported backdrop of increasing secularisation, the real picture is probably very different.

These poll findings were confirmed in a study by Sociologist Stanley Presser of the University of Maryland and research assistant Linda Stinson of the U.S. Bureau of Labor Statistics. They studied thousands of time-use diaries completed from the mid-1960s through to the 1990s.

---

[88] (Hadaway & Maler, Did You Really Go To Church This Week? Behind the Poll Data, 1998)
[89] (Hadaway, Marler, & Chaves, What the Polls Don't Show: A Closer Look at U.S. Church Attendance, 1993)

One of the time-use studies used had been conducted by the US Environment Protection Agency to determine what chemicals people had been exposed to. These diaries revealed that only twenty-six had actually attended a place of worship. Using this data Presser and Stinson estimated that actual church attendance in the USA had fallen from forty-two percent in 1965 to twenty-six percent in 1994.

> *Presser suspects that Gallup and NORC respondents felt the need to inflate their church attendance to impress the interviewers. (Social scientists call this phenomenon "social desirability bias.") Since those in the diary study were asked only to account for how they spent their time and not whether they went to church, they likely didn't feel pressure to fudge their reports, he contends.* [90]

It seems fairly clear from these studies then that in the USA, many Christians – as many as half – lie to try to be seen to conform to social norms and expectations. It is difficult to reconcile this readiness to lie with a genuine belief that a god who values truth, honesty and personal integrity, and who specifically forbids bearing false witness, is watching and making note with the intention of calling them to account later.

I suspect that there are two things going on here:

1. People assume religion is a good thing so will exaggerate their faith and exaggerate its importance to them when, in truth, they have never really thought about it very much but have simply adopted the default cultural identifier they were labelled with as children.
2. Maintaining this cultural identifier gives group affiliation and fills their psychological need for the esteem of others.

The former is very easy to demonstrate by simply asking them to explain what evidence convinced them that they had the one true god and the one true faith. There will be none, of course and the reasons given will be vague assertions, insistence that 'it is all around you', and appeals to the validity of faith itself. Almost invariably there will be a demand to prove them wrong, so trying to divest themselves of any burden of proof, and the insistence that your disbelief is a fault with you. The problem will be externalised but rarely internalised.

---

[90] (Marin, 1998)

The latter can be explained by basic motivational psychology as outlined by Maslow with his *Hierarchy of Needs*, which is generally accepted by motivational psychologists as the basic model of motivation in sentient animals like humans.

Briefly, in 1943, Abraham Harold Maslow identified five levels of need which he arranged in a hierarchy with basic physiological needs like the need for food, shelter, etc. being at the bottom, moving up to 'self-actualisation' at the top. Maslow proposed that the bottom needs must be filled before the higher ones become significant motivators. For example, people will be less strongly motivated to be social if they are hungry, and will even risk safety for food.

This basic hierarchy has since been modified and refined to expand the levels to eight with:[91]

1. Biological and Physiological needs – air, food, drink, shelter, warmth, sex, sleep, etc.
2. Safety needs – protection from elements, security, order, law, stability, etc.
3. Love and belongingness needs – friendship, intimacy, affection and love, – from work group, family, friends, romantic relationships.
4. Esteem needs – self-esteem, achievement, mastery, independence, status, dominance, prestige, managerial responsibility, etc.
5. Cognitive needs – knowledge, meaning, etc.
6. Aesthetic needs – appreciation and search for beauty, balance, form, etc.
7. Self-Actualization needs – realizing personal potential, self-fulfilment, seeking personal growth and peak experiences.
8. Transcendence needs – helping others to achieve self-actualization.

The need for love and belongingness is low down on this list and comes even below esteem needs such as self-esteem; and a long way below cognitive needs (the need for knowledge and learning, etc.).

So is it surprising then that a person will lie about their cultural identifier which fits them into a particular social group and probably (or at least they might think so) earns them the love and affection of their friends and family,

---

[91] (McLeod, Maslow's Hierarchy of Needs, 2014)

before they even think about their own need for self-esteem? Is it 'better' to be loved and belong than to have self-respect? Biologically, it would seem that the drive for group affiliation can and does entail the sacrifice of one's own self-worth and self-respect. In other words, intellectual dishonesty is a price worth paying and particularly with people inculcated with a low sense of self-worth anyway.

The church invented 'sin' so it could monopolise the cure whilst the clergy act like people with Munchausen's By Proxy. They make you think you are sick so they can be the heroes who cure you – and you will love them for it and give them power over your life.

Why bother with those cognitive needs when they appear to be satisfactorily filled because 'God did it!' answers any need for knowledge, at least when it comes to scientific explanations.

I should say at this point that Maslow's Hierarchy does not just apply to religious people of course. It applies to all humans, whether they think it does or not. It certainly applies just as much to scientists, rationalists and atheists. Atheists need to work particularly hard to try to eliminate bias from their thinking (which is probably why free-thinkers and rational thinkers tend to be atheists in the first place).

The need for affiliation may well explain the success of the Sunday Assembly[92] movement which has rapidly grown from a single 'church' in London to a world-wide movement in just a few years. Atheists, just like everyone else for the most part, like to be part of a group and to join in communal activities.

Religious people, of course, get their group affiliative needs met in large part by going to church and joining in.

The needs for affiliation then, combined with the cultural assumption that being religious is a good thing, combine to give powerful reasons why people lie about their faith. This provides reason to think that religious delusion is actually not as deep or as widespread as it might appear at first sight. Hence there is actually not a very strong inhibition against lying for Jesus or Allah.

---

[92] (SundayAssembly)

Freedom of Intellectual Honesty

Where then is the danger to the individual and to society in the intellectual dishonesty apparently needed by such a large number of people in order to appear to be religious? Why is there a good reason to lose faith if it increases group cohesion and makes people feel wanted and part of something bigger than themselves?

Is a society a healthy one when it is based on a mass delusion that involves people in so much irrational intellectual dishonesty?

To answer this question we only need look at what societies were like when they were much more religious that most are today and to compare the difference. It is also useful to look at what some fundamentalist groups such as ultra-orthodox Jewish communities, fundamentalist Christian, Mormon and Scientology cults and radical Islamist states are like and ask, to an outsider, what have these to offer? Why do other people's cults look wacky, sinister and more than a little dangerous?

To take a basic example, most people in most of Europe and certainly in the United Kingdom, would not only **not** object to evolution being taught in science lessons in our schools but would insist on it being taught. It would provoke a degree of outrage were it permitted for creationism and its pseudo-scientific version, Intelligent [sic] Design, to be taught as valid scientific theories.

By contrast, in the USA many science teachers are actually afraid to teach evolution because of the reaction it will provoke. School children are primed to disrupt the class with prepared questions, shouting bible verses while demanding their First Amendment right to do so, or by simply shouting and screaming about Satan, etc. Teachers will often be subject to verbal and physical abuse, and may even receive death threats, to the extent that evolution is not taught effectively nor the evidence for it objectively assessed.

Consequently many American children remain largely ignorant of it or believe the theory to be some incomprehensibly infantile parody of it that no sane person would believe anyway. Some even believe it to be some sort of satanic plot by 'Sciencists' or Communists.

Yet understanding evolution is fundamental to any real understanding of biology or appreciation of the world of nature above and beyond the infantile wonder of a child looking at a conjuring trick and thinking it must be magic.

The consequences for this anti-science, anti-evolution religiously inspired culture are, as Francis Collins in *The Language of God* warned:

> *This image of God as a cosmic trickster seems to be the ultimate admission of defeat for the Creationist perspective. Would God as the great deceiver be an entity one would want to worship? Is this consistent with everything else we know about God from the Bible, from the Moral Law, and from every other source— namely, that He is loving, logical, and consistent?*
>
> **Thus, by any reasonable standard, Young Earth Creationism has reached a point of intellectual bankruptcy, both in its science and in its theology.** *Its persistence is thus one of the great puzzles and great tragedies of our time. By attacking the fundamentals of virtually every branch of science, it widens the chasm between the scientific and spiritual worldviews, just at a time where a pathway toward harmony is desperately needed. By sending a message to young people that science is dangerous, and that pursuing science may well mean rejecting religious faith, Young Earth Creationism may be depriving science of some of its most promising future talents.*
>
> *But it is not science that suffers most here. Young Earth Creationism does even more damage to faith, by demanding that belief in God requires assent to fundamentally flawed claims about the natural world. Young people brought up in homes and churches that insist on Creationism sooner or later encounter the overwhelming scientific evidence in favor of an ancient universe and the relatedness of all living things through the process of evolution and natural selection. What a terrible and unnecessary choice they then face! To adhere to the faith of their childhood, they are required to reject a broad and rigorous body of scientific data, effectively committing intellectual suicide. Presented with no other alternative than Creationism, is it any wonder that many of these young people turn away from faith, concluding that they simply cannot believe in a God who would ask them to reject what science has so compellingly taught us about the natural world?* [93] [My emphasis]

Freedom of Intellectual Honesty

Francis Collins, as we saw in Chapter 4, is not averse to using fallacies, intentionally or otherwise, but here he is warning that, by opposing the teaching of evolution and trying to undermine the basis of science itself, creationists are possibly depriving the USA of some of the best scientific talent. This also means, although Collins does not point it out, that creationism is also depriving very many potential young scientists of the pleasure he and countless other scientists get from doing good science; getting, in Richard Feynman's words, the pleasure of finding things out.

The US economy may be strong enough to forego growing and developing its own scientific talent and simply importing it from other countries such as India, Japan, South Korea or Malaysia where children learn to be proper scientists. Second and third world talent can be bought up by US corporations and universities for less than it would cost to educate them in the USA, but is this fair to American children?

Perhaps more importantly, is it moral to parasitise the education systems of relatively poor countries so that fundamentalist Christian Churches and the creationist website owners can amass huge fortunes from the donations they receive? Donations from those who end up feeling obliged to say thank you for not learning science well enough to get a decent job doing it?

"Thank you for fooling me and depriving me of a good job and the pleasure of finding things out Mr Ham and Mr Comfort! Here! Have some of the money I earned flipping burgers so you can use it to mislead even more people!"

It is not just in the personal tragedy of those individuals deprived of the pleasure of a proper understanding of the world around them – and they do not even need to stop believing in an imaginary friend to do that. The real danger of habitual intellectual dishonesty comes from the vulnerability of these individuals to manipulation by people who specialise in it. They sell them spurious reasons to suppose they are leading useful lives and really making a difference, when all they are doing is spreading more delusion, more disinformation and more encouragement to be intellectually dishonest.

Any objective outside observer looking at American politics over the last half century will have noticed something rather strange and sinister happening

---

[93] (Collins, 2007) (p. 176-178).

especially on the right. It is also filtering across into the centre and left, such as it is. In the early 1960s, a great deal of Christian fundamentalism was channelled into fighting injustice and inequality and especially to the cause of integration and emancipation of poor, mostly Black, people.

There were some extremist White Protestant groups who opposed integration and supported segregation and even disenfranchisement but the moral argument was overwhelmingly with the integrationists. The White right Christian supremacists quickly lost what little political influence they had outside the White ghettos of the Bible belt.

Now things look different. The fundamentalist Christian Churches have become closely aligned and almost synonymous with the conservative extreme right in the USA. Now no Republican candidates for office can be anything other than self-declared born-again, fundamentalist Christians, usually Bible-waving Young Earth Creationists. They will have constantly assured the voters that God personally told them to run for office. Even all but a few Democrat candidates will have publicly declared their love for God and undying gratitude to God for having created and specially blessed America.

George Walker Bush, having announced that he was now a born again fundamentalist Christian and no longer the dissolute, over-privileged, alcoholic waster he had been in his draft-dodging, drunk-driving, drug and alcohol befuddled youth, was deemed fit to 'lead the Free world' because Jesus had 'washed away his sins'. He then ordered the invasion of Iraq 'because God told him to'. This same God however seemed powerless to tell him there were no weapons of mass destruction capable of being launches in forty-five minutes – the official excuse for the invasion.

It goes without saying that it is the duty of every Jesus-loving Christian to turn out to vote for Jesus' personally-selected candidates. Maintaining the God delusion and rewarding the intellectual dishonesty of those who just want to fit in somewhere is now essential to American politics. This in a nation that was specifically founded as a secular state because those who founded it knew full well the monstrous conception that would result from pastors jumping into bed with politicians.

A religion supposedly founded by a man who told us to care for the sick, to feed the poor, to give away all our possessions to relieve poverty and hardship, to forgive our enemies and to visit prisoners in prison, is now supporting an extremist political cause which has precisely the opposite aims. If elected, Republican candidates will cut welfare programs, end affordable health care, kill even more enemies in Syria and Iraq and implement economic strategies that depend on a few immensely rich individuals becoming vastly richer.

Of course they will also throw more people into already overcrowded prisons because the 'most Christian' developed country has one of the highest crime rates and the highest *per capita* prison population in the developed world. Most of these people will be poor, black, dispossessed and fundamentally Christian people. In 1963, people like Martin Luther King sought to harness the power of this group to liberate them from the same predominantly White Christians they now support. If elected, they will ensure Black people stay poor, dispossessed and, if possible, disenfranchised.

So much for living the dream!

All of this is possible because people want to go along with the crowd and to fit in. The god delusion provides an excellent cover for the required abandonment of personal responsibility and intellectual honesty. Blaming God, a holy book and the pastors, imams, rabbi's and gurus, often in collective acts so grotesquely inhuman that only the most deprave psychopath would perform them alone.

Never in the history of human conflict has a god ever failed to be on one side or the other, or more usually both. Rarely, if ever, has any organised abuse of power or systematic victimisation of any minority been 'justified' without a reference to what God wants. Every argument for hate, every purge, every pogrom, every witch-burning and massacre will have had a god skulking somewhere in the background and pretending to be moral, such is the power of the clergy to manipulate those who have abandoned personal responsibility and self-reliance.

As Voltaire reputedly said, those who can make you believe absurdities can make you commit atrocities.

With a loss of faith comes a loss of delusion and a loss of the excuse for intellectual dishonesty. It also brings with it the liberating freedom to form your own opinions, to be led by the evidence wherever it may lead, the freedom to dissent from the mob and the empowerment of taking personal responsibility.

With loss of faith you are free to exercise true moral judgements and not to feel you have to conform to the 'morality' of a repugnant act such as genocide or infanticide, as highly-paid fundamentalist evangelical apologists such as Dr. William Lane Craig would have you do. Nor do we need to conform to the group norms and traditions of our particular faith group as a condition for belonging to it. Responding directly to Dr William Lane Craig's morally bankrupt defence of infanticide I addressed in Chapter 2, Dan Barker, in *Life Driven Purpose: How an Atheist Finds Meaning*, has this to say:

> *Those of us who do not saddle ourselves with such perverse purpose— who are no longer toddlers— are free to say to parents and authority figures: "You did wrong." No one can prevent me from exercising my ethical judgment whenever and however I choose. If I think my Dad or the president or the pope screwed up, I will say so. If I think the god character depicted in the bible acted like a monster, I have the freedom and the right to condemn such actions. To do less would be to abdicate moral responsibility. Blasphemy is a moral impulse. Blasphemy is insulting or attributing evil intentions to God, which I just did. It is clear why church leaders would invent such a crime. Blasphemy undermines their authority. The old joke that "blasphemy is a victimless crime" doesn't go far enough. Blasphemy is no crime at all. It arises from healthy human judgment. When the Church made blasphemy illegal they were actually acknowledging our natural human ethical impulses and conclusions. When someone accuses me of blasphemy— and this does happen from time to time— I usually reply: "Wow! Thank you for the compliment!" No authoritarian father can tolerate a bratty child who challenges his commands. Biblical morality says: "Shut up and don't ask questions. God is good, good, good, no matter what you think. God said it, I believe it, and that settles it." No matter what crimes he commands or commits, including gross genocide against human families unknowingly trespassing on his holy property, we are to pretend, against all we consider decent and moral, that "God is love."* [94]

---

[94] (Barker, Life-Driven Purpose: How an Atheist Finds Meaning, 2015)

I would echo Dan Barker's comments here; if a religious person finds they cannot bring themselves to say, 'If my religion says that, then my religion is wrong!', when their religion requires them to do something they would not do otherwise, they are not a moral person. They have given up the thing that should make them human – their ability to empathise and act in ways another person would want them to act, and to adjust their behaviour according to the needs of others.

They may believe they defer to 'God' but even if they do, it is a deference more akin to the way a toddler defers to a strict and frightening father in case it makes him angry or displeased. In all probability however, they have actually given over the power to decide their own actions to authority figures of their faith or to the peer-pressure of the group. They have given up freedom for the servitude of slavery and have betrayed the millions of their ancestors who survived the sieve of natural selection by getting it right and by doing the right thing by their fellow man. No benevolent god would require them to do that. To tell themselves that this is the right way to behave, despite the effect it has on others, is supreme intellectual dishonesty.

But does not the thought that all the beauty and wonder in nature and that our own existence is the creation of a god, make it all seem more wonderful?

This has always struck me as a particularly self-centred view, as though there is some comfort in the thought that everything is here for you and was simply made for you to enjoy. The notion that the entire world and everything in is at Man's disposal is deeply engrained in Western cultures. It is probably reinforced and given the gloss of a divine mandate by the biblical claim that God gave man dominion over the earth and every living thing (Genesis 2:26-28) although pre-biblical and non-biblical cultures seem to have taken it for granted too.

This notion has led to what amounts with hindsight to have been an abuse of the planet and its natural resources to the extent that we may be on the verge of a catastrophic climate changes which could have very serious long-term consequences for the planet. While writing this book, climate scientists announced that the month of February 2016 was almost certainly the warmest on record and may have exceeded the threshold above which climate change may become dangerous.

We are currently seeing a mass extinction of species which has only ever before been seen on Earth following major geological or cosmological events. The only previous example of a life-form having such a massive effect on life on Earth was the effect of oxygen production by cyanobacteria when oxygen was toxic to most living things.

Mankind is exterminating species at a rate unprecedented since the extinction of the dinosaurs, now widely believed to have been caused by radical climate change following a comet strike. Most of this is being done by environmental destruction. We are taking the trees of natural forests for timber without replacing them. We are clearing more and more acres of land to devote to the monocultures of food production on an industrial scale.

We are still pushing millions of tons of non-biodegradable plastics into the oceans. Our industries are burning fossil fuels and pumping carbon dioxide into the atmosphere at a hugely faster rate than plant growth can take it up and turn it back into plant material, and resources of coal, oil and natural gas, are rapidly being depleted.

Quite simply, there are more humans demanding a technological lifestyle (and why would they not?) than the planet can cope with. We are overpopulating and polluting our space-ship Earth, the only life-support system we have in a hostile Universe.

Despite all the dangers to mankind and the rest of life on Earth, and despite the notion that mankind has guardianship of it all, what do religions contribute to a solution? The answer is little or nothing. In many cases they actually add to the problem and oppose moves to solve it.

The Catholic Church actively campaigns against effective contraception on the superstitious grounds that every human baby is made by God and that it is for God alone to decide how many babies a woman should have. Contraception is officially interfering with the will of an omnipotent god!

The only permitted family planning method permitted for married couples is the so-called rhythm method where the couple must try to estimate if the woman is in her fertile period and abstain otherwise. This method is known to be the least effective method of family planning. Even *coitus interruptus* is prohibited and of course, a sex-obsessed God will be watching carefully to make sure not a drop of semen ever fails to be deposited in the vagina of a lawfully married female partner.

Yet you only need consider the fact that to produce a human baby several million sperms are launched at a single egg in a competitive race to get there first. If it was the intention of a magic man in charge of all this to produce one specific, pre-destined individual according to an eternal divine plan, why not simply send one sperm with the right genes to fertilise that particular egg?

Meanwhile, the powerful evangelical Christian lobby in the USA is so convinced that their particular god is going to return to Earth in the near future, so the long-term future does not matter. Anyway, Earth was given to mankind to do with exactly as we wish, so climate change, if it is happening at all, is all part of their particular god's plan.

In the end, this particular god can be relied on to sort it all out for the greater good. A 'greater good' which incredibly often involves killing billions of people while saving a 'righteous' few who can then have it all for themselves. Naturally, these righteous few will all be members of a particular church who worship a particular god in a particular way.

How have we managed our 'God-given stewardship' of life on Earth?

I remember as a child being horrified at the many gamekeepers' 'pantries' I used to find in the woods around the hamlet where I live. The role of a gamekeeper was then, and probably still is in many places, to ensure a supply of 'game' species for the landowner and his guests to kill for 'sport'. To that end he was expected to kill just about everything else that was not game. The attitude then was that, because mankind had dominion, if you could not eat an animal, wear its skin for clothing or otherwise make use of it, it was vermin and should be exterminated like weeds in a vegetable patch.

So, these gamekeepers' 'pantries' were where the gamekeeper displayed his kills for the landowner to see that he was doing his job properly. They were a wonderful source of skulls for my collection which included assorted owls, buzzards, kestrels and other raptors such as peregrine falcons, stoats, weasels, badgers, squirrels (both red and grey). In fact just about anything that could not be eaten.

This slaughter brought several birds of prey to the point of extinction just for the 'sport' of standing in a line across a field with a couple of double-barrelled shot-guns and having beaters flush the pheasants and partridges out of the woods towards you. Your assistant would load the guns as fast as you could fire them and the dead pheasants would be piled high. The pheasants of course had been bred by the gamekeeper in special pens with a bantam hen to incubate the eggs, to ensure a plentiful supply.

At annual intervals in the 1950s and probably before, a special otter hunt was organised along the River Evenlode until otters had been exterminated entirely. On one occasion I asked one of the green-jacketed hunters if they had caught anything. 'Nothing! We haven't caught one for about five years now! Don't think there are any!' and yet they were still looking just in case… Apart from the perverted 'fun' of doing it, the reason otters were exterminated on the Evenlode was because an exclusive gentlemen's fishing club had bought the fishing rights and was trying to turn it into a trout stream. Otters of course were vermin.

Otters are now protected species in the UK and otter hunting is illegal. They have still not returned to the Evenlode. As people throughout much of Europe have lost their faith so they have become more environmentally aware and aware that other species have a right to exist. The irony is that the notion of a divine mandate led to our cavalier attitude; only now do we take seriously our responsibility to minimise our own impact on the planet. We now realise that we do not have a divine mandate but a moral one which has nothing to do with a deity and no magic daddy is going to rescue us from our folly.

The notion that we should only do right and avoid wrong because a watching strict father figure wants us to, gives a false sense of security. If we screw up too badly, the father figure will step in to make it all right again, like any decent real loving father would, – won't he? It does not make us more responsible; it makes us less so.

This change, as we abandon the Medieval and Bronze Age tribal morality of the Abrahamic religions, is what has produced much of the gentler, kinder, more egalitarian and inclusive European culture of today. As Richard Dawkins said in an interview with George Pell in 2012:

> *The absolute morality that a religious person might profess would include what; stoning people for adultery, death for apostasy, punishment for breaking the Sabbath? These are all things which are religiously based absolute moralities. I don't think I want an absolute morality. I think I want a morality that is thought out, reasoned, argued, discussed and based upon, I'd almost say, intelligent design [pun intended]. Can we not design our society, which has the sort of morality, the sort of society that we want to live in – if you actually look at the moralities that are accepted among modern people, among 21st-Ccentury people, we don't believe in slavery anymore. We believe in equality of women. We believe in being gentle. We believe in being kind to animals. These are all things which are entirely recent. They have very little basis in Biblical or Quranic scripture. They are things that have developed over historical time through a consensus of reasoning, of sober discussion, argument, legal theory, political and moral philosophy. These do not come from religion. To the extent that you can find the good bits in religious scriptures, you have to cherry pick. You search your way through the Bible or the Quran and you find the occasional verse that is an acceptable profession of morality and you say, 'Look at that. That's religion,' and you leave out all the horrible bits and you say, 'Oh, we don't believe that anymore. We've grown out of that.' Well, of course we've grown out it. We've grown out of it because of secular moral philosophy and rational discussion.*

To me, to attribute anything and everything to the work of a deity which, being omnipotent and omniscient therefore capable of anything', needed minimal effort, is to negate and minimise nature. It is like dismissing the careful skill and practice of a good conjurer as 'magic' or the skill of a surgeon as a 'miracle'.

It can only be with a huge amount of intellectual dishonesty that people settle for the easy answers of religion or more likely simply go along with the crowd and accept what they have been told, even subscribing to the view that to question the dogma and doctrine is wrong. How can it be intellectually honest to claim to be in awe of 'God's Creation' and yet not want to learn as much about it as possible or be willing to dismiss it lightly as divine magic? How can it be intellectually honest to subscribe to the view that knowledge is the enemy of faith; that somehow learning and seeking answers outside a holy book is akin to blasphemy?

A question the devoutly religious never address, especially those with an anti-science agenda, is, "What if God created science so you could discover the lies Satan wrote in your holy book?" To date I have never seen a coherent answer or anything that comes close to addressing this question. I invite religious readers to answer it now. In all probability, most religious people, as they do when asked how they know Satan (or an evil god) did not write their holy book, will simply put this question out of their mind and refuse to address it. The problem is, if you put your faith in a holy book you have no external basis by which to judge its validity, so your entire basis for faith is what someone else told you.

It takes a profound form of arrogant intellectual dishonesty to put those questions to one side whilst telling others to follow the Bible or Qur'an, or to ignore the evidence when it conflicts with the holy book when you have abdicated all responsibility for your own beliefs. Yet this propensity to put aside difficult questions, and questions that would undermine the foundations of belief, are common place, not just in religions but in other areas where a degree of magical thinking is required.

Many people earn a living from so-called 'paranormal' phenomena such as mind-reading, fortune-telling, spiritualism, etc., and very many people are gullible enough to believe it and even pay for it. It is, of course, no different to faith healing. It is a trick; a fraud.

If a person really had the powers to heal the blind, make a paraplegic walk, or cure cancer with a touch, some magic hand movements and words, why are they not touring the world curing the blind, making the paraplegics walk and curing cancer? Why does it all have to be done in a carefully managed environment, often with dimmed lighting? Surely, if these people are as holy as they pretend and have the powers they claim, they have a moral duty to use their power as widely as possible to do the maximum good, not just to take as much money as they can wring out of the gullible people who pay to see them.

To truly read a mind by telepathy they would require a new force hitherto unknown to science. The discoverer of this new force would deserve a Nobel Prize at least. Yet they never subject themselves to rigorous scientific tests designed to prove their claims which, if proven, would guarantee their place in scientific history. Somehow, when the spotlight of science is shone on these magical 'forces' they seem to magically evaporate or steal away like a thief in the night.

It takes but a moment's rational thought to see through these fraudulent claims, yet the questions are never asked or are waved aside and meanwhile people recommend the frauds to their friends and bask in the pretence of secret knowledge. As with religion, the dishonesty lies with not addressing the 'wrong' questions in case the wrong answers are discovered.

9. Freedom from Fear.

As Sam Harris said:

> *Tell a devout Christian that his wife is cheating on him, or that frozen yogurt can make a man invisible, and he is likely to require as much evidence as anyone else, and to be persuaded only to the extent that you give it. Tell him that the book he keeps by his bed was written by an invisible deity who will punish him with fire for eternity if he fails to accept its every incredible claim about the universe, and he seems to require no evidence whatsoever.*[95]

In very many ways, religion resembles an acute anxiety disorder. It is no coincidence that a synonym for a devout Christian is a God-fearing Christian. Fear of God or Allah is a major theme in Christianity and Islam and almost always the fall-back argument when all else fails. A God-fearing Christian is supposed to be trustworthy and deserving special respect is he or she not?

But what if we substitute the word 'spider' for God? What if we talk about spider-fearing people? How about closed spaces, or open spaces; how about lifts or flying; walking through doorways or using new technology? Would we consider those who feared any of these things rational and worthy of special respect because of their fear, or would we maybe see their condition as a problem which they need help and support to overcome? Would we see it as something which they could, given time and the right treatment, eventually overcome and return to living a normal life?

What I am talking about here is morbid phobia; irrational, life-changing fears. The sort of fear which becomes part of the sufferer's identity and around which they and their family may have to fit their life and take special measures to accommodate.

---

[95] (Peters, 2012)

The United Kingdom NHS website, NHS Choices, has the following definition of a phobia:

> *A phobia is an overwhelming and debilitating fear of an object, place, situation, feeling or animal.*
>
> *Phobias are more pronounced than fears. They develop when a person has an exaggerated or unrealistic sense of danger about a situation or object.*
>
> *If a phobia becomes very severe, a person may organise their life around avoiding the thing that's causing them anxiety. As well as restricting their day-to-day life, it can also cause a lot of distress.*
>
> **Anxiety disorder**
>
> *A phobia is a type of anxiety disorder. You may not experience any symptoms until you come into contact with the source of your phobia.*
>
> *However, in some cases, even thinking about the source of a phobia can make a person feel anxious or panicky. This is known as anticipatory anxiety.* [96]

How much of a religious person's life is conditioned by God-fearing, or theophobia to give it its correct medical name? How much of a religious person's time is spent thinking about their god and how to avoid upsetting it and keeping it friendly? How much time is spent seeking its forgiveness or its approval for fear of the consequences of not doing so? How much time do they spend assuring it of their 'love and obedience' and otherwise trying to placate, reassure and mollify it?

The answer of course is a great deal of it. Their 'faith' often defines them as people. Asked to describe themselves, most fundamentalists will immediately identify with their religion. "I am a Christian/Muslim who..."

Unlike other phobias, where the response is avoidance and even fleeing the scene, with an omnipresent god this is simply not an option. The only recourse is to bargain and try to placate and curry favour with it. Watch the reaction of

---

[96] (NHS Choices, 2016)

a seriously arachnophobic person to the suggestion that they come close and examine a harmless spider to see for themselves that there is nothing to worry about. Try talking to them about how a spider's eyes work, or how their silk is made. I have done this several times. The fear of the object prevents them from appreciating something wonderful and fascinating about it.

Now compare that to the reactions of a seriously devout religious fundamentalist when you ask them to examine a few simple questions about their god. Questions like, "Can it create an object so heavy it cannot lift it?", or "How do you know Satan didn't write the Bible to fool you?" Forced to confront questions of this sort, many religious people can become extremely aggressive, often resorting to verbal abuse and threats. They frequently use avoidance techniques, and even cast protective spells in the form of quotes from their hand-book of 'faith'. They may attempt to mollify their god by telling you they will 'pray for you'; even calling on others to assist in this ritual.

They clearly perceive these harmless philosophical questions as a serious threat much as an arachnophobe perceives a harmless house spider or garden spider not as a thing of interest and intrigue but as an object of terror; and so show symptoms of irrational fear.

Dr Marlene Winell is a human development consultant and a recovering former Christian fundamentalist, who has identified what she terms, 'Religious Trauma Syndrome'[97]. This group of psychological disorders is felt particularly acutely by people leaving (especially) fundamentalist religions. It has several similarities to post-traumatic stress disorder.

The fact that many former fundamentalists suffer these symptoms is indicative of the harm religion does to the believer. Broadly, these fall into the following major headings:

> **Foundation of fear**. All fundamentalist religions use fear as the main method of ensuring compliance and conformity. A horrifying picture is painted, using biblical or qur'anic texts, of a future of everlasting pain and torture with no relief possible. The 'salvation formula' is offered as the only possible way to avoid this terrifying future. This is inculcated

---

[97] (Winell, Religios Trauma Syndrome)

into the immature minds of children who lack the critical thinking skills to evaluate it yet there is never any certainty that 'salvation' will be achieved. The only hope it to try continually to be 'saved'.

Believers see the world as an unsafe, 'fallen' place ruled by Satan until Jesus comes back to save the world. Children are raised to fear and distrust anything outside the closed religious subculture of their parents as 'worldly' and unworthy.

Sufferers report:

> *I feel like much of my life was lived in fear. I am reading all I can to continue to find peace from what I've been taught. I still fear and I am 65.*
>
> *I feel little hope, because I don't know how it is remotely possible for me to ever let go of my fear of hell. If I give up my belief system, I'll go to hell. Even though my whole life has been so unhappy in the church--it has brought me nothing but turmoil and heartbreak and disappointment and unanswered questions and dissatisfaction.*
>
> *During my freshman year in college, I started having nightmares. In my dreams, the rapture would happen and I would be left behind, or worse, sent to hell. Several times I woke up just before I was tossed into the flames, my mouth open, ready to scream. My mind was crying out, 'Please, Jesus! Forgive me! I'm sorry I wasn't good enough! I'm sorry!'*
>
> *After twenty-seven years of trying to live a perfect life, I failed... I was ashamed of myself all day long. My mind battling with itself with no relief... I always believed everything that I was taught but I thought that I was not approved by God. I thought that basically I, too, would die at Armageddon.*

Self as bad. Next to the doctrine of Hell, the self-loathing that comes from being born with original sin is perhaps the most toxic fundamentalist doctrine. It is entirely essential to even the most moderate and liberal of Christian and Islamic sects. Yet you can never measure up. Any pride you might have in your achievements or abilities is itself sinful. Anything good must be attributed to God but anything bad; anything which does not work out perfectly, is due to your personal failing.

In fundamentalist religions, demons and djinn are real and looking for an opportunity to possess you; to take over your mind and put evil thoughts in it – thoughts such as doubt and scepticism. Independent thought is evil and at best the sin of pride; at worst a sign of possession and moral weakness and rejection of God's love.

Sufferers report:

> *When your parents exorcised you and said you had 'unclean' spirits that was very very wrong. To believe a child can have demons just shows how seriously deluded your parents really were. You have spent your whole life being scared...being scared of your dad, of God, of hell, the rapture, the end of the world, death as well as more 'normal' fears such as the dark.*

> *I've spent literally years injuring myself, cutting and burning my arms, taking overdoses and starving myself, to punish myself so that God doesn't have to punish me. It's taken me years to feel deserving of anything good.*

> *I spent most of my life trying to please an angry God and feeling like a complete failure. I didn't pray enough, read enough, love enough, etc.*

> *I have tried to use this brand of Christianity to free myself from the depression and addictions that I have struggled with from childhood, and have done all the things that 'Christianity' demanded I do. I have fasted, prayed, abstained from secular things, tithed, received the spirit, baptized in the spirit, read the Bible, memorized Scripture, etc. etc. None of it has worked or given me any lasting solution... I have become so desperate at times, that I have wanted to take my own life.*

Cycle of abuse. The relationship between the believer and God is similar to that between an abused spouse and an abusive partner. A 'personal relationship' is one of complete dominance and submission. The believer is convinced that he or she should be ever grateful for complete dominance by an authoritarian, potentially violent and ever threatening God as a kind of special 'love' because the believer is barely worthy of it. The believer needs to constantly repent and rededicate to the relationship and the temporary relief from anxiety keeps the cycle of abuse going.

Sufferers report:

> *I prayed endlessly to be delivered from those temptations. I beat my fists into my pillow in agony. I used every ounce of faith I could muster to overcome this problem. 'Lead me not into temptation, but deliver me from evil' just didn't seem to be working with me. Of course, I blamed it on myself and thought there was something wrong with me. I thought I was perverted. I felt evil inside. I hated myself.*

> *I do not want to give up my faith in Christ or God but I have NEVER been able to hold onto my own decisions or to make them on my benefit without IMMENSE PAIN re: God's will which I was supposed to seek out but could not find.*

Don't think, don't feel. Fundamentalist religions specifically warn against trusting one's own judgement but requires uncritical acceptance of far-fetched claims. Questioning dogma is discouraged with threats of Hellfire. Children learn to distrust even their own thoughts and feelings and so lose the ability to make their own moral judgements, making them prey to the whims of the authority figures in their closed community.

Sufferers report:

> *Fundamentalism makes people crazy. It is a mixture of beliefs that do not make sense, causing the brain to keep trying to understand what cannot be logical.*

> *I really don't have much experience of decision making at all. I never made any plans for my adult life since I was brought up to believe that the end of the world would come.*

> *I suppressed a lot of my emotions, I developed cognitive difficulties and my thinking became increasingly unclear. My whole being turned from a rather vibrant, positive person to one that's passive and dull.*

Abuses of power. Unchecked authoritarianism allows sexual, emotional and physical abuses to be widespread. Combined with sexual repression, a God-approved patriarchal power structure, and a culture of secrecy, this leads to abuse of both women and children. Severe homophobia often leads to depression and suicides.

Sufferers report:

> *I had so many pent up emotions and thoughts that were never acknowledged. Instead of protecting me from a horrible man, they forced me to deny my feelings and obey him, no matter what. It's no wonder I developed an eating disorder.*[98]

These symptoms and experiences described by Dr Winell relate essentially to the more cult-like fundamentalist churches, of course, but this is only a matter of degree. The central dogma of original sin; of the believer being unworthy and in need of constant forgiveness and redemption only earned by prayer and adherence to church doctrine, is still a feature of most mainstream Christian and Islamic sects.

There is still the same hierarchical structure and discouragement of doubt and original thought. Enjoyment of sex and sexuality is still seen as inherently evil, except in carefully prescribed conditions and a source of shame and guilt otherwise. There is still the same oppression of having an imaginary, potentially violent and vengeful God with impossibly high standards to measure up to, watching every thought. There is still the terrifying prospect of Hellfire for failing to measure up

Extreme examples of the manifestation of the mind-control that religious leaders can exercise over their followers can be seen in two mass suicides by extremist cults; the Heaven's Gate cult and the People's Temple cult.

---

[98] (Winell, Understanding Religious Trauma Syndrome: Trauma from Religion)

Based on the Christian Bible Book of Revelations, Heaven's Gate was the last in a series of renamed and reinvented cults invented by Marshall Applewhite and Bonnie Nettles. Following a heart attack during which Applewhite claimed to have had a near death experience, he decided that he and his nurse, Bonnie Nettles, were the 'two witnesses' in the following:

> *And I will give power unto my two witnesses, and they shall prophesy a thousand two hundred and threescore days, clothed in sackcloth.* (Revelations 11:3)

The cult taught a mixture of apocalyptic Christianity, science fiction, inspired partly by the TV Series 'Star Trek', and a bastardised version of evolution. Marshall claimed to be directly related to Jesus and so to be a member of an "Evolutionary Kingdom Level Above Human". Apparently, their mission was to warn that earth was about to be cleansed, renewed and refurbished prior to recycling.

In three batches over the three days 24, 25 & 26 March 1997, Marshall and thirty-eight Heaven's Gate cultists committed suicide so they could be taken to the 'Next Level' aboard the spaceship Marshall had told them was behind the Hale-Bop comet. Only one member survived, having left the commune a few days before so he could continue the cult's work.

The People's Temple cult was led by Rev James Warren Jones (Jim Jones) who preached a curious mixture of Christian biblical literalism and perverse Marxism. Taking Marx's and Engle's view from the Communist Manifesto that religion is the opium of the people, Jones decided this meant the way to true socialism was through the enlightenment of drugs.

Having tried several different locations the cult settled down to build their Utopian commune, Jonestown, in Guyana, then still a British colony. As is usual with closed cults, contact with the outside world was limited. Jones controlled the only means of communication and was therefore the commune's sole source of information about the outside world.

As his mental and physical health began to deteriorate he became more and more paranoid that the CIA and others were conspiring to close the commune down. In a series of votes, the members of the commune were presented with just four options: flee to the Soviet Union, commit 'revolutionary suicide', stay and fight or flee into the jungle. The commune apparently voted for 'revolutionary suicide'.

After a rehearsal in which members were told to line up to be given a beaker of red liquid to drink, having been told it was poison and that they would die in forty-five minutes. All members, including children, complied with the instruction.

After this 'successful' test of faith, and following a phoney 'six day siege' of the commune, and as the commune began to break up, Jones ordered the rest to commit 'revolutionary suicide'. Mothers squirted syringes of cyanide into their children's mouths before killing themselves. In all, nine hundred and nine people died, including Jones who shot himself in the head. Until the 9/11 attack, this was the largest ever single loss of American civilian life in a single incident.[99]

These two examples of the dangers of giving up personal responsibility and giving control of your mind to cult leaders and religious dogma are, as I said, extreme examples but what evidence there is suggests that children especially are at risk from certain less extreme Christian cults, at least in America. In her book, *Breaking Their Will: Shedding Light on Religious Child Maltreatment*, Janet Heimlich lists the following examples of research into child abuse in religious groups:[100]

> *A 1984 study reviewing the "health status" of children in religious cults shows that these groups have unusually high incidences of physical abuse, sleep deprivation, and medical neglect.[101] Another 1984 study on cults details appalling abuses, leading researchers to conclude that "there is a primacy of ideology over biology" in that "childcare may be seen as a disposable superfluity."[102]*
>
> *A 1984 survey of Quaker families reveals that Quaker fathers reported more acts of violence toward their children than did fathers nationally, and Quaker sibling violence was significantly higher than sibling violence rates reported nationally.[103]*

---

[99] (Wikipedia, 2016)
[100] (Heimlich, 2011) (p. 27-28).
[101] (Langone & Eisenberg, 1993)
[102] (Markowitz & Halperin, 1984)
[103] (Brutz & Ingoldsby, 1984)

A 1995 study examined surveys sent to mental health professionals asking about patients' allegations of childhood abuse involving ritualistic, ceremonial, supernatural, religious, or mystical practices. In the findings, abuses largely fell into three categories: torturing or killing a child to rid him or her of evil, withholding needed medical care for religious reasons, and abusing a child under the cover of a religious role.[104]

A 1998 study that looked at 172 child deaths occurring in church groups that strongly promote faith healing found that most of the victims would likely have survived had they received timely medical care.[105]

A 1999 study shows that Christian fundamentalist parents hinder their children's efforts to go to college if those children do not subscribe to fundamentalist beliefs.[106]

A 1999 study shows that individuals who are extrinsically religious are at greater risk for being perpetrators of child physical abuse than those who are intrinsically religious.[107]

A 2002 report detailing physical and sexual abuses that took place in a missionary boarding school in Africa— a school overseen by an American religious institution— notes that the long-term psychological effects of those abuses were "of staggering proportions."[108]

A 2003 study shows that adults who experienced "religion-related" abuse (defined in the study as abuse by religious authorities, denial of medical care on religious grounds, and beatings to rid children of evil) in childhood suffered from more serious psychological problems than those who experienced abuse that was not "religion-related."[109]

A 2008 paper published in the Southern Medical Journal concludes that conservative Protestants, particularly those who believe in biblical literalism or inerrancy, spank and/ or physically abuse their children more than other Christian denominations.[110]

---

[104] (Bottoms, Shaver, Goodman, & Qin, 1995)
[105] (Asser & Swan, 1998)
[106] (Skerkat & Darnell, 199)
[107] (Jackson, et al., 1999)
[108] (Stearns, Beardslee, Edmund, Evinger, & Poling, 2002)
[109] (Bottoms, Neilson, Murray, & Filipas, 2004)

> *Most of the approximately twenty states that have laws permitting corporal punishment in schools are located in the southern* United States, an area commonly called the Bible Belt.

So casual, incidental child maltreatment seems to be widespread in religious families, not necessarily as sadistic or exploitative abuse but because the faith of the parents tells them that this is the God-approved way to treat children.

In addition to this, we have the multiple examples of systematic, predatory abuse; especially but not exclusively, homosexual paedophile abuse of boys by mainly but not exclusively, Catholic priests. The cataloguing of these alone would probably occupy a small army of compilers and researchers. This abuse was not limited to male teachers in boarding school but included nuns in for example the Magdalen Laundries in Ireland.[111] There, girls were treated as slave labour, were at the disposal of local Catholic priests and were often subjected to emotional and physical abuse by the nuns in charge of them.

This abuse was tolerated for so long because of the cultish code of silence inside and outside the Catholic Church, coming from deference to the authority of priests and bishops and fear of the threat of damnation for upsetting them. The knowledge that a priest can, without any accountability to anyone, refuse to give absolution to a 'sinner' and might even condemn them from the pulpit was, and still is, a constant threat hanging over the heads of devout Catholics.

But of course, abuse of children, serious though that is, is not the only way in which religions rules through fear. In his 1927 lecture, *Why I am not a Christian,* the mathematician, philosopher and atheist, Bertrand Russell said:

> *You will find that in the Gospels Christ said, "Ye serpents, ye generation of vipers, how can ye escape the damnation of Hell." That was said to people who did not like His preaching. It is not really to my mind quite the best tone, and there are a great many of these things about Hell There is, of course, the familiar text about the sin against the Holy Ghost: "Whosoever speaketh against the Holy Ghost it shall not be forgiven him neither in this World nor in the world to come." That text has caused an unspeakable amount of misery in the world, for all sorts of people have imagined that they have committed the sin against the Holy Ghost, and*

---

[110] (Socolar, Cabinum-Foeler, & Sinal, 2008)
[111] (Wikipedia, 2016)

> *thought that it would not be forgiven them either in this world or in the world to come. I really do not think that a person with a proper degree of kindliness in his nature would have put fears and terrors of that sort into the world.*
>
> *[...]*
>
> *Religion is based primarily and mainly upon fear. It is partly the terror of the unknown and partly the wish to feel that you have a kind of elder brother who will stand by you in all your troubles and disputes. Fear is the basis of the whole thing – fear of the mysterious, fear of defeat, fear of death. Fear is the parent of cruelty, and therefore it is no wonder if cruelty and religion have gone hand in hand. It is because fear is at the basis of those two things.*[112]

Russell then went on to recommend that:

> *We want to stand upon our own feet and look fair and square at the world -- its good facts, its bad facts, its beauties, and its ugliness; see the world as it is and be not afraid of it. Conquer the world by intelligence and not merely by being slavishly subdued by the terror that comes from it. The whole conception of God is a conception derived from the ancient Oriental despotisms. It is a conception quite unworthy of free men. When you hear people in church debasing themselves and saying that they are miserable sinners, and all the rest of it, it seems contemptible and not worthy of self-respecting human beings. We ought to stand up and look the world frankly in the face. We ought to make the best we can of the world, and if it is not so good as we wish, after all it will still be better than what these others have made of it in all these ages. A good world needs knowledge, kindliness, and courage; it does not need a regretful hankering after the past or a fettering of the free intelligence by the words uttered long ago by ignorant men. It needs a fearless outlook and a free intelligence. It needs hope for the future, not looking back all the time toward a past that is dead, which we trust will be far surpassed by the future that our intelligence can create.*

---

[112] (Russell, 1927)

Freedom from Fear

At first sight, actually loving the object of your fear and something from which no escape is possible, may seem strange or maladaptive. Surely, if religion was based on fear, religious people would hate their god, or at least see its demands and behaviour not as a perfect role model, but as an example of behaviour to be avoided. However, the phenomenon of loving your captor is a well-documented psychological process, first identified in 1973 following a bank robbery in Stockholm, Sweden. After being held hostage for five days, the hostages began to identify with their captors and even defended them when the siege was over.

An extreme example of this phenomenon was seen in the case of Patty Hurst, granddaughter of American press tycoon, William Randolph Hurst, who, in 1974 was kidnapped and held for ransom by a small radical student urban revolutionary group calling itself the Symbionese Liberation Army. Eventually, after being subjected to physical abuse and death threats, she joined the group, making propaganda broadcasts for them and even taking part in an armed robbery. After nineteen months as a fugitive she was arrested and convicted of bank robbery. She was eventually pardoned by President Clinton.

'Stockholm Syndrome', as it is now known, might have an origin in human adaptive evolution as hunter-gatherers. Israeli military historian and sociologist, Azar Gat, who studied the few remaining hunter-gatherer societies, observed:

> *Deadly violence is also regularly activated in competition over women... Abduction of women, rape... are widespread direct causes of reproductive conflict ...*[113]

It would follow naturally from this that those women who not only did not resist their captors but actively cooperated with them, would willingly or otherwise produce more living descendant than those who resisted.

Of course, this phenomenon could have originated in a pre-human, tribal society dominated by an alpha male such as I suggested in Chapter 7.

We even get echoes of this behaviour in the Late Bronze Age from the Bible, with the following tale from Hebrew origin myths in which 'the children of Israel' had defeated the 'children of Benjamin' in battle and had driven them

---

[113] (Gat, 2000)

into 'the rock Rimmon', killing all their women in the process. They now wanted to make peace with an offering of a gift of 'wives' but were forbidden from giving them their own women:

> *And the children of Israel repented them for Benjamin their brother, and said, There is one tribe cut off from Israel this day. How shall we do for wives for them that remain, seeing we have sworn by the LORD that we will not give them of our daughters to wives?*
>
> *And they said, What one is there of the tribes of Israel that came not up to Mizpeh to the LORD? And, behold, there came none to the camp from Jabeshgilead to the assembly. For the people were numbered, and, behold, there were none of the inhabitants of Jabeshgilead there.*
>
> *And the congregation sent thither twelve thousand men of the valiantest, and commanded them, saying, Go and smite the inhabitants of Jabeshgilead with the edge of the sword, with the women and the children. And this is the thing that ye shall do, Ye shall utterly destroy every male, and every woman that hath lain by man.*
>
> *And they found among the inhabitants of Jabeshgilead four hundred young virgins, that had known no man by lying with any male: and they brought them unto the camp to Shiloh, which is in the land of Canaan.*
>
> *And the whole congregation sent some to speak to the children of Benjamin that were in the rock Rimmon, and to call peaceably unto them. And Benjamin came again at that time; and they gave them wives which they had saved alive of the women of Jabeshgilead: and yet so they sufficed them not.*
>
> *And the people repented them for Benjamin, because that the LORD had made a breach in the tribes of Israel. Then the elders of the congregation said, How shall we do for wives for them that remain, seeing the women are destroyed out of Benjamin?*
>
> *And they said, There must be an inheritance for them that be escaped of Benjamin, that a tribe be not destroyed out of Israel. Howbeit we may not give them wives of our daughters: for the children of Israel have sworn, saying, Cursed be he that giveth a wife to Benjamin.*

Then they said, Behold, there is a feast of the LORD in Shiloh yearly in a place which is on the north side of Bethel, on the east side of the highway that goeth up from Bethel to Shechem, and on the south of Lebonah. Therefore they commanded the children of Benjamin, saying, Go and lie in wait in the vineyards; And see, and, behold, if the daughters of Shiloh come out to dance in dances, then come ye out of the vineyards, and catch you every man his wife of the daughters of Shiloh, and go to the land of Benjamin.

And it shall be, when their fathers or their brethren come unto us to complain, that we will say unto them, Be favourable unto them for our sakes: because we reserved not to each man his wife in the war: for ye did not give unto them at this time, that ye should be guilty.

And the children of Benjamin did so, and took them wives, according to their number, of them that danced, whom they caught: and they went and returned unto their inheritance, and repaired the cities, and dwelt in them. (Judges 21:6-23)

This story is not told as a morality tale to illustrate the evil of kidnap and rape of women. It is a simple account of how people then might have solved the problem of not having enough women, in a society in which women were mere commodities and assumed not to have any rights in the small matter of who had sex with them and whose children they bore.

There are numerous other examples in the Bible of rape being regarded as an almost normal way to get a wife. For example, in Numbers 31:7-18 we are told how Moses had ordered the complete destruction of all the Midianites but the force he sent against them returned with all the women and children. Moses was angry with this but relented, telling his soldiers that, so long as they killed all the male children and all the women who were not virgins, they could keep the virgins for themselves to do with as they wished.

In Deuteronomy 22:28-29 we are told that if a man is caught in the act of raping a woman who is not already betrothed, he can keep his victim as his wife if he pays her father fifty shekels. Of course, she has no say in the matter being a mere chattel.

269

In the Late Bronze Age Middle East, they solved the problem of not having enough women by kidnapping some from a neighbouring tribe or by raping a virgin. Obviously virgins were best to avoid the risk of rearing another man's child. In the evolutionary model proposed by Azar Gat, this form of society would have resulted in an evolutionary environment with intense selection pressure in favour of those who quickly form a bond with their captors.

It is not just in the Stockholm Syndrome that we can see how a 'loving' relationship can also be an abusive one where the victim of abuse feels responsible. We also see it in the abusive spouse/abused spouse relationship where guilt also plays a major role, as it does with the Abrahamic religions, in the relationship. The parallels between religion and an abusive relationship are quite stark:

The website Help.org, list twenty-three signs of an abusive relationship[114]. A relationship does not need to involve all twenty-three but any of them can indicate an abusive relationship of one degree or another. By simply substituting the words, 'your god' for 'your partner' there are a clear ten which typify a devoutly religious Christian's relationship with their god:

Do you:

- Feel afraid of your god much of the time? (Psalms 19:9 The fear of the LORD is clean, enduring for ever.)
- Avoid certain topics out of fear of angering your god? (Psalms 19:14 Let the words of my mouth, and the meditation of my heart, be acceptable in thy sight, O LORD.)
- Believe that you deserve to be hurt or mistreated? (Ezra 9:13 And after all that is come upon us for our evil deeds, and for our great trespass, seeing that thou our God hast punished us less than our iniquities deserve, and hast given us such deliverance as this.)

Does your god:

- Blame you for its own abusive behaviour? (Leviticus 26:14-46.)

---

[114] (HelpGuide.org, 2016)

- Have a bad and unpredictable temper? (2 Chronicles 30:8 ...and serve the LORD your God, that the fierceness of his wrath may turn away from you.)
- Hurt you or threaten to hurt you or kill you? (Deuteronomy 30:19 I call heaven and earth to record this day against you, that I have set before you life and death, blessing and cursing: therefore choose life, that both thou and thy seed may live.)
- Threaten to take your children away or harm them? (Exodus 20:5 ...for I, the Lord your God, am a jealous God, visiting the iniquity of the fathers on the children, on the third and the fourth generations of those who hate Me.)
- Act excessively jealous and possessive? (Exodus 34:14 For thou shalt worship no other god: for the LORD, whose name is Jealous, is a jealous God.)
- Control where you go or what you do? (Deuteronomy 6:2 That thou mightest fear the LORD thy God, to keep all his statutes and his commandments, which I command thee, thou, and thy son, and thy son's son, all the days of thy life; and that thy days may be prolonged.)
- Constantly check up on you? (Psalms 94:11 The LORD knoweth the thoughts of man.)

The similarity between the relationship between abuser and abuse victim in an abusive relationship, and that between captive and captor in Stockholm Syndrome, is clear. The difference is that while the captor uses physical means to keep the captive in captivity, an abusive partner uses mostly psychological strategies such as guilt or threats. Of course, the latter can also include physical restraint too. Possibly, the same evolutionary pressures could have produced women (especially, but not exclusively) who are vulnerable to an abusive relationship.

We can see then how fear underpins much of religion and how, due to the evolutionary pressures in a hunter gatherer society and societies which regarded women as property rather than full human being in their own right, even those who fear their god and have no escape from it, can persuade themselves that they love it. They can also persuade themselves that, somehow, it loves them because it does not hurt them, even though the threat is ever-present. Of course, by their innate guilt and need for forgiveness, the relationship is all the fault of the victim. All the abuser wants to do is love his victim.

I'll expand on this idea of religion being used for control in the next and final chapter.

In April 2014, the online news magazine, Huffington Post, published the results of a detailed survey of the religious views and attitudes of Britons[115]. An astonishing sixty percent of Brits said they considered that religions do more harm than good. The same survey found that a majority (fifty-five percent) of Brits now think atheists are at least as moral as religious people.

The Huffington Post quoted the sociologist, Professor Linda Woodhead, of Lancaster University as saying:

> [It is] *striking" to see the number of people professing no religion. This confirms something I've found in my own surveys and which leads me to conclude that religion has become a 'toxic brand' in the UK. What we are seeing is not a complete rejection of faith, belief in the divine, or spirituality, though there is some to that, but of institutional religion in the historic forms which are familiar to people.*

Citing sex scandals involving Catholic priests and rabbis, to conflict in the Middle East and Islamist terror attack as the cause of this rejection of religion in Britain, Professor Woodhead said:

> *I'd add religious leaderships' drift away from the liberal values, equality, tolerance, diversity,* [which is] *embraced by many of their own followers and often championed by non-religious and atheist people more forcefully.*

It is clear then that, in Britain at least, religion is being increasingly seen as harmful both in being the cause of divisions and conflict between people, but in the opportunities for cynical abuses of the power and authority it gives to certain people.

Increased familiarity and contact with atheists has shown that you do not need religion to be good people. Indeed, over twelve percent thought atheists were

---

[115] (Elgot, 2014)

more moral than religious people. This is in stark contrast to the USA, incidentally, where atheists often come below Islamic terrorists in surveys of how people view our trustworthiness. In the USA, atheists are still regarded by large sections of the population as Satanic, despite the fact that most of those with such views have probably never consciously met an atheist.

Amazingly, a large majority of Americans seem to think the only reason other people would behave well towards their fellows is because of the promise of a reward or the threat of punishment. I have so far never encountered a self-professed Christian, even one who claims that morality comes from God, who admits he or she lacks the ability to empathise and to understand how his or her behaviour might affect others. Yet they assume that everyone else is what amounts to a psychopath. This is an incredibly pessimistic view of humanity held by people whose religion supposedly tells them love and respect all people.

What I would say to any religious person who genuinely believes it is his or her theophobia which is keeping their psychopathy in check, then please stay theophobic for your own sake and for the sake of the rest of society!

It would be difficult to argue with the current situation in the Middle East and across the world, where fundamentalist Islamic terrorists are committing atrocities, often simply to create terror as a means of control, that religion is not the fundamental cause of conflict. The situation between Muslims and Jews in Palestine is a tale of two people (who before 1947 coexisted peacefully for the best part of 1500 years, incidentally) having been driven apart by religiously-inspired politics. These politics themselves had their origins in the religiously-inspired politics in Europe a generation earlier.

Fear of what God or Allah will do to you later if you do not subscribe fully to everything the clerics tell you, or what is ordered in your holy book, drives people into opposing camps unable to compromise and accommodate because God or Allah demands everyone's complete obedience. A Muslim who believes Allah, through the Qur'an, has ordered the beheading of 'infidels'[116] and apostates and anyone who has 'insulted' Muhammad[117] or Islam[118] (what

---

[116] When your Lord revealed to the angels: I am with you, therefore make firm those who believe. I will cast terror into the hearts of those who disbelieve. Therefore strike off their heads and strike off every fingertip of them (Quran 8:12)
[117] Those who annoy Allah and His Messenger - Allah has cursed them in this World and in the

defines an insult?) cannot afford to **not** carry out that instruction. The alternative is an eternity in Hell.

The fear of what believers think awaits them after death, and of course the other side of that coin – the promise that those who do not suffer eternal torture will get eternal life and happiness – is a powerful tool in the hands of those who wish to manipulate and control populations for their own ambitions. As Voltaire said, those who can persuade you to believe absurdities can persuade you to commit atrocities. Armies of individuals, who on their own might be paragons of virtue, can commit acts of barbaric savagery especially when persuaded that God is on their side and hates the enemy.

The Bible and the Hadiths are full of stories of God or Allah, or more likely God's or Allah's messenger, ordering massacres, genocides and land theft. Of course a loving and merciful God supposedly committed the greatest act of mass genocide – the Noahcian flood. Did the authors of that tale intend us to heed the warning about what God could do if so minded, or was it a story designed to show how much God loves his creation?

For example, this charming little tale from the Old Testament

> *And Moses sent to spy out Jaazer, and they took the villages thereof, and drove out the Amorites that were there. And they turned and went up by the way of Bashan: and og the king of bashan went out against them, he, and all his people, to the battle at edrei. And the Lord said unto Moses, Fear him not: for I have delivered him into thy hand, and all his people, and his land; and thou shalt do to him as thou didst unto Sihon king of the Amorites, which dwelt at Heshbon. So they smote him, and his sons, and all his people, until there was none left him alive: and they possessed his land.* (Numbers 21:32-35).

The lesson from these bloodthirsty and triumphalist Old Testament tales of war, conquest and casual genocide, is what they tell us about the times in which they were written, regardless of whether they are real history, embroidered history or pure inventions. It was assumed that soldiers and their

---

Hereafter, and has prepared for them a humiliating Punishment. (Quran 33:57)

[118] Truly, if the Hypocrites, and those in whose hearts is a disease, and those who stir up sedition in the City, desist not, We shall certainly stir thee up against them: Then will they not be able to stay in it as thy neighbours for any length of time: They shall have a curse on them: whenever they are found, they shall be seized and slain (without mercy). (Quran 33:61)

commanders would go and do this sort of thing when they were told God required it! Nowadays of course, a modern-day Moses and probably his senior generals would be liable to arrest and trial by a War Crimes Tribunal under International Law. The events described in the Christian 'book of objective morals' are considered amongst the most depraved actions of which humans are capable.

And yet, in July 1995, having been told that the Orthodox Christian Church is the one true religion and that God requires it, a Serbian militia, aided by Greek volunteer irregulars, massacred 7000 Muslim Bosniak men and boy from the town of Srebrenica, Bosnia.[119] They also forcibly expelled 20,000 civilians from the town. This was just one of a series of religiously-inspired atrocities, during the series of wars, ethnic cleansings and land-grabs, following the breakup of former Yugoslavia.

This is the conflict to which Christopher Hitchens was alluding when he told of his temporary membership of the Greek Orthodox Church to please his soon-to-be in-laws with:

> *I was a member of the Greek Orthodox Church, I might add, for a reason that explains why very many people profess an outward allegiance. I joined it to please my Greek parents-in-law. The archbishop who received me into his communion on the same day that he officiated at my wedding, thereby trousering two fees instead of the usual one, later became an enthusiastic cheerleader and fund-raiser for his fellow Orthodox Serbian mass murderers Radovan Karadzic and Ratko Mladic, who filled countless mass graves all over Bosnia.* [120]

The Balkans is a patchwork of different ethnic and rival religious groups, often speaking the same language but insisting on writing it in either the Cyrillic script (Orthodox Christian) or Latin script (Catholic Christian). There are also Muslim people of Turkic origins (Albanians) and Slavic Muslim converts (Bosniaks) from the time of the Ottoman Empire.

Despite many centuries of living side by side and for some fifty years in a single state, religion had managed to keep all the different peoples living in

[119] (Smith, 2015)
[120] (Hitchens, God is Not Great: How Religion Poisons Everything, 2011) (p. 26).

mutual mistrust and hostility. Only in a few places such as Sarajevo was there any semblance of peaceful coexistence. As soon as the central authority that had been established by the Communists under Tito at the end of World War II collapsed, the different ethnic groups resorted to their traditional faith-based, murderous hostility and pursued vendettas going back to the thirteenth and fourteenth centuries.

On the day when the final touches were being put to this book, former Bosnian leader, Radovan Karadzic, was convicted of war crimes, including genocide, committed during the 1992-95 Bosnian war by a war-crimes tribunal at The Hague. He was sentenced to 40 years imprisonment. He has announced he will be appealing. A verdict is still awaited on his main general, Ratko Mladic.

This genocide has been described as the worst genocide in Europe since World War II. The plan by Orthodox Christian forces was to eradicate the entire male Muslim population of Sarajevo.

The driving force behind religiously-inspired massacres is invariably fear: fear of what God will do if you do not carry out 'God's will' (as related by the priests and politicians), and fear of what those with the 'wrong god' will do to you because they stupidly believe their false god wants them to do it.

Not only do religious hopes and fears make individuals and populations susceptible to manipulation so that they will commit atrocities, they can also have a deep and lasting, often a lifelong, effect on individuals. I am not thinking here of the clinical mental illness of religious paranoia but of a general background of fear and anxiety which can condition a victim's entire approach to life and relationships.

In January 2013, the Richard Dawkins Foundation for Science and Reason published a selection of personal accounts of how religious fears had affected people. Bear in mind that these are almost invariably from those who have deconverted to atheism. It is likely that very many religious people will be suffering from even worse examples of this religious metal abuse. These accounts included the following:

> [LR] *I was brought up by a conservative Southern Baptist mother and atheist father. As a child I was indoctrinated into a "hellfire and brimstone" religion that taught me anyone that didn't accept Christ as*

276

lord and savior would burn in eternal damnation. Every night for years I laid awake praying that god would convince my dad to become Christian so when I died we would be together in eternity. I remember having nightmares about his damnation. It wasn't until high school I was able to leave the church and denounce all the nonsense I'd been fed as a child. To this day I consider myself a recovering Christian and as a result do not allow my child to be involved in Christian churches or organizations. No child should have to suffer the abuse of organized religion and carry lifelong scars from it

[ABW] *I was told to never bring home toys or books that belonged to my school friends and never to purchase things second-hand (like at yard sales, the Good Will, etc.) because the owner or previous owner could be involved in spiritistic [sic]practices and attached a demon to the object. Once the demon has entrance to the home, it would torment and rape me, my mother, and sister. I was 6 when I was told this.*

[TB] *I was invited to watch a Church production called "Hell's Fire and Heaven's Gates", depicting the deaths of several people. Those who were believers were shown to ascend to heaven where Angels sang, those who were not, were hauled down underneath the stage by a man dressed as the devil with flames shooting up and terrifying music. I accepted Christianity out of pure fear. It was a horrible experience.*

[PR] *I was "born into" the evangelical church in Germany, and for many years was told exactly that, that I would burn in hell for eternity and suffer terrible pain if I were to reject the church's teachings. As if those words were not enough, we (in Sunday school) were shown horrific pictures that depicted human suffering in hell, resulting in many nightmares as I grew up. When I was 14 I was forced to participate in the traditional ritual of being "confirmed," because it was what was expected from me by my family. Two weeks after that, I rode my bike to the courthouse and filed papers that I was officially leaving the church. As a mother, I have encountered one child in particular, who has told my boys that they would go to hell if they don't believe in Jesus, had their character attacked for knowing about religion but not being religious (which would ultimately be their choice). As a result of this taunting or religious bullying, my younger son was afraid to go to sleep and had nightmares. Needless to say, they are not playing with this child anymore.*

[LT] *I went through 10 years of undiagnosed Bipolar Hell. My parents took me to Christian counsellors instead of psychiatrists, who told me that my depression came from sin and that if I truly repented in my heart, I would be healed. I began cutting and branding myself with hot metal in an attempt to prove to God that I was willing to suffer like Jesus suffered. When I attempted suicide at age 22 I was finally properly diagnosed in the psych ward. My church excommunicated me. I now lead a happy, stable life with medication and without God.* [121]

If these personal accounts are typical, there must be huge numbers of people who have not been able or willing to leave their religion and so see their fears as artificial and something told to them to keep them compliant and unquestioning. This fear is invariably instilled in early childhood when, with very good evolutionary reasons, as we saw in Chapter 7, they will believe just about anything their parents or authority figures tell them.

In many, if not all cases, the parents who abuse their children with these horror stories and threats do so because they think it right. They **too** were abused as children, and part of their inculcated fear will be fear of what will happen to their children if they are not made afraid to question and to doubt, and afraid to have sexual desires and normal human emotions. They will also fear for their own future if they do not inculcate their children.

Like a cycle of physical abuse, where abused children are more likely to physically abuse their own children, so religiously abused children are highly likely to religiously abuse their own children with these horror stories. The real malevolence of religion can be seen in the fact that it makes people think mental abuse of children is an act of love. Children carry these fears, often subconsciously, into adult-hood and can still suffer from them even if they realise it was all nonsense and had no more truth than childhood stories about Santa and tooth fairies.

There is not a general consensus amongst psychologists and psychiatrists on the benefits or otherwise of religious faith or 'spirituality' on mental health.

---

[121] (RDFSR, 2013)

Most of the studies have been done on American Christians as the subject group so this may or may not be a representative sample of religions in general and across several different human cultures and environments. Some studies have shown some benefit from being religious in, for example, recovering from depression, possibly due to closer community support. However, it is also recognised that some sects might have a harmful view of mental illness, seeing it as possession or something to be ashamed of.

The UK-based mental health charity, Rethink Mental Illness, lists the following help and harm from 'spirituality' which it distinguishes from 'religion' as including religion but being wider and more general.

Can spirituality be helpful during mental illness?

Spirituality may improve your mental health. Researchers are not totally sure why[122]. There are a few ways that spirituality may help your mental health.

- *If you are part of a spiritual community you may have more support and friendship.*
- *Spirituality may help you feel connected to something bigger than yourself. It may help you to make sense of your experiences.[123]*
- *You may feel strength or hope from your spirituality that helps to get you through times when you are unwell.*
- *You may feel more at peace with yourself and other people around you.*

Can spirituality be harmful during mental illness?

Some religious beliefs may not be helpful if you are unwell. They may lead you to feel guilty or in need forgiveness. This may impact on your mental health.

Some religions may say that people with mental illness are possessed by demons or spirits. Others say that someone has a mental illness because

---

[122] (Dein, Cook, Powell, & Eagger, 2010)
[123] (Mental Health Foundation)

they have done something wrong. These beliefs might stop people from getting professional help. Religious groups may suggest different things to help the person such as exorcisms, herbal remedies or witchcraft. These approaches may be more harmful than helpful.

If you are vulnerable, members of faith communities may try to exploit you. You may be more open to people who want to impose their views on you. You may feel more vulnerable in times of difficulty and emotional distress. Extreme religious groups may look for vulnerable people and draw them into their cult or group. They get people to follow their practices and their set ways of thinking. People that are isolated or lonely may be more vulnerable to this type of situation. [124]

Taking these reported benefits as given, and accepting that this factsheet is dealing with spirituality rather than religion *per se*, there is nothing there that is especially unique to religions. The growing Sunday Assembly movement, for example, shows that atheists too can and do form mutually supportive communities. Wanting to belong to a group is a basic human desire, as we saw in Chapter 8. Religion is merely the excuse for forming a community of like-minded individuals, although many people had no real choice in being members. It is not the reason for it.

The feeling of connectedness can come from a scientific understanding of just how we are connected by shared ancestry with, and mutual interdependency on, other life forms. I know I get a tremendous sense of being part of something much larger when I realise that I am made of the same stuff the Universe is made of, not as something separate from it but as part of the whole.

Who can fail to marvel at how evolution has created a human brain through which, because it is part of the Universe, has made the Universe self-aware? To me, this is a wonderfully spiritual and uplifting thought. Who can fail to be impressed with the thought that for 3.5 billion years, not a single one of your ancestors failed the fitness test?

What these studies show however, is not so much the harm that can come from religious delusion, as how they may or may not help in certain forms of mental

---

[124] (Rethink Mental Illness, 2015)

illness. There is also general agreement that some, especially fundamentalist, religions are actually harmful to those suffering mental illness.

Speaking at the Hay Literary Festival in May 2013, the neurophysiologist, Dr Kathleen Taylor, a research scientist at Oxford University's Department of Physiology, Anatomy and Genetics, in reply to a question about future developments in neuroscience in coming years, said:

> *One man's positive can be another man's negative. One of the surprises may be to see people with certain beliefs as people who can be treated. Someone who has for example become radicalised to a cult ideology – we might stop seeing that as a personal choice that they have chosen as a result of pure free will and may start treating it as some kind of mental disturbance.*
>
> *In many ways it could be a very positive thing because there are no doubt beliefs in our society that do a heck of a lot of damage. I am not just talking about the obvious candidates like radical Islam or some of the more extreme cults. I am talking about things like the belief that it is OK to beat your children. These beliefs are very harmful but are not normally categorised as mental illness.*[125]

This link between extreme faith and mental illness is not something newly discovered. Writing in Mental Health, Religion & Culture in 2002, past president of the Royal College of Psychiatrists, Dr Dinesh Bhugra, warned that psychiatric clinicians and researchers need to be aware that changing religious beliefs, especially to more extreme ones, is an early sign of developing psychosis.[126]

There is however, another class of mental illnesses in which religion plays a major role. This is the mental illness known as paranoia, of which schizophrenia is a part. In these illnesses, the perceived role of gods is a major influence on the behaviour of the sufferer and the course of the illness, and can impact seriously on the management of it. As the German philosopher, Friedrich Nietzsche, observed, "A casual stroll through the lunatic asylum shows that faith does not prove anything".

---

[125] (Taylor, 2013)
[126] (Bhugra, 2002)

The psychiatrist, Professor Andrew Sims, in his essay on religious delusions, relates a, perhaps extreme, example of religious delusion and what it can cause, in the case of William Hadfield.[127] Hadfield shot at; intending to miss, George III on 15 May 1800, in a bizarre form of suicide, believing this would save the world:

> *Hadfield's madness was associated with, or precipitated by, severe brain damage from sabre wounds to the head sustained in Flanders in 1794, when he was one of the Duke of York's bodyguards. He had outbursts of extreme violence, during one of which he had threatened the life of his own child because, he said, he had been commanded by God to do so. He had a delusion that he must die to save the world but, because of his religious beliefs, this must not be from suicide. Therefore, in order to be hanged, he staged an elaborate mock-assassination attempt on the King at Drury Lane Theatre by firing a pistol at close range; an expert marksman, he missed by 12 inches! He was disarmed, arrested and charged with high treason.*
>
> *Thomas, later Lord, Erskine defended him, and Dr Crichton of Bethlehem Hospital gave medical evidence; the enlightened Lord Chief Justice 'stopped the trial and directed the jury to find Hadfield 'Not Guilty: he being under the influence of Insanity at the time the act was committed''. The case of Hadfield changed thinking, and hence the law, on criminal responsibility. Later that same year, the law was changed so that Hadfield, as an insane person, and therefore not guilty of murder, could be detained indefinitely at Bethlehem, and so his religious delusion effectively initiated the practice of forensic psychiatry and subsequent framing of the Mental Health Act.* [128]

Although the immediate cause of Hadfield's delusional state might have been brain trauma, possibly involving the temporal lobes, rather than fear instilled as a child, never the less, the act to which it led was regarded by the court as the act of an insane person. Hadfield believed God was commanding him to devise a way to die without killing himself, 'to save the world'. In less enlightened times and in slightly different circumstances, Hadfield might well have been regarded as a martyr, fit for elevation to the Communion of Saints.

---

[127] (Sims, 2012)
[128] Forshaw D & Rollin H (1990) *The history of forensic psychiatry in England.* In (Buglass & Bowden, 1990) pages 83-85.

Freedom from Fear

The Communion of Saints contains any number of individuals, such as Teresa of Ávila, whose behaviour and intensity of religious conviction betray the symptoms of insanity or extreme mental anguish bordering on, if not crossing over into, psychosis.

Teresa of Ávila, born Teresa Sánchez de Cepeda y Ahumada (28 March 1515 – 4 October 1582) was born in Ávila , Spain, the granddaughter on her father's side of a forced convert from Judaism to Christianity, Juan Sánchez de Toledo. Her father, Alonso Sánchez de Cepeda, bought a knighthood to assimilate himself into Spanish Catholic society. Her mother, Beatriz de Ahumada y Cuevas, was keen that her children were raised as devout Catholics. It is clear that religion, or at least an overt display of Christian piety, was central to Teresa's childhood and upbringing and a dominant part of her self-identity.

At the age of seven she ran away with her brother, intending to become a Christian martyr by fighting the Moors, but was discovered by her uncle just outside the city gates and brought back home. At the age of fourteen her mother died and she turned instead to the Virgin Mary as a surrogate mother figure. At about this time she began taking an inordinate interest in romantic novels which would then have been mostly about gallant knights, and taking an interest in her own appearance. It seems very likely that she was experiencing something of an obsessive sexual awareness and experiencing sexual desires. At any rate, so concerned did her father become that he sent her to an Augustinian nunnery at Ávila.

So Theresa was a devoutly pious girl from a family in which Catholicism played a central role as they tried to show how truly they had been converted; but she was also highly aware of sex and her own (unfulfilled) sexual desires. Not surprisingly, she began to have hallucinations such as this one which she recorded for posterity:

> *I saw in his hand a long spear of gold, and at the point there seemed to be a little fire. He appeared to me to be thrusting it at times into my heart, and to pierce my very entrails; when he drew it out, he seemed to draw them out also, and to leave me all on fire with a great love of God. The pain was so great, that it made me moan; and yet so surpassing was the sweetness of this excessive pain, that I could not wish to be rid of it...*

The sexual metaphor and the description of a powerful female orgasm in that 'vision' can scarcely be missed. These 'visions' continued for much of her life.

Can anyone regard these as the normal fantasies of a normal young woman? They practically shout out as the sad fantasies of a sexually repressed woman who should be enjoying her sexuality, not the visions of a mystic in touch with God. Instead, she was shut away and denied a normal life because her interest in sex was considered sinful and the threat of everlasting torture hung over her and her family.

What normal, healthy mind would come up with the following words, attributed to John Calvin, the founder of Calvinism?

> *We take nothing from the womb but pure filth [meras sordes]. The seething spring of sin is so deep and abundant that vices are always bubbling up form it to bespatter and stain what is otherwise pure.... We should remember that we are not guilty of one offense only but are buried in innumerable impurities.... all human works, if judged according to their own worth, are nothing but filth and defilement.... they are always spattered and befouled with many stains.... it is certain that there is no one who is not covered with infinite filth.* [129]

Or this little gem attributed to Tertullian, the 'father of Latin Christianity' and 'founder of Western theology':

> *Woman is a temple built over a sewer, the gateway to the devil. Woman, you are the devil's doorway. You should always go in mourning and in rags. Do you not know that you are Eve? The judgment of God upon this sex lives on in this age; therefore, necessarily the guilt should live on also. You are the gateway of the devil; you are the one who unseals the curse of that tree, and you are the first one to turn your back on the divine law; you are the one who persuaded him whom the devil was not capable of corrupting; you easily destroyed the image of God, Adam. Because of what you deserve, that is, death, even the Son of God had to die.*

---

[129] (Bouwsma, 1988) p. 36.

It is perhaps worth quoting Christopher Hitchens on the matter of religion and sex here. He says it better than most, and it probably needs a few words of sanity at this point:

> *The relationship between physical health and mental health is now well understood to have a strong connection to the sexual function, or dysfunction. Can it be a coincidence, then, that all religions claim the right to legislate in matters of sex? The principal way in which believers inflict on themselves, on each other, and on nonbelievers, has always been their claim to monopoly in this sphere. Most religions (with the exception of the few cults that actually permit or encourage it) do not have to bother much with enforcing the taboo on incest. Like murder and theft, this is usually found to be abhorrent to humans without any further explanation. But merely to survey the history of sexual dread and proscription, as codified by religion, is to be met with a very disturbing connection between extreme prurience and extreme repression. Almost every sexual impulse has been made the occasion for prohibition, guilt, and shame. Manual sex, oral sex, anal sex, non–missionary position sex: to name it is to discover a fearsome ban upon it. Even in modern and hedonistic America, several states legally define "sodomy" as that which is not directed at face-to-face heterosexual procreation.* [130]

As atheist and Humanist, Stephen Fry, pointed out in an Intelligence² debate in Methodist Central Hall, Westminster, in October 2009, on the motion, 'The Catholic Church is a force for good in the world':

> *It's the strange thing about this* [Catholic] *Church; it is obsessed with sex, absolutely obsessed. Now, they will say we with our permissive society and our rude jokes, we are obsessed. No, we have a healthy attitude, we like it, it's fun, it's jolly, because it's a primary impulse it can be dangerous and dark and difficult, it's a bit like food in that respect only even more exciting. The only people who are obsessed with food are anorexics and the morbidly obese, and that in erotic terms, is the Catholic Church in a nutshell.* [131]

---

[130] (Hitchens, God is Not Great: How Religion Poisons Everything, 2011) (pp. 91-92).
[131] (Intelligence Squared, 2009)

The Catholic Church in particular amongst Christian churches, although there may well be some even more obsessive cults, often resembles less a church about God, salvation and redemption, and more a sex cult in which the aim is to maximise the guilt and minimise the pleasure of sex. The chosen means for this repression is naturally, that time-honoured fall back weapon for those with no real arguments, threats.

Not surprisingly, when priests and nuns were able to exercise power without responsibility over children and vulnerable adults, this repressed sexuality very frequently manifested itself as sexual abuse. Almost all Catholic institutions where children were at the disposal of priests and nuns were rife with predatory paedophiles. Most Catholic seminaries have a history of sexual activity between trainees and trainers to the extent that, when the trainees themselves went on to abuse, the impulse was to cover it up rather than risk having past abuses brought out into the open. The whole Catholic establishment became a criminal conspiracy with a code of silence that would do credit to any Mafia family.

Just about every Catholic Diocese in the Western world now has a large number of abuse allegations against priests, bishops and institutions in its jurisdiction and accusations of complicity, cover-up and obstruction of justice. Several diocese in the USA have filed for bankruptcy, such is the scale of compensation claims. Yet a pope who supposedly dedicated himself to reform, openness and eradication of this culture of abuse and complicity, faces the stiffest opposition from within his own Vatican civil service, his college of cardinals and his convocation of archbishops and bishops.

An obsession with sex and repression of sexuality then is perhaps the worst aspect of the fear of God so far as it affects individuals. Guilt about perfectly natural thoughts and feelings, and especially about acting on them, has probably led to more anxiety and depression and more obsessive attempts to rid oneself of it, than any other field of human activity and all because at the heart of it lies a morbid phobia about what God might do to you one day.

Just in case readers get the impression that it is only the Abrahamic religions which can control through fear, the following example from the Hindu Bhagavad Gita should suffice to correct matters. It relates how when Arjuna was worried about the coming battle between the Pandavas and their cousins the Kauravas, sects of the Indian house and rivals for the vacant throne, he told

Krishna about it. At the time Krishna was in one of his manifestations as Arjuna's charioteer. Krishna reassured him that killing people is just fine because:

> *Great warrior, carry on they fight. If any man thinks he slays, and if another thinks he is slain, neither knows the ways of truth. The Eternal in man cannot kill: the Eternal in man cannot die. He is never born, and he never dies. He is in Eternity: he is for evermore... When a man knows him as never-born, everlasting, never-changing, beyond all destruction, how can that man kill a man, or cause another to kill?...*
>
> *Think thou also of thy duty and do not waver. There is no greater good for a warrior than to fight in a righteous war. There is a war that opens the doors of heaven, Arjuna! Happy the warriors whose fate is to fight such war. But to forgo this fight for righteousness is to forgo thy duty and honour: is to fall into transgression... And to a man who is in honour, dishonour is more than death... Can there be for a warrior a more shameful fate?*
>
> *In death thy glory in heaven, in victory thy glory on earth.* [132]

So, just as with Dr William Lane Craig's spirited defence of Israelites killing people when God wants them to, presumably because God could not do it himself, and anyway, death is not the end so it is not really killing people, Krishna tells Arjuna to put aside his worries; he has a job to do. Of course, as you might expect there is a reward. It will get him into Heaven and, in the Hindu religion, avoid the inconvenience of being born again as a beetle or a slug. Well worth killing a few baddies for.

Perhaps no treatise on the societal harm of religion would be complete without a quotation from Emma Goldman, writing in 1913:

> *Both Nietzsche and Stirner saw in Christianity the leveller of the human race, the breaker of man's will to dare and to do. They saw in every movement built on Christian morality and ethics attempts not at the emancipation from slavery, but for the perpetuation thereof. Hence they opposed these movements with might and main.*

---

[132] Bhagavad Gita 2:18-21, 31-4, 37.

Whether I do or do not entirely agree with these iconoclasts, I believe, with them, that Christianity is most admirably adapted to the training of slaves, to the perpetuation of a slave society; in short, to the very conditions confronting us to-day. Indeed, never could society have degenerated to its present appalling stage, if not for the assistance of Christianity. The rulers of the earth have realized long ago what potent poison inheres in the Christian religion. That is the reason they foster it; that is why they leave nothing undone to instil it into the blood of the people. They know only too well that the subtleness of the Christian teachings is a more powerful protection against rebellion and discontent than the club or the gun.

No doubt I will be told that, though religion is a poison and institutionalized Christianity the greatest enemy of progress and freedom, there is some good in Christianity "itself." What about the teachings of Christ and early Christianity, I may be asked; do they not stand for the spirit of humanity, for right and justice?

It is precisely this oft-repeated contention that induced me to choose this subject, to enable me to demonstrate that the abuses of Christianity, like the abuses of government, are conditioned in the thing itself, and are not to be charged to the representatives of the creed. Christ and his teachings are the embodiment of submission, of inertia, of the denial of life; hence responsible for the things done in their name.

I am not interested in the theological Christ. Brilliant minds like Bauer, Strauss, Renan, Thomas Paine, and others refuted that myth long ago. I am even ready to admit that the theological Christ is not half so dangerous as the ethical and social Christ. In proportion as science takes the place of blind faith, theology loses its hold. But the ethical and poetical Christ-myth has so thoroughly saturated our lives that even some of the most advanced minds find it difficult to emancipate themselves from its yoke. They have rid themselves of the letter, but have retained the spirit; yet it is the spirit which is back of all the crimes and horrors committed by orthodox Christianity. The Fathers of the Church can well afford to preach the gospel of Christ. It contains nothing dangerous to the régime of authority and wealth; it stands for self-denial and self-abnegation, for penance and regret, and is absolutely inert in the face of every indignity, every outrage imposed upon mankind.

Here I must revert to the counterfeiters of ideas and words. So many otherwise earnest haters of slavery and injustice confuse, in a most distressing manner, the teachings of Christ with the great struggles for social and economic emancipation. The two are irrevocably and forever opposed to each other. The one necessitates courage, daring, defiance, and strength. The other preaches the gospel of non-resistance, of slavish acquiescence in the will of others; it is the complete disregard of character and self-reliance, and therefore destructive of liberty and well-being.

Whoever sincerely aims at a radical change in society, whoever strives to free humanity from the scourge of dependence and misery, must turn his back on Christianity, on the old as well as the present form of the same.

Everywhere and always, since its very inception, Christianity has turned the earth into a vale of tears; always it has made of life a weak, diseased thing, always it has instilled fear in man, turning him into a dual being, whose life energies are spent in the struggle between body and soul. In decrying the body as something evil, the flesh as the tempter to everything that is sinful, man has mutilated his being in the vain attempt to keep his soul pure, while his body rotted away from the injuries and tortures inflicted upon it.

The Christian religion and morality extols the glory of the Hereafter, and therefore remains indifferent to the horrors of the earth. Indeed, the idea of self-denial and of all that makes for pain and sorrow is its test of human worth, its passport to the entry into heaven.

The poor are to own heaven, and the rich will go to hell. That may account for the desperate efforts of the rich to make hay while the sun shines, to get as much out of the earth as they can: to wallow in wealth and superfluity, to tighten their iron hold on the blessed slaves, to rob them of their birth-right, to degrade and outrage them every minute of the day. Who can blame the rich if they revenge themselves on the poor, for now is their time, and the merciful Christian God alone knows how ably and completely the rich are doing it.

And the poor? They cling to the promise of the Christian heaven, as the home for old age, the sanatorium for crippled bodies and weak minds. They endure and submit, they suffer and wait, until every bit of self-respect has been knocked out of them, until their bodies become emaciated and withered, and their spirit broken from the wait, the weary endless wait for the Christian heaven. [133]

---

[133] (Goldman, 1913)

10. Freedom to Choose.

The Iranian atheist, who writes under the pseudonym, Kavah Mousavi, has this to say about how atheism and loss of religious superstition freed him, referencing Winston Smith, in George Orwell's *1984*, who thought the only thing that was his own was a few cubic centimetres inside his skull:

> *So this is what good atheism has done for me: atheism has enabled me to wage a war to liberate those "the few cubic centimeters inside my skull". It is ultimately a war destined to be lost – I will never not be the child of my time and my place, and I will never be entirely free in my thought. But it is a worthy war to wage nevertheless, for every battle won is a great victory in itself.*

> *As I strive to think free and live free and to carve out my own path in the unforgiving terrain of life, atheism has enabled me to avoid many obstacles to freedom that although not always but often are inseparable from religion. Freedom from superstition, freedom from meaningless taboos, freedom from celestial and earthly authorities, freedom from bigotries against those who do not belong to the same tribe as mine.*

> *Not all atheists are free from these bounds and not all religious people are bound by them, undoubtedly. But I am sure of myself that absence of religion has helped me greatly, and I am sure there are others have a similar experience.*

> *Because of atheism I can support democracy, oppose theocracy, support the equal rights for women and LGBT+ people without having to hold sacred a book which embodies the opposite of all these values and I do not have to resolve the mental dissonance of such an intellectual contradiction.*

> *Because of atheism I can easily accept science and not be forced to choose between my dogma and the facts on issues such as evolution or circumcision or masturbation or abortion.*

> *Because of atheism I can laugh at Mohammad and all else that is sacred, and save my outrage for the real injustices in the world, instead of getting angry at harmless satire targeting warlords of the past.*
>
> *Because of atheism I can indulge in my harmless desires and to consider the naked human body beautiful, not something to be covered in shame.*
>
> *Because of atheism I can think about the great questions without a God vetoing certain areas and certain concepts. I am not aware of all my unconscious biases and failings of critical thinking, but at least religious ones are not among them.*
>
> *Atheism is freedom. Atheism does not equal critical thinking, or tolerance, or a truly liberated mind. But atheism is an opportunity, an option, a potential blank slate. To me atheism means that on this Saganian speck of dust we inhabit I find my own destination and I walk my own road and all my accomplishments and all my failures are ultimately my own, no idol is my god and no lord is my shepherd*
>
> *And this is something I relish, something that makes all those traumas and abuses worth it.*[134]

I challenge anyone to read the above and not feel that sense of liberation and freedom the writer experienced not just of thought but of action, when he realised what losing faith had made available to him. He felt free to learn, to love, to think, to appreciate people for who they are, not what they are. He felt free from the cognitive dissonance that would have come from trying to fit his learning into a pre-defined and woefully inadequate model of reality in case it offended Allah.

It is not insignificant that for everyday life, and for any activity where material reality has to be taken into account, the only way to make rational decisions is to behave atheistically. The simple task of crossing a road is the same for an atheist as for a theist, even though a theist might want to mutter a few prayers as well. In the end, it is the physical evidence that the road is safe to cross that determines the appropriate action.

---

[134] (Mousavi, 2015)

Atheists and theists leaving a sinking ship must go through exactly the same process of getting into a lifeboat even though the theist might spend a moment in prayer. Only the most insane of theist would decline to get in a lifeboat believing a god would be along to save them shortly. In effect, theists crossing a road or theists getting into a lifeboat are behaving just like atheists. Even Christians have a saying, 'God helps those who help themselves', to explain why people need to behave like atheists in everyday life. That rather begs the question though of why the Christian god would favour people who behave like atheists.

Even the most religious of scientists must behave in science as though the material world is all that there is. No science is made possible or the answer made more reliable by including a god or something supernatural in the hypothesis because these things are untestable, unfalsifiable and hence unusable in real world science. A good scientist must behave *as though* he or she were an atheist when it comes to doing good science. Any religious beliefs must be excluded and discounted as surely as any personal bias. In effect, science is atheistic even if the scientist is not.

Science only started to make any real process when scientists discovered the scientific method which requires them to behave like atheists when they do science. When, like creationists do today, scientists were expected to start from a religious view by for example taking the Bible as their starting point, science never progressed beyond that of the Bronze Age people who wrote the Bible. In effect, science was a pointless attempt to confirm Bronze Age superstitions, including a flat Earth, a geocentric Universe, the Sun and Moon as lamps hanging from a dome and the heart as the seat of emotions and thought.

The following were posted in response to a request in the Facebook debate group, 'Why Atheism?'[135] for people to explain how they felt atheism liberated or empowered them:

> [ML] *Atheism, for me, has liberated me from the Ideas of sin and guilt, as well as self-delusion. The choices I make now are more thoughtful. I see life as not as some temporary journey until transcending to an afterlife, but rather as my only journey. This idea that ALL OF THIS! being*

---

[135] https://www.facebook.com/groups/whyatheism/

something I will only experience once and once only, gives new meaning to the phrase, "Once in a lifetime opportunity." Every day, hour, and minute is a once in a lifetime opportunity for me.

I feel more compassion for all things around me. I understand now that every living thing on this beautiful blue dot is experiencing a once in a lifetime opportunity. But, with that, I also see lost opportunities increasingly piling up. My life is inescapable and finite, and that, is what humbles me to my bones. Without faith in a higher being, I am forced to examine and re-examine my part in the now. The pendulum of my judgments of others, over time, has moved toward a reservation for myself. Good with God, humanism, self-growth, and self-awareness, have become my foundation.

Historically the human race has gone from the invention of polytheism, to now primarily a monotheistic society. This shift from many to one in conjunction with the growth of Atheism gives me hope that one day all god's will only live in our history books and not in our hearts.

[KC] *Being atheist, I am no longer befuddled by interpreting what is good to mean doing what is good by the 'Good Book'. It may have taught me to think for myself but it has passed its best before date. I now judge what is good by what provides the greatest happiness to the most people. Not limited to Hebrews or Christians as the bible seems to favour.*

[DG] *In a word, liberated. It was as though some great weight was lifted off my shoulders. I was a doubter for many years and finally I was no more.*

From the first contributor, there is knowledge of connectedness with all other life. It comes from freeing the mind to consider that we are **not** a special creation, separate from other living things, in a way which is more than just the difference between species. Freedom from fear and freedom from the need to cope with cognitive dissonance because the facts do not fit, allows this contributor to explore biological science and be led by the evidence, where ever it may lead. Real-world evidence no longer has to be shoehorned into a primitive, superstitious model of reality. Reality shines with a much brighter light than does superstition and slavish compliance to dogma.

The second contributor feels that atheism empowers (and requires) him to make his own moral judgements and to consider the effects his actions have on others and on society at large to produce the most happiness. Nowhere in the Bible or in the Qur'an is there any exhortation or instruction or even a polite request to consider your actions so as to maximise the sum total of human happiness.

Where moral actions are mandated, they are frequently simply because God says so. It is not until we get to the New Testament in the Bible that there is any suggestion that we should do good simply because it **is** good, with for example the story of the Good Samaritan where the 'goodness' of the act is immediately obvious to anyone who already knows what goodness is (and so do not need a parable to tell them).

As Sam Harris explained:

> *If you think that it would be impossible to improve upon the Ten Commandments as a statement of morality, you really owe it to yourself to read some other scriptures. Once again, we need look no further than the Jains: Mahavira, the Jain patriarch, surpassed the morality of the Bible with a single sentence: "Do not injure, abuse, oppress, enslave, insult, torment, torture, or kill any creature or living being." Imagine how different our world might be if the Bible contained this as its central precept. Christians have abused, oppressed, enslaved, insulted, tormented, tortured, and killed people in the name of God for centuries, on the basis of a theologically defensible reading of the Bible.* [136]

But why even look in holy 'scriptures' for morality anyway? Morality can be found in the plays of William Shakespeare, the poems of Byron and Robert Frost, the writing of John Steinbeck, Charles Dickens, the Bronte sisters, Mary Ann Evans and Thomas Hardy – and those are just a small selection from the English literary world. I could have chosen a list from French, Spanish,

---

[136] (Peters, 2012)

German and Italian, and no doubt Japanese and Chinese writers. There is more morality in a few pages of Thomas Paine, David Hume, Leo Tolstoy, Lao Tsu or K'ung Fu-tzu than in the entire New Testament.

It is not just the Abrahamic religions which repress and condition individuals into conforming to dogma rather than forming their own opinions either. The following is from a Hindu contributor to the Indian youth website, Youth Ki Awaaz:

> *My family believed in Hinduism at the time of my birth. My mother used to be a lot more religious then. My dad, on the other hand, battled with conflicting ideologies. I grew up watching him chant Hindu prayers on a daily basis to please his god. I also watched him read and expose himself to atheist literature and science. He is now an atheist. My parents never force fed me their beliefs. I was encouraged to ask questions and seek answers.*
>
> *As I asked questions, I found answers, and as I found answers, I had new questions. It was during my teenage that I let myself unlearn the religious teachings that my family and the society had thrust upon me and I let myself choose. Then, the transformation began. I started seeing things more clearly. It was as if my vision was corrected. I dared to leave behind my fears of offending my imaginary friend (read God), and got rid of the religious mental conditioning.*
>
> *I became sensitive to the numerous social injustices that are part and parcel of every religion. Initially, I became aware of the social inequality of the caste system in Hinduism and the various forms of patriarchal subjugation that were disguised as customs and culture, intertwined with religion. I only had to look with an open mind to see that organised religion was merely a tool to control the masses, and delude them into giving up their reasoning capacity to stop them from questioning the supposedly 'sacred' authority. Most of the past and present wars of the world have had religion as their causes. Most of the world's riots have been ethnic cleansing based on religion. Organised religion, though most would argue that it encourages the spirit of community, has only divided human beings, rather than uniting them.*

> *Once the belief in the system of organised religion was shattered, it wasn't long before my belief in the concept of God was lost too. Becoming an atheist has been the most liberating experience I've ever had in my life. It happened slowly and steadily.*[137]

Like the Iranian blogger, Kaveh Mousavi, this contributor found that losing the mental straightjacket of religious dogma and the need to conform in order to belong and please an imaginary god, he was able to see the social injustices inherent in his former religion. He was no longer able to dismiss them as somehow the will of God and something to be accepted as having some mysterious hidden purpose, but real and above all solvable injustices.

An atheist is free to pick and choose and decide for himself or herself if these writers were right or wrong or whether the morality they include is relevant to today or not. A devout, God-fearing Christian or Muslim is basically stuck with what the Late Bronze and Early Iron Age authors of their respective holy books considered right for their times.

Religion is of course, primarily about control. There are two basic ways religions seek to control people: they seek to impose their beliefs through the government in the form of laws reflecting religious beliefs rather than laws maximising freedom of conscience, and they seek special privileges for themselves and their followers

As Austin Kline, writing in the About.com Atheist and Agnostic blog explained:

> *The underlying principle behind this is the belief that all proper or just morality, law, standards of conduct, ethics, and authority ultimately derives from God. When civil authorities fail to execute what one believes to be the wishes or standards of God, then those civil authorities have failed to live up to the standards which justify their existence. At this point the religious believer is justified in ignoring them and taking God's wishes into their own hands. There is no such thing as a justified civil authority independent of God and thus no valid civil laws which can excuse godless, immoral behavior.*[138]

---

[137] (Shanmugasundaram, 2014)
[138] (Kline)

An example of religions seeking to impose their religious views on other people is perhaps most readily found today in the marriage laws. Until recently, all Christian countries defined marriage as the union of one man with one woman for life, to the exclusion of all others. Sexual relationships outside marriage were regarded as the 'sin' of adultery and are still regarded as criminal offences in some Christian countries and many Islamic countries. In Islamic countries, when a man may lawfully have more than one wife, 'adultery' is often a capital offence, especially for the woman.

Despite this, as any sociological study into human sexual behaviour shows, extra-marital sex is commonplace for both genders, and pre-marital sex is the norm in developed nominally Christian countries. For a bride to be a virgin on her wedding night would now be regarded as unusually and maybe even a little bit strange. Both couples would now expect their partner to be sexually experienced. Sociologically, humans are neither monogamous nor especially faithful to a partner. They have been described variously as 'slightly polygamous' and 'ambiguously monogamous'.

Freed from the straightjacket of religious superstitions, people are reverting to a more natural state of human relationships. This evolved over millions of years as we diverged from the other apes, starting their sexual strategies. No doubt Christians and Muslims will publicly condemn Western sexual freedom as immoral or 'wanton' (while quietly craving it and probably privately practicing it when they can) but what they are condemning is something perfectly natural and which they believe their creator created. What they really regret is that they are not controlling peoples' private lives.

In many societies, polygamy is common. Polyandry is also known, though much less so. Very clearly, a life-time commitment to a single sexual partner is not the 'normal' human sexual state and yet religions try to impose an artificial morality on us not because it is natural but because it gives them control over even our personal, private relationships. It is probably not surprising that when Late Bronze Age tribal leaders tried to codify human morals in order to maintain control, on the list was 'Though shalt not commit adultery' and 'Thou shalt not covet thy neighbour's wife'.

If someone can explain to me one good reason why marriage should even be the union of two people to the exclusion of all others, and not an agreed union between three, four or more people who have agreed freely to enter into a legal union of some sort, provided there are full safeguards for the interests of any children, I would be grateful to hear of it. On the face of it, this arrangement might even produce a more stable environment for children than the present 'nuclear family' arrangement, where a breakdown in relationships means children lose half their full-time adult role-models and carers, and one parent is often left to carry the burden of childcare and fill all parental roles.

Here is how some Bible literalist Christian groups see marriage. Although quite lengthy, the following statement of the 'complementary' roles of men and women in a household is worth reading if only to see how religion can shape the human mind and the obsessive degree of control over our private lives religious leaders can try to exercise. It is taken from AllAboutGOD.com, a Christian social networking site.

A very similar statement appeared in the now defunct Vision Forum Ministries, which closed down when it was found that a board member and a married woman were having an illicit relationship while telling everyone else how they should conduct themselves

It is worth bearing in mind as you read it that this view of gender role is not from the third century, but is held by some modern Americans in 2016:

Role of Husband in the Bible

Role of the Husband in the Bible – Leader
The role of the husband in the Bible starts with leadership. Scripture makes it very clear that a husband must be a leader of his home and have healthy control of his life. 1 Timothy 3; in speaking of two church leadership positions traditionally filled by men, teaches that an Overseer and Deacon must manage their family well. Verse 5 specifically says, "If anyone does not know how to manage his own family, how can he take care of God's church?"

Furthering this understanding, Ephesians 5:21-24 says, "Submit to one another out of reverence for Christ. Wives, submit to your husbands as to the Lord. For the husband is the head of the wife as Christ is the head of the church, his body, of which he is the Savior. Now as the church submits to Christ, so also wives should submit to their husbands in everything." Again, in 1 Corinthians 11:3, Scripture says, "But I want you to realize that the head of every man is Christ, and the head of the woman is man, and the head of Christ is God."

One of the primary roles of a husband in the Bible, then, is to lead. Leadership simply means influence. Therefore, a biblically-based husband should influence his family. Husbands are not dictators, they should not demand, they should not rule over their wives. Instead, husbands should influence their wives and families in accordance with biblical teaching. They should exemplify, with their voice and their actions, attributes that bring glory to God and value to their spouse and family. The fruit of a good biblically-based husband is a strong, confident, spiritually mature wife and family.

Two very specific ways a husband influences his home is through his provision and protection.

Role of the Husband in the Bible – Provider and Protector

The role of the husband in the Bible starts with leadership, but encompasses provision and protection. A husband will never influence his wife if he does not care for her. He can demand and she may follow as a result, but he will never truly have her heart unless he provides for her needs, cares for her well-being, and protects her both physically and spiritually. For as Scripture says:

> *"Anyone who does not provide for their relatives, and especially for their own household, has denied the faith and is worse than an unbeliever" (1 Timothy 5:8).*

> *"Husbands, love your wives and do not be harsh with them" (Colossians 3:19).*

> *"Husbands, in the same way be considerate as you live with your wives, and treat them with respect as the weaker partner and as heirs with you of the gracious gift of life, so that nothing will hinder your prayers" (1 Peter 3:7).*

God loves His daughters and the children they bear. When He gives one of His daughters to a man, He desires that the man cares for her. In no place does Scripture teach or endorse that women and children be considered second rate or inferior to men. Instead, He finds them so precious that He asks for special care to be given them; a care that only biblically-based men can provide. Women are very capable of taking care of themselves. However, God did make men and women different and thus due to the physical nature and strength God gave men, He has charged them with the provision and protection of their families.

The physical nature and strength of a man is to be managed with grace and gentleness. God did not create men to lord over women nor did he create women to simply wait on men. He made them both to complement each other through healthy companionship.

Role of the Husband in the Bible – Companion
The role of the husband in the Bible is fulfilled through the heart of companionship. Ephesians 5:25-33 says, "Husbands, love your wives, just as Christ loved the church and gave himself up for her to make her holy, cleansing her by the washing with water through the word, and to present her to himself as a radiant church, without stain or wrinkle or any other blemish, but holy and blameless. In this same way, husbands ought to love their wives as their own bodies. He who loves his wife loves himself. After all, no one ever hated his own body, but he feeds and cares for it, just as Christ does the church—for we are members of his body. 'For this reason a man will leave his father and mother and be united to his wife, and the two will become one flesh.' This is a profound mystery—but I am talking about Christ and the church. However, each one of you also must love his wife as he loves himself, and the wife must respect her husband."

The relationship between a husband and a wife is meant to be one of love, respect, and support. They are to help each other. This idea is introduced at the beginning of the Bible in the story of the creation of Eve. Adam needed a companion, a suitable helper, yet one could not be found until God created Eve. Genesis 2:20-24 says, "...But for Adam no suitable helper was found. So the LORD God caused the man to fall into a deep sleep; and while he was sleeping, he took one of the man's ribs and then closed up the place with flesh. Then the LORD God made a woman from the rib he had taken out of the man, and he brought her to the man. The man said, 'This is now bone of my bones and flesh of my flesh; she shall be called "woman," for she was taken out of man.' That is why a man leaves his father and mother and is united to his wife, and they become one flesh."

This also leads to another understanding of companionship. God created men and women with natural, physical, and emotional differences. Usually where one is weak, the other is strong. Therefore, a husband and wife can help each other by meeting the other person's needs through physical and emotional intimacy. 1 Corinthians 7:2-5 addresses this, "But since sexual immorality is occurring, each man should have sexual relations with his own wife, and each woman with her own husband. The husband should fulfil his marital duty to his wife, and likewise the wife to her husband. The wife does not have authority over her own body but yields it to her husband. In the same way, the husband does not have authority over his own body but yields it to his wife. Do not deprive each other except perhaps by mutual consent and for a time, so that you may devote yourselves to prayer. Then come together again so that Satan will not tempt you because of your lack of self-control." When the needs of our spouse are properly met through healthy companionship, the two can help each other and can live a successful life together.

Lastly, through their companionship a husband and wife work together as a team to develop and grow a family. God's plan was that every home operate under the specific roles of both a husband and a wife and that through this they raise healthy children who honor God with their lives. Ephesians 6:1-3 says, "Children, obey your parents in the Lord, for this is right. 'Honor your father and mother' —which is the first commandment with a promise— 'so that it may go well with you and that you may enjoy long life on the earth.'" Children are blessed through the honor of their mother and father working in unison to train them up in the way they should go.

The companionship between a man and a woman is directed by the influence of the husband through his provision and protection and is covered by his caring, gentle, and graceful love for his wife and family. Without the biblical roles of a husband being fulfilled by a strong man of God, the family unit risks the difficulties brought on by sin and spiritual distortion. Satan desires the destruction of the family, but through Christ

> *and proper understanding of biblical roles, the family is a strong and safe place to grow in God.* [139]

Note the entire 'justification' for men declaring the role of women, and for abrogating to themselves the right to do so with no reference to women's opinions. It is wholly and solely that they can find excuses for it in a book of highly dubious provenance, which some people assert is the inspired word of an invisible magic man for which there is not an iota of definitive evidence.

The stories in the Bible were written by people with a Late Bronze Age Middle Eastern tribal misogyny who saw women as goods, not people. The cultural norms, prejudices and assumptions in that society are expected to be appropriate for today and half the world's population are expected to meekly comply, because some men say so – and they have a book they can blame.

Religion puts women under the control of, and at the disposal of, men and there is a good biblical foundation for this, so we are told. It almost goes without saying that these rules were written by the same people who assumed that rape was a perfectly legitimate way to get wives, even as gifts for others, and that women were men's possessions, to be bought and sold at will.

This is perhaps put more succinctly and brutally by that doyen of early Christian philosophy and moral righteousness, the founder of Western theology, Saint Augustine of Hippo, who said:

> *Any woman who acts in such a way that she cannot give birth to as many children as she is capable of, makes herself guilty of that many murders.*

But of course it is not just women who have been controlled and forced into allotted roles by religion or using the excuse religion provides. I mentioned in Chapter 7 how the teaching of the Anglican Church in Britain was used to maintain the English class system with its rigid social stratification – something that still pervades the United Kingdom's culture to the extent that we hardly notice it ourselves but which quickly becomes apparent to visitors.

The second way religions seek to control other people is by a demand to be accorded special privileges. These invariably allow the religious leaders or members of their particular faith to restrict the actions of others or to

---

[139] (All About God)

discriminate others and deny them freedom of action or choice. This has manifested itself in the United Kingdom, for example, with several cases where rights guaranteed to others under the Human Rights Act have meant Christians providing goods and services or those involved in the public services have had to provide services to those with whom they disagree. Homosexual couples staying in a guest house run by Christians; a Christian registrar having to perform a marriage ceremony for same sex marriage, etc.

In all of these cases, it has provoked shrieks of outrage from other Christians, including some very senior figures in the Church, about not being allowed to discriminate being a violation of a Christian's human rights. The argument is invariably that, being Christian, their right to deny human rights to others is a privilege to which they are entitled. The Human Rights Act guarantees rights to people regardless of their gender or sexual orientation but Christians believe they should have the right to restrict it and to deny it altogether to those of whose lifestyle they disapprove, based on what their favourite holy book says.

Consequently, in a nation state in which the Head of State is also head of the established church; where certain Anglican bishops are granted automatic membership of the senior house in our bicameral parliament and where the Church of England is heavily involved in the education of our children, Christians feel persecuted by this denial of special privileges. So, they wish to see the Human Rights Act abolished altogether.

They would rather people did not have any human rights if they cannot have special ones for themselves! It is probably no coincidence that, when Christianity reigned supreme throughout Europe, there was no Human Rights Act and little concept even of human rights.

As a young left-wing political activist in the 1960s and 1970s, one of the things we tried to do constantly was to raise the 'class-consciousness' of working people. We tried to persuade people that they could see political issues as class issues which were preventing working people from developing their potential to the full. How much more quickly would the four minute mile have been broken if all working class children had owned running shoes and had access to the training facilities Roger Banister had as a student at the elite Oxford University?

Freedom to Choose

How many potential Einsteins, Mozarts, Monets or Darwins were struggling to make ends meet to feed a family by working on an assembly line at Cowley or Longbridge and going home exhausted with little to look forward to but a few drinks down the pub and a football match on Saturday?

It was not that working people were leading useless or unproductive lives or that their chosen recreations and lifestyles were anything to decry, but that they lacked real choices and the opportunity to get out of that cycle of drudge, tolerated only because they never believed they were entitled to anything more.

I knew people who could play chess games in their heads, who could quote Shakespeare at length, who could tell you every football result from the entire Football League fixture list for the previous Saturday or calculate instantly where they needed to aim their next dart as their previous one hit the dartboard. Yet they had never been abroad for a holiday, tasted wine or been to an art gallery or the theatre because 'that's not for the likes of us!'

The greatest difficulty political activists faced was in trying to persuade people that they did not have an allotted position in life and that ambition and aspiration was not 'getting above themselves' – an expression we heard all too often, intended as an insult. The same problem was faced by Civil Rights activists in the USA in the 1950s and 1960s where raising the consciousness and aspirations of Black and disenfranchised peoples was perhaps the major task. Again, a decade later, the feminist movement had the task of raising the consciousness of women; later still the issue was raising the consciousness of homosexuals and transgender people to believe that they too were entitled to equal opportunities and freedom from discrimination.

I particularly loved my mother because she stood up for me against my father who, despite being a dedicated Trades Unionist and Socialist all his life, never-the-less had limited ambitions and limited ambitions for my siblings and me. He wanted me to leave school at fifteen years old to 'get a job and earn some money' like a good working class child should, but my mother insisted I remain at school for another (voluntary) year to take what were called 'O' Levels (General Certificate in Education, Ordinary Level). These few 'O' Levels were enough to open the door for me to higher education in Biology.

It was not easy and it was certainly not automatic, and I still suffered all my working life from what is known as 'Imposter Syndrome' in that I sometimes felt I had no right to be in certain management roles or to give instructions to the staff I managed. At the age of twenty-three I was faced with the possibility of committing to a two-year science PhD (or DPhil as it is known in Oxford). It is one of the great regrets of my life that I took the cowardly decision because I found the idea of moving into that social circle too daunting.

The English class system I had been inculcated with and which had been impressed on us as young children growing up in rural Oxfordshire, had conditioned me to think some things were out of my reach and 'that is not for the likes of us'.

Now the issue for atheism and Humanism is to raise the consciousness of everyone to see that they can be free from generations of faith-based control which has limited their choices in life and their freedom to think for themselves. Like the gays of the 80s and 90s, the feminists of the 70s and 80s, the Blacks of the 50s and 60s, atheists should be free to proudly declare their atheism and watch as their fellow atheists come pouring out of the closet. Tens of millions more will realise that they have been atheist all along, if only they had had the courage and permission to think about it.

Dan Barker's mother, who had never really realised atheism was an option until her son announced he was an atheist, and who having realised she was actually allowed to think about whether religions were true or not, decided they were a lot of baloney. Being openly atheist gives other people permission to be atheist too.

To me, the issue is what it always had been – that of people liberation. Freeing people from the mental shackles they have become comfortable with and which they may even believe they should be wearing. To be truly free the slave must feel he or she is entitled to freedom and be willing and able to take back control for their own lives. It does not bother me in the least what people believe, so long as they do not try to make me conform to their beliefs; what bothers me is that people are truly free to choose for themselves.

I hope this tour through the common fallacies and false logic that passes for religious apologetics that themselves are a poor substitute for evidence, has contributed to this debate.

Freedom to Choose

I hope too that the benefits I have outlined from a loss of faith in terms of individual liberties, personal responsibility and a less divided, more inclusive and Humanist society will help convince people that faith is not a virtue but a sin.

Faith is not harmless. Faith is a harmful delusion. It is harmful to the individual, to the community and to humanity. It is a clear and present danger and should be opposed by all those who want to build a better future not just for themselves but for our children and our children's children.

Before all that we have to ensure there is a future at all and that it has not all been sacrificed by morbidly paranoid theophobics on the faith-based delusion that there will be something better for them when they've killed everyone else to mollify and please their imaginary friend because it wants them to.

Bibliography.

A Brief Illustrated Guide to Understanding Islam. (n.d.). *Chapter 1: Some Evidence for the Truth in Islam.* Retrieved March 6, 2016, from A Brief Ilustrated Guide to Understanding Islam: http://www.islam-guide.com/ch1-1.htm

All About God. (n.d.). *Role of Husband in the Bible.* Retrieved from All About God: http://www.allaboutgod.com/role-of-husband-in-the-bible.htm

American Association for the Advancement of Science. (1990). *Chapter 1: The Nature of Science.* Retrieved March 5, 2015, from Science For All Americans Online: http://www.project2061.org/publications/sfaa/online/chap1.htm

AnswersInGenesis. (2015, August 10). *Statement of Faith.* Retrieved March 6, 2016, from Answers in Genesis: https://answersingenesis.org/about/faith/

Asser, S. M., & Swan, R. (1998, April). Child Fatalities From Religion-motivated Medical Neglect. *Pediatrics, 101*(4), 625. Retrieved March 1, 2016, from http://pediatrics.aappublications.org/content/101/4/625

Attenborough, D. (1979). *Life on Earth: A Natural History.* William Collins & Sons. Retrieved from http://www.amazon.co.uk/Life-On-Earth-Natural-History/dp/0002190915

Azimov, I. (1989, Fall). The Relativity of Wrong. *The Skeptical Inquirer, 14*(1), pp. 35-44. Retrieved March 5, 2016, from http://chem.tufts.edu/answersinscience/relativityofwrong.htm

Barker, D. (2009). *Godles: How an Evangelical Preacher Became on of America's Leading Atheists.* Perseus Books Group.

Barker, D. (2015). *Life-Driven Purpose: How an Atheist Finds Meaning.* Pitchstone Publishing.

Bhugra, D. (2002). Self-concept: Psychosis and attraction of new religious movements. *Mental Health, Religion & Culture, 5*(3). doi:10.1080/13674670110112703

Blackmore, S. (2007, November 13). A dangerous delusion. *Guardian – Opinion.* Retrieved March 5, 2016, from http://www.theguardian.com/commentisfree/2007/nov/13/adangerous delusion

Blanken, I., Van de Ven, N., & Zeelenberg, M. (2015). A Meta-Analytic Review of Moral Licensing. *Personality and Social Psychology Bulletin, 41*(4), 540-558. doi:10.1177/0146167215572134

Boghosian, P. (2013). *A Manual for Creating Atheists.* Pichstone Publishing.

Bottoms, B. L., Neilson, M., Murray, R., & Filipas, H. (2004). Religion-Related Child Physical Abuse: Characteristics and Psychological Outcomes. *Journal of Aggression, Maltreatment & Trauma, 8*(1-2), 87-114. doi:10.1300/J146v08n01_04

Bottoms, B. L., Shaver, P. R., Goodman, G., & Qin, J. (1995). In the Name of God: A Profile of Religion-Related Child Abuse. *Journal of Social Issues, 51*(2), 1540-4560. doi:10.1111/j.1540-4560.1995.tb01325.x

Bouwsma, W. (1988). *John Calvin: A Sixteenth Centuary Portrait.* Oxford: Oxford University Press.

Brañas-Garza, P., Bucheli, M., Espinosa, M. P., & García-Muñoz, T. (2013, July 11). Moral Cleansing and Moral Licenses: Experimental Evidence. *Economics and Philosophy*, 199-212. doi:10.1017/S0266267113000199

Brutz, J. L., & Ingoldsby, B. B. (1984, February). Conflict Resolution in Quaker Families. *Journal of Marriage and Family, 46*(1), 21. Retrieved March 1, 2016, from http://www.jstor.org/stable/351859

Buglass, R., & Bowden, P. (1990). *Principles and Practices of Forensic Psychiatry.* Edinburgh: Churchill Livingstone.

Bibliography

Collins, F. (2007). *The Language of God: A Scientist Presents Evidence for Belief.* London: Simon & Schuster UK Ltd.

Conant, J. B. (1950). *The Overthrow of Phlogiston Theory: The Chemical Revolution of 1775-1789.* Cambridge: Harvard University Press.

Crabtree, S. (2007, August 30). *Book Uncovers a Lonely, Spiritually Desolate Mother Teresa.* Retrieved March 6, 2016, from Christianity Today: http://www.christianitytoday.com/ct/2007/augustweb-only/135-43.0.html

Crabtree, S. (2010, August 31). *Religiosity Highest in World's Poorest Nations.* Retrieved August 31, 2016, from Gallup: http://www.gallup.com/poll/142727/religiosity-highest-world-poorest-nations.aspx

Dawkins, R. (2001). *Sadly, an Honest Creationist.* Retrieved February 14, 2016, from Scepsis: https://scepsis.net/eng/articles/id_2.php

Deem, R. (2013, March 26). *Science and the Bible: Does the Bible Contradict Scientific Principles?* Retrieved February 22, 2016, from Evidence for God: http://www.godandscience.org/apologetics/sciencebible.html#n04

Dein, S., Cook, C. C., Powell, A., & Eagger, S. (2010, February). Religion, spirituality and mental health. *The Psychiatrist, 34*(2), 63-64. Retrieved March 6, 2016, from http://pb.rcpsych.org/content/34/2/63

Department of Justice and Equality. (2011). *The Cloyne Report.* Government of the Republic of Ireland. Dublin: Department of Justice and Equality. Retrieved from http://www.justice.ie/en/JELR/Cloyne_Rpt.pdf/Files/Cloyne_Rpt.pdf

Dunbar, R. (2006, July). *Professor Robin Dunbar.* Retrieved March 1, 2016, from Durham University. https://www.dur.ac.uk/ias/news/race_religion_inheritance/dunbar/

Elgot, J. (2014, November 20). Half Of Brits Say Religion Does More Harm Than Good, And Atheists Can Be Just As Moral. *The Huffington Post.* Retrieved February 24, 2016, from http://www.huffingtonpost.co.uk/2014/11/03/religion-beyond-belief_n_6094442.html

Festinger, L. (1957). *A Theory of Cognitive Dissonance.* Stanford University Press. Retrieved from http://www.amazon.co.uk/Books-Theory-Cognitive-Dissonance-Leon-Festinger/dp/0804709114

Finkestein, I., & Silberman, N. A. (2002). *The Bible Unearthed: Archaeology's New Vison of Ancient Israel and the Origins of Sacred Texts.* Free Press.

Foster, K. R., & Kokko, H. (2009, January 7). The evolution of superstitious and superstition-like behaviour. *Proceedings of the Royal Society B, 276,* 31-37. doi:10.1098/rspb.2008.0981

Freedom From Religion Foundation, National Convention Address (2012). [Motion Picture]. Retrieved February 24, 2016, from https://youtu.be/dJTQiChzTNI

Front Matter. (2005, June). Candor in Science. (L. M. Guenin, Ed.) *Synthese, 145*(2). Retrieved from http://www.jstor.org/stable/20118588

Gat, A. (2000, April). The Human Motivational Complex: Evolutionary Theory and the Cause of Hunter-Gatherer Fighting, Part II: Proximate, Subordinate, and Derivative Causes. *Antropological Quarterly, 73*(2), pp. 74-88. Retrieved March 6, 2016, from http://www.jstor.org/stable/3317188

Glaeser, E., & Sacerdote, B. (2008). Education And Religion. *Journal of Human Capital,* 188-215. doi:10.1086/590413

Goldman, E. (1913). *The Failure of Christianity.* Retrieved March 1, 2016, from http://www.positiveatheism.org/hist/goldman413.htm

GotQuestions?org. (n.d.). *Why does God require faith? Why doesn't God "prove" Himself to us so there is no need for faith?* Retrieved February 22, 2016, from GotQuestions?.org: http://www.gotquestions.org/God-require-faith.html

Bibliography

Hadaway, K. C., & Maler, P. L. (1998, May 6). Did You Really Go To Church This Week? Behind the Poll Data. *Christian Century, 115*(14), 472-475. Retrieved from Christian Century: http://connection.ebscohost.com/c/articles/564355/did-you-really-go-church-this-week-behind-poll-data

Hadaway, K. C., Marler, P. L., & Chaves, M. (1993, May). What the Polls Don't Show: A Closer Look at U.S. Church Attendance. *American Sociological Review, 58*(6), 741-752. Retrieved from http://www.jstor.org/stable/2095948

Heimlich, J. (2011). *Breaking Their Will: Shedding Light on Religious Child Maltreatment.* Prometheus Books.

HelpGuide.org. (2016, March). *Understanding domestic violence and abuse.* Retrieved from Domestic Violence and Abuse: http://www.helpguide.org/articles/abuse/domestic-violence-and-abuse.htm

Hitchens, C. (2007). *The Portable Atheist: Essential Reading for the Nonbeliever.* Perseus Books Group.

Hitchens, C. (2011). *God is Not Great: How Religion Poisons Everything.* Atlantic Books Ltd.

Hitchens, C. (2011, April 22). *Hitchens' address to American Atheists.* Retrieved February 22, 2016, from Phayngula: http://scienceblogs.com/pharyngula/2011/04/22/hitchens-address-to-american-a/

Hume, D. (1776). *Dialogues Concerning Natural Religion.* London: Project Guttenburg (Kindle Edition).

Intelligence Squared. (2009). *Intelligence Squared Catholic Church Debate – Transcrit.* Retrieved from http://www.amindatplay.eu/en/2009/12/02/intelligence%C2%B2-catholic-church-debate-transcript/

Irish Times. (2015, May 2). Same-sex Marriage Referendum. *Irish Times*. Retrieved March 5, 2016, from http://www.irishtimes.com/news/politics/marriage-referendum

IslamWeb.net. (2012, December 30). *The Islamic concept of faith*. Retrieved February 22, 2016, from IslamWeb.net: http://www.islamweb.net/en/article/134445/the-islamic-concept-of-faith

Jackson, S., Thompson, R. A., Christiansen, E. H., Coleman, R. A., Wyatt, J., Buckendahl, C. W., . . . Peterson, R. (1999). Predicting Abuse-Prone Attitudes and Discipline Practices in a Nationally Representative Sample. *Child Abuse & Neglect, 23*(1), 15-29. doi:10.1016/S0145-2134(98)00108-2

Jehovah's Witnesses. (n.d.). *Awake! How Did Life Begin?* Retrieved from Jehovah's Witnesses: https://download-a.akamaihd.net/files/media_magazines/8c/g_E_201501_01.rtf

Kline, A. (n.d.). *Religious Conflicts over Neutral, Civil Laws. Why Do Religious Believers Put Private, Religious Morality Over Civil Law?* Retrieved February 24, 2016, from About.com – Atheism: http://atheism.about.com/od/secularismseparation/a/SecularLaw.htm

Lane Craig, W. (n.d.). *If ISIS's God Were Real, Would I Be Obliged to Follow Him?* Retrieved March 6, 2016, from Reasonable Faith: http://www.reasonablefaith.org/if-isis-god-were-real-would-i-be-obliged-to-follow-him

Lane Craig, W. (n.d.). *Slaughter of the Canaanites*. Retrieved March 6, 2016, from Reasonable Faith: http://www.reasonablefaith.org/slaughter-of-the-canaanites

Langone, M. D., & Eisenberg, G. (1993). Children in Cults. In M. D. Langone (Ed.), *Recovery from Cults: Help for Victims of Psychological and Spritual Abuse* (p. 330). New York: W. W. Norton.

Laurens, K. R., J., H. M., Sunderland, M., Green, M. J., & Mould, G. L. (2012). Psychotic-like experiences in a community sample of 8000 children aged 9 to 11 years: an item response theory analysis.

Bibliography

Psychological Medicine, 42, 1495-1506. doi:10.1017/S0033291711002108

Lewis, C. S. (1942, June 8). *The Weight of Glory*. Retrieved March 6, 2016, from http://www.verber.com/mark/xian/weight-of-glory.pdf

Loftus, J. W. (2006, November 2). *The Outsider Test...* Retrieved March 6, 2016, from Debunking Christianity!: http://debunkingchristianity.blogspot.co.uk/2006/02/outsider-test.html

Marin, R. (1998, May 23). *Bearing False Witness To Thy Pollster*. (U. P. Syndicate, Producer) Retrieved March 5, 2016, from Hartford Courant: http://articles.courant.com/1998-05-23/features/9805230112_1_diaries-church-attendance-social-scientists

Markowitz, A., & Halperin, D. A. (1984). Cults and Children: The Abuse of the Young. *Cultic Sudies Journal*, 145.

McLaughlin, M. (2012). *Creation Myths and Tales of Origin*. McLaughlin Group.

McLeod, S. (2014). *Cognitive Dissonance*. Retrieved February 18, 2016, from Simply Psychology: http://www.simplypsychology.org/cognitive-dissonance.html

McLeod, S. (2014). *Maslow's Hierarchy of Needs*. Retrieved February 17, 2016, from Simply Psychology: http://www.simplypsychology.org/maslow.html

McPhillips, B. (2007, September 23). *Einstein Proves the Existence of God*. Retrieved March 1, 2016, from http://brendanmcphillips.com: http://brendanmcphillips.com/2007/09/23/einstein-proves-the-existence-of-god/

Mehta, H. (2015, August 21). *Atheists Now Make Up 0.1% of the Federal Prison Population*. Retrieved March 5, 2016, from Friendly Atheist: http://www.patheos.com/blogs/friendlyatheist/2015/08/21/atheists-now-make-up-0-1-of-the-federal-prison-population/

Mental Health Foundation. (n.d.). *Spirituality*. Retrieved February 22, 2016, from https://www.mentalhealth.org.uk/a-to-z/s/spirituality

Mousavi, K. (2015, April 24). *"Atheism is Freedom" Why I Love Being an Atheist Even Though I Live in Iran*. Retrieved February 27, 2016, from Alternet: http://www.alternet.org/belief/atheism-freedom-why-i-love-being-atheist-even-though-i-live-iran

Mukesh, R., Pandiyarajan, R., Selvakumar, U., & Lingadurai, K. (2012). Influence of Search Algorithms on Aerodynamic Design Optimisation of Aircraft Wings. *Procedia Engineering, 38*, 2155-2163. doi:10.1016/j.proeng.2012.06.259

National Academies Press. (1999). *Introduction*. Retrieved from Science and Creationism: A View from the National Academy of Sciences: http://www.nap.edu/read/6024/chapter/2

Navabi, A. (2014). *Why There Is No God: Simple Responses to 20 Common Arguments for the Existence of God*. Atheist Republic.

NHS Choices. (2016, January 14). *Phobias*. Retrieved March 1, 2016, from Health A-Z: http://www.nhs.uk/Conditions/Phobias/Pages/Introduction.aspx

Owen, Katy. (n.d.). *Religion and the Great British Public – Survation for Huffington Post UK*. Retrieved March 5, 2016, from Survation: http://survation.com/religion-and-the-great-british-public-survation-for-huffington-post-uk/

Oyama, A., Obayashi, S., & Nakamura, T. (n.d.). *Real-Coded Adaptive Range Genetic Algorithm Applied to Transonic Wing Optimization*. Retrieved March 5, 2016, from Institute of Fluid Scienceg, Tokyo University: http://www.ifs.tohoku.ac.jp/edge/publications/Ppsnvi.pdf

Pearce, J. M. (2015). *The Problem with "God": Classical Theism under the Spotlight*. Onus Books.

Peters, T. (2012, Setember 9). *Sam Harris explains the term Atheism*. Retrieved March 5, 2016, from Soundcloud: https://soundcloud.com/tommypeters-1/sam-harris-explains-the-term

Bibliography

Pew Research Center. (2014). *Religious Landscape Study – Views about human evolution.* Retrieved March 5, 2016, from Religion & Public Life: http://www.pewforum.org/religious-landscape-study/views-about-human-evolution/

Pew Research Center. (2015, January 29). *Chapter 3: Attitudes and Beliefs on Science and Technology Topics.* Retrieved March 5, 2016, from Internet, Science & Tech: http://www.pewinternet.org/2015/01/29/chapter-3-attitudes-and-beliefs-on-science-and-technology-topics/

Pew Research Center. (2015, January 29). *Internet, Science & Tech.* Retrieved March 5, 2016, from Public and Scientists' Views on Science and Society: http://www.pewinternet.org/2015/01/29/public-and-scientists-views-on-science-and-society/

Popper, K. (1963). *Conjecture and Refutations.* London, UK: Routledge and Kegan Paul.

RationalWiki. (2015, December 26). *Main Page.* Retrieved March 6, 2016, from RationalWiki: http://rationalwiki.org/wiki/Main_Page

RationalWiki. (2016, January 28). *Life — How Did It Get Here? By Evolution or by Creation?* Retrieved Maech 6, 2016, from RationalWiki: http://rationalwiki.org/wiki/Life_%E2%80%94_How_Did_It_Get_Here%3F_By_Evolution_or_by_Creation%3F

RationalWiki.org. (n.d.). *Argument from incredulity.* Retrieved March 6, 2016, from RationalWiki.org: http://rationalwiki.org/wiki/Argument_from_incredulity#Personal_incredulity

RDFSR. (2013, January 2). *Facebook: What fears you faced based on religion.* Retrieved February 21, 2016, from Richard Dawkins Foundation for Science and Reason: https://richarddawkins.net/2013/01/facebook-what-fears-you-faced-based-on-religion/

Rees, T. J. (2009). Is Personal Insecurity a Cause of Cross-National Differences in the Intensity of Religious Belief? *Journal of Religion and Society, 11*. Retrieved March 5, 2016, from Creighton Digital

Repository (CDR):
https://dspace.creighton.edu/xmlui/bitstream/handle/10504/64442/2009-17.pdf

Research Gate. (2015, June 12). *What is intellectual honesty?* Retrieved February 14, 2016, from ResearchGate: https://www.researchgate.net/post/What_is_intellectual_honesty/3

Rethink Mental Illness. (2015, July). *Sprituality, Religion and Mental Illness – Factsheet.* Retrieved March 6, 2016, from Rethink Mental Illness: file:///C:/Users/DELL/Downloads/Spirituality%20_And%20_Mental%20_Illness%20_Factsheet%20(1).pdf

Reuters. (2007, August 24). *Letters reveal Mother Teresa's doubt about faith.* Retrieved March 6, 2016, from Reuters USA: http://www.reuters.com/article/us-teresa-letters-idUSN2435506020070824

Root, J. (2010). *C. S. Lewis and a Problem of Evil: An Investigation of a Pervasive Theme.* James Clarke & Co Ltd.

Russell, B. (1927, March 6). Why I Am Not A Christian. Retrieved from http://www.users.drew.edu/~jlenz/whynot.html

Schafersman, S. D. (1997, January 15). *An Introduction to Science – Scientific Thinking and the Scientific Method.* Retrieved March 5, 2016, from State University of New York at Stony Brook, Department of Geosciences – Earth Science Research Project: http://www.geo.sunysb.edu/esp/files/scientific-method.html

Schick, T. (2000). *Readings in the Philosophy of Science.* (T. Schick, Ed.) Mountain View, California: Mayfield Publishing Company.

Shanmugasundaram, M. (2014, September 10). *Why Becoming An Atheist Has Been The Most Liberating Experience Of My Life.* Retrieved February 24, 2016, from Youth Ki Awaaz: http://www.youthkiawaaz.com/2014/09/becoming-atheist-liberating-experience-life/

Bibliography

Sims, A. (2012). *Religious Delusion.* Royal College of Psychiatrists. Retrieved March 5, 2016, from http://www.rcpsych.ac.uk/pdf/Religious%20delusions%20Andrew%20Sims.pdf

Singer, P. (2009). *The Life You Can Save: How to Play Your Part in Ending World Poverty.* Picador.

Skerkat, D. E., & Darnell, A. (199). The Effects of Parents' Fundamentalism on Children's Educational Attainment: Examining Differences by Gender and Children's Fundamentalism. *Journal for the Scientific Study of Religion, 38*(1), 28. Retrieved March 1, 2016, from http://wcfia.harvard.edu/files/wcfia/files/511_sherkat_2.pdf

Slick, M. (2011). *The Transcendental Argument for the Existence of God.* Retrieved March 1, 2016, from Christian Apologetics and Research Ministry: https://carm.org/transcendental-argument

Smith, J. R. (2015, November 30). *Srebrenica massacre.* Retrieved February 22, 2016, from Encyclopaedia Britannica: http://www.britannica.com/event/Srebrenica-massacre

Snow, J. (1854, September 23). *The Cholera Near Golden Square, and at Deptford [To the Editor of the Medical Times and Gazette].* Retrieved from UCLA Department of Epidemiology, School of Public Health: http://www.ph.ucla.edu/epi/snow/choleragoldensquare.html

Socolar, R., Cabinum-Foeler, E., & Sinal, S. (2008, July). Is Religiosity Associated with Corporal Punishment or Child Abuse? *Southern Medical Journal, 101*(7), 707-710. doi:10.1097/SMJ.0b013e3181794793.

St Augustine of Hippo. (5th Century CE). Whether We are to Believe in the Atipodes. In *De Civitate Dei (City of God)* (M. D. Rev, Trans., Vol. XVI). Calvin College (Christian Classics Ethereal Library).

Stearns, G., Beardslee, H., Edmund, L., Evinger, J., & Poling, N. (2002). *Final Report of the Independent Committee of Inquiry Prebyterian Church (USA).* Louisville, KY. Retrieved February 24, 2016, from http://www.pcusa.org/media/uploads/ici/pdfs/ici-report.pdf

SundayAssembly. (n.d.). *Celebrating Life Together – Inspiring Events and Caring Communities in 60+ Cities Worldwide.* Retrieved March 6, 2016, from SundayAssembly: http://www.sundayassembly.com/

Taylor, K. (2013, May 30). Religious Fundamentalism 'May Be Catagoriesed as Mental Illness & Cured By Science'. *The Huffington Post.* Retrieved February 25, 2016, from http://www.huffingtonpost.co.uk/2013/05/30/religious-fundamentalism-categorised-mental-illness-cured-_n_3359267.html

The Clergy Project. (2015). *Welcome to the Clergy Project.* Retrieved March 6, 2016, from The Clergy Project: http://clergyproject.org/

The National Academy of Sciences. (2008). *Is Evolution a Theory or a Fact?* Retrieved March 5, 2016, from Evolution Resources: http://nationalacademies.org/evolution/TheoryOrFact.html

Theotokos Catholic Books. (n.d.). *Nine Major Approved Apparitions.* Retrieved from Theotokos Catholic Books: http://www.theotokos.org.uk/pages/appdisce/nineapps.html

Wikipedia. (2016, February 29). *Jonestown.* Retrieved March 6, 2016, from Wikipedia: https://en.wikipedia.org/wiki/Jonestown

Wikipedia. (2016, February 7). *Great Disappointment.* Retrieved March 6, 2016, from Wikipedia: https://en.wikipedia.org/wiki/Great_Disappointment

Wikipedia. (2016, March 5). *Great Famine (Ireland).* Retrieved March 6, 2016, from Wikipedia: https://en.wikipedia.org/wiki/Great_Famine_(Ireland)

Wikipedia. (2016, February 20). *Journey to the Seventh Heaven.* Retrieved March 6, 2016, from Wikipedia – Buraq: https://en.wikipedia.org/wiki/Buraq#Journey_to_the_Seventh_Heaven

Wikipedia. (2016, February 16). *Kitzmiller v. Dover Area School District.* Retrieved March 6, 2016, from Wikipedia: https://en.wikipedia.org/wiki/Kitzmiller_v._Dover_Area_School_District

Bibliography

Wikipedia. (2016, February 23). *Kurt Wise.* Retrieved March 6, 2016, from Wikipedia: https://en.wikipedia.org/wiki/Kurt_Wise

Wikipedia. (2016, March 6). *Magdalene laundries in Ireland.* Retrieved March 6, 2016, from Wikipedia: https://en.wikipedia.org/wiki/Magdalene_laundries_in_Ireland

Wikipedia. (2016, February 6). *Sabra and Shatila massacre.* Retrieved March 6, 2016, from Wikipedia: https://en.wikipedia.org/wiki/Sabra_and_Shatila_massacre

Wikipedia. (2016, March 4). *Srebrenica.* Retrieved March 6, 2016, from Wikipedia: https://en.wikipedia.org/wiki/Srebrenica_massacre

Winell, M. (n.d.). *Religios Trauma Syndrome.* Retrieved March 1, 2016, from British Association for Behavioral and Cognitive Psychotherapies: http://www.babcp.com/Review/RTS.aspx

Winell, M. (n.d.). *Understanding Religious Trauma Syndrome: Trauma from Religion.* Retrieved March 1, 2016, from The British Association for Behavioural and Cognitive Psychotherapies: http://www.babcp.com/Review/RTS-Trauma-from-Religion.aspx

Winther, R. G. (2015, March 5). *The Structure of Scientific Theories.* Retrieved March 5, 2016, from Stanford Encyclopedia of Philosophy: http://plato.stanford.edu/entries/structure-scientific-theories/

Wise, K. P. (n.d.). *In Six Days – Why 50 Scientists Choose to Believe in Creation.* Retrieved February 14, 2016, from Creation Miniteries International: http://creation.com/kurt-p-wise-geology-in-six-days

About the Author.

Firstly, Rosa Rubicondior is not my real name. It is from the Latin, *rosa rubicundior, lilo candidior, omnibus formosior, semper in te glorior* (redder than the rose, whiter than the lilies, lovelier than all others, I will always glory in thee). The only significance of it is that, when I was a radical lefty I wrote a weekly column in a magazine and wanted something red for a pen name. I found it in the lyrics on the sleeve of a vinyl recording of *Carmina Burana*, a mediaeval poem in German and Latin, set to music by Carl Orff and which was very popular in the 1960s.

I toyed with Rufa Tunica (Red Shirt), which is also in the lyrics, but in the end settled for Rosa Rubicondior. The name lay dormant for some 35 years until I resurrected it for my blog. It was only later that I realised I had misspelled it slightly; it should have been Rosa Rubicundior.

My reason for wishing to be anonymous was that I originally intended my *Rosa Rubicondior* blog to be about UK politics. As a part-time employee of an NHS Trust and a former member of an NHS Trust's senior management team, I wanted to be free to comment on the NHS without compromising my employers and jeopardising my position. It was only later, as I got pulled more and more into the atheism versus religious fundamentalism and creationism debates, especially in their right-wing political forms that I discovered blogging about atheism, Humanism, religious apologetics and biological science was actually closer to my interests.

The decision to be anonymous has since been vindicated by the threats and campaign of lies and vilification to which I have been subjected by a small number of religious extremists, psychopaths, obsessively psychotic stalkers and inadequate characters with self-evident personality disorders, on Twitter and elsewhere. The people at Twitter Support seem unable or unwilling to take effective action to prevent the antics of these characters.

Religion, it seems, is a fertile breeding-ground for inadequate nutters looking for an excuse for their antisocial behaviour and a justification for their hate campaigns, as they try to make their own little lives have some sort of relevance by constant attention-seeking and pathetic displays of what power the Internet gives them. In pre-Internet days, these sad individuals and failures of the mental health services would have been restricted to standing at their windows shouting abuse at strangers in the street, stealing underwear off washing lines at night or posting anonymous poison-pen letters to neighbours.

Then of course there are the seriously dangerous individuals who believe they know what their god thinks, who it hates and who it wants punished, and have decided it requires their help to hand out the punishments. I have no intention of exposing my family to these deranged individuals whose 'love' for humanity involves cutting heads of.

Anyway, enough of why I use a pseudonym.

I was born and brought up in a small North Oxfordshire village during the post-war baby boom and have had a love of nature since before I can remember. I was one of five children of the daughter of a Cotswold shepherd of some renown, and a car factory worker and former soldier who was rescued from Dunkirk and spent the last three years of World War II in India where he learned to speak fluent Hindi.

By any standards we were poor and grew most of the food we ate in our garden and on an allotment on the edge of the village. In some respects we were close to hunter-gatherers and along with other villagers, never passed over a chance to gather firewood from the woods and fields when a large elm tree fell or shed a branch, to collect watercress from the River Evenlode and to gather mushrooms and wild fruit from the fields and hedgerows in autumn.

I don't remember learning to read – I was probably about five or six years old – but I read anything I could get my hands on, especially anything to do with nature. I realised I was an atheist when I was nine years old when it suddenly dawned on me that not all religions could be right, but they could all be wrong. Since there was no more reason to suppose only ours was right while all the others, ancient and modern, were wrong, the most sensible view was that they were all wrong. I have been an atheist ever since.

On leaving school with a few 'O' levels, I worked as a laboratory technician for Oxford University on a Medical Research Council grant, working my way up to Senior Research Technician and gaining an ONC in Science, HNC in

About the Author

Applied Biology and state registration as a Medical Laboratory Technician. I co-authored a paper on reproductive physiology in guinea pigs in the process.

After eleven years I was made redundant when the government cut back on research spending and our small unit was disbanded. Disillusioned and needing a job to support a new family, I decided on a change of career and joined the Ambulance Service. With the advantage my medical and biological knowledge gave me I became one of the first UK Paramedics and an instructor, eventually working my way through the ranks to become a Control Room Manager.

I gained a Diploma In Management Studies at Oxford Brookes University, taught myself computer programming and became the Trust's Information Manager, Freedom of Information and Data Protection Officer. I formally retired two years early but was asked to return part-time as a performance information analyst and deployment planning consultant.

I have been a socialist and trades unionist since my teens and have been a member of the Labour Party for about thirty years. Briefly, during the early 1970s, I was a member of the Communist Party of Great Britain but left after a couple of years when I realised it was as dogmatic and cult-like as a fundamentalist religion; quite incapable of holding rational debates about policy or changing to meet the changing needs of a post-industrial economy.

Within twenty years, Communist regimes in Eastern Europe were collapsing under their own inertia and irrelevance and the people of Eastern Europe were taking their countries back. Like religions, Communism was never anything more than a promise of jam tomorrow.

So that's me: a materialist rationalist who never consciously decided to be led by evidence but who has always assumed that it is the only honest thing to do. I think the Universe is wonderful enough without magic and mystery.

To me, being an evolved ape, 3.5 billion years in the making, is infinitely more marvellous than being the unworthy product of a magician who made me out of dirt just to worship him.

Other books by Rosa Rubicondior.

The Light of Reason: And Other Atheist Writings.
Irreverent essays, thought-provoking articles and humorous items on atheism, religion, science, evolution, creationism and related issues.

(Paperback) ISBN-10: 1516906888, ISBN-13: 978-1516906888   £9.95 (US $14.95)
(Kindle) ASIN: B014N0IPVI   £3.95 (US $5.99)

The Light of Reason: Volume II – Atheism, Science and Evolution.
Thought-provoking essays on the conflict between fundamentalist religion and science, and exposing the anti-science, extremist political agenda of the modern creationist industry.

(Paperback) ISBN-10: 1517105188, ISBN-13: 978-1517105181   £9.95 (US $14.95)
(Kindle) ASIN: B014N0IR16   £3.99 (US $5.99)

The Light of Reason: Volume III – Apologetics, Fallacies, and Other Frauds.
Thought-provoking essays and articles on religion and atheism, dealing with religious apologetics, fallacies, miracles and other frauds

(Paperback) ISBN-10: 151710761X, ISBN-13: 978-1517107611   £6.95 (US $9.95)
(Kindle) ASIN: B014N0IRE8   £2.99 (US $3.99)

The Light of Reason: Volume IV - The Silly Bible.
Exposing the absurdities, contradictions and historical inaccuracies in the Bible and advancing the case for atheism and against religion. This volume, the fourth in the Light of Reason series, deals with contradictions and absurdities in the Bible.

(Paperback) ISBN-10: 1517108209, ISBN-13: 978-1517108205   £8.95 (US $13.95)
(Kindle) ASIN: B014N0IR8E   £3.99 (US $4.99)

The Light of Reason: And Other Atheist Writing. (all 4 volumes in one e-book)
Based on the Rosa Rubicondior science and Atheism blog, this is a collection of Atheist and science articles, some short, others lengthier, exploring the interface between religion and science and which have been published over some four years.

(Kindle only) ASIN: B013DYOK32   £6.34 (US $9.95)

An Unprejudiced Mind: Atheism, Science & Reason.
Essays on science and theology from a scientific atheist perspective, exploring particularly evolution versus creationism.

(Paperback) ISBN-10: 1522925805, ISBN-13: 978-1522925804   £9.95 (US $14.95)
(Kindle) ASIN: B019UGXPM4   £3.99 (US $5.95)

Printed in Great Britain
by Amazon